U0578007

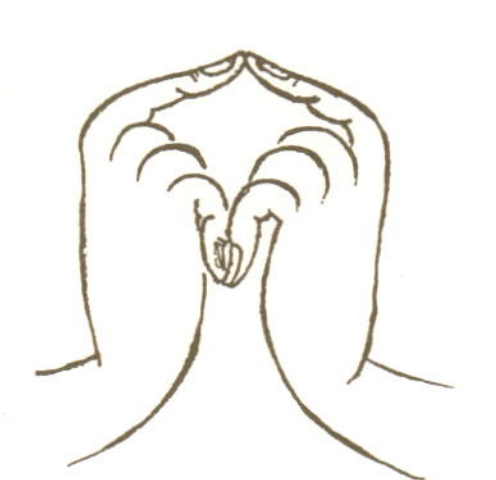

漢藏交融

金銅佛像集萃

主　編　王家鵬
副主編　沈衛榮

རྒྱ་བོད་ཆོས་ལུགས་མཉམ་འདྲེས།

གསེར་ཟངས་སྐུ་བརྙན་གཅེས་བསྡུས།

中華書局

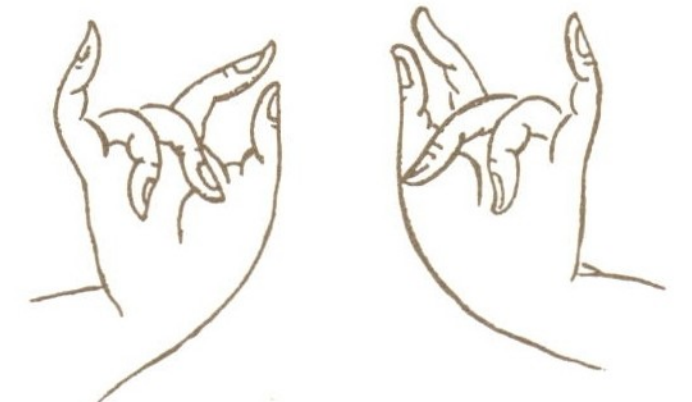

Sino-Tibetan Buddhist Interactions

A Treasury of Gilt Copper Buddhist Statues

Edited by Wang Jiapeng
and Shen Weirong

Zhonghua Book Company

總籌劃　屈全繩

總顧問　季羨林　馮其庸　王　堯　拉巴平措　屈全繩

顧　問　談錫永　金維諾　步連生　孫國璋　陳慶英

主　編　王家鵬

副主編　沈衛榮

編　委　王家鵬　沈衛榮　謝繼勝　吉美桑珠
賈壯苗　李　巍　李舒迦

Chief Design

Qu Quansheng

Chief Consultants

Ji Xianlin　Feng Qiyong　Wang Yao　Lhapa Phuntsogs　Qu Quansheng

Consultants

Tan Xiyong　Jin Weinuo　Bu Liansheng　Sun Guozhang　Chen Qingying

Chief Editor

Wang Jiapeng

Deputy Editor

Shen Weirong

Associate Editors

Wang Jiapeng　Shen Weirong　Xie Jisheng
Jigme Samdrub　Jia Zhuangmiao　Li Wei　Li Shujia

支持單位

故宫博物院

中國國家博物館

Endorsed by

The Palace Museum

National Museum of China

李巍金銅佛造像鑒藏

ལིས་ཝེ་ཡིས་ཉར་ཚགས་བྱས་པའི་ཟངས་སྐུ།

Li Wei's Collection of Gilt Copper Buddhist Statues

目録

Contents

爲中華文化增輝

季羨林敬題

二〇〇八年六月二十六日

季羨林（北京大學資深教授、國際著名東方學家、印度學家、梵語文學家、文學翻譯家、教育家）

八聲甘州

爲李巍先生藏漢藏金銅佛像珍品集題

望巍巍雪域麗西天，卓立幾千秋。仰布宮莊肅，峥嶸殿閣，玉宇瓊旒。更寶相萬千態，佛法詎邊疇。參妙諦無上，萬世同修。

聞説佛劫三千，看十年小劫，桑海西州。嘆沉淪寶相，鉛淚銅仙流。法輪轉、天龍護法，盡神功、大施金剛鈎。覓聖像，虔誠呵護，聚萬佛樓。

己丑四月寬堂馮其庸敬題八十又七

馮其庸（中國人民大學資深教授、著名紅學家、文史學家）

怒目低眉看種種慈悲爲
念此心同慧根豈辨華夷
界寶相堪融漢藏風且證
文明嬗演史仍窺藝事去
來蹤今朝諸佛一堂萃盛
會當應謝李公

賀漢藏交融金銅佛像集萃出版
北京故宮博物院院長 鄭欣淼作 盧中南錄

怒目低眉看種種，
慈悲爲念此心同。
慧根豈辨華夷界，
寶相堪融漢藏風。
且證文明嬗演史，
仍窺藝事去來踪。
今朝諸佛一堂萃，
盛會當應謝李公。

賀漢藏交融金銅佛像集萃出版
北京故宮博物院院長鄭欣淼作 盧中南錄

鄭欣淼（故宫博物院院長、中國魯迅研究會會長、中國作家協會會員）

盧中南（中國革命軍事博物館研究館員、中國書法家協會理事）

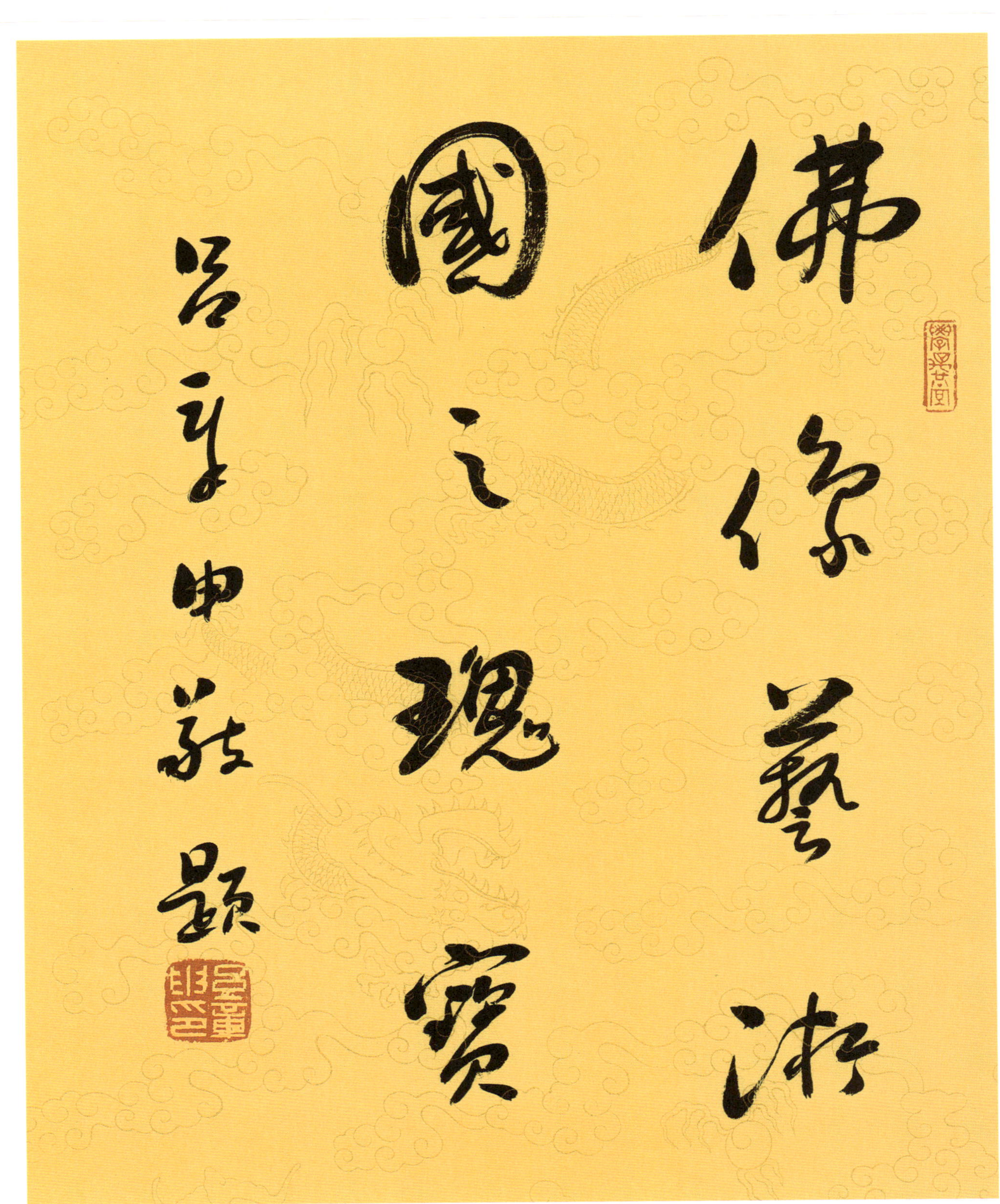

佛像藝術
國之瑰寶
呂章申敬題

呂章申（中國國家博物館館長、高級建築師、中國國際書畫研究會顧問）

佛教傳到雪域高原，
佛像請到聖地拉薩；
佛祖被尊稱爲「覺悟」，
佛殿被叫做「覺康」。
先輩大師們叮嚀再三；
貢巴繞色接受比丘戒，
師徒三尊加兩位漢比丘，
聚集安多點燃佛教餘火。
弘傳佛法的各個時期，
出現了無數的上師大德；
彼此不分教派和民族，
共同建造了輝煌的殿堂。

以恭敬的心情
於二〇〇九年吉祥月日

拉巴平措（中國藏學研究中心總干事）

八聲甘州

和寬堂詞丈　為

李巍先生珍藏漢藏

金銅佛像出版精選圖册題

記初時萬里作孤征，心期未成秋。鷲莊嚴法界，諸尊海會，銀冕金旒。一爾大千震動，寶相落田疇。垂盡銅偬淚，玉殿誰修。

却喜於今歲月，許春工費盡，裝點神州。縱靈光百折，漢藏兩交流。未推遷、金剛界裏，轉年光、鎖索集鈴鈎（鎖索鈴鈎為四大勾召天女）。從今後，人天一册，共禮梵樓。

己丑六月

無畏金剛阿闍梨談錫永并書

談錫永（北美漢藏佛學研究會會長、寧瑪派傳人、香港漢藏佛學家）

序

漢藏佛教交融　漢藏佛像輝映

王堯

兩年前，我有幸在馮其庸先生的介紹下，偕同我的學生沈衛榮、謝繼勝、王家鵬等一行藏學研究新鋭，參觀了北京東方瑰寶公司的藝術精品展示室，親眼目睹了李巍先生個人收藏的數以百計的明清金銅佛像。年過八十的我，從事藏傳佛教學習研究已近六十年，有老一輩師尊于道泉教授和王森教授引導，並有幸親近了貢嘎上師和東噶・洛桑赤列先生。在他們的關懷指導下，我踏入藏傳佛教門檻，平生走訪參拜過的佛教名刹已很難確切記憶，也曾於歐美、日本等地參觀過不少著名的博物館、藝術館，觀賞並參與過規模盛大的藏傳佛教藝術展覽，本以爲麟鳳龜龍，已無緣再覽。可當我置身於李巍先生嘔心瀝血收集、珍藏的這批明清金銅佛像之中時，頃刻之間我仿佛到了一個別有洞天的藝術殿堂。李巍先生一人的收藏在數量上差不多抵得上我平生所見到的，而且留下難忘記憶的同類金銅佛像的總和，而其造像樣式之豐富、鑄造技術之精美，更是遠遠超出了我的期待。這始料不及的事情明白地告訴我，明清兩代鑄造的金銅佛像不但數量之多難以估量，且其形制之精美、造像風格之多樣，都給人耳目一新的感覺。這不但讓我大開了眼界，而且也令我不由得對漢藏佛教藝術交流的那段美好年代生起無限的向往和緬懷之情，並對爲保存這批國寶級的佛教藝術珍品付出了辛勤勞動的李巍先生生發出由衷的敬意。

自上個世紀七十年代末開始，我有幸多次在歐美和日本不少著名學術機構中從事藏學研究和教學工作，並代表中國藏學家參與了許多國際性的藏學學術研究活動。其間曾多次碰到過一些可能是出於無知，或者別有用心的人，他們舌燦蓮花，不顧歷史事實地否認明代漢藏兩個民族間十分緊密的政治和宗教關係，愣説明朝缺乏其前朝蒙古人所擁有的那種摧枯拉朽的軍事力量，所以對西藏事務涉及不深。這顯然是對中華民族文明發展的歷史，特別是對明代漢藏關係史缺乏起碼的了解而自以爲是的謬論。事實上，由於元朝對西藏地方近百年的有效統治，西藏與中原的關係在行政、經濟和文化等方面都已經緊密相連，不可分割。元、明政權的更迭，並沒有影響到西藏與中原王朝間的行政隸屬關係，從元朝在西藏地區劃分的三個宣慰司到明朝在同一地區設立的三個行都指揮使司，名稱雖然起了變化，但中央政府對西藏地方的有效統治却没有任何改變。明朝的軍事力量雖不及元朝，但明廷與西藏之間在宗教、文化等方面的交流則遠勝於前朝，漢藏兩個民族在大明王朝的統治之下和平共處，根本無須兵戎相見。繼元之後，明廷國策是「衆建多封」。漢藏關係史上有著名的「明封八王」（即大寶、大乘、大慈三大法王和闡化、闡教、護教、輔教、贊善五大教王）。他們是明初應邀來朝廷弘法和依例入貢，並受到朝廷敕封「法王」、「教王」名號的西藏喇嘛中的著名代表。不僅如此，實際上明代西藏各個地區、教派和大小寺院都曾派出僧俗代表來朝廷入覲，接受明廷對

他們的敕封和賞賜，當時到內地或入貢、或弘法、或參訪、或朝山的西藏喇嘛總數或當以千、萬計。李巍先生藏品中出現的大量明代金銅佛像，特別是那些刻有「大明永樂年施」或者「大明宣德年施」六字款的精品正是這段歷史的有力見證。當時晉京入朝的喇嘛每每將在西藏鑄造的金銅佛像作爲向朝廷獻禮的貢品，而朝廷也經常將宮廷製作的金銅佛像作爲禮品賞賜給絡繹不絶來京入朝的喇嘛們。金銅佛像於漢藏之間的這種雙向流動，正是明代漢藏兩個民族間十分緊密的政治、宗教和文化關係的象徵。

長期以來，國外的許多研究佛學的專家學者，通常更多地注意印度佛教和藏傳佛教之間的聯繫，偏重於作印藏佛學研究。可能是由於他們對漢藏、藏漢佛教間的互動、交流和融合的歷史缺乏深刻的了解，往往忽視漢藏佛學之間存在的歷史聯繫。近年來，中國學者在漢藏佛學比較研究方面取得了突出的成績，特別是通過故宮寶藏中的許多實物展示和研究成果公布，尤其是對敦煌文獻和黑水城文獻中有關漢藏佛學的多種文字資料的開發和利用，使得漢藏佛教交流史的面貌變得越來越清晰。這些文獻資料表明，漢傳佛教曾經是藏傳佛教的兩大源頭，漢傳禪宗佛教不但在前弘期的藏傳佛教信衆中深得人心，而且也在後弘期藏傳佛教各派，特別是寧瑪派和噶舉派的教法中留下了明顯的印記。而藏傳佛教從西夏開始，歷經元、明、清、民國等時期，形成一股熱潮，不斷東傳在漢地得到了廣泛的傳播，其影響不但見於宮廷，亦散見於全國各地，如北京、承德和蒙古。即使在我們國家經歷了十年浩劫之後，李巍先生依然能够從全國各地收集到如此衆多的明清時代藏傳佛教金銅佛像，這充分説明藏傳佛教曾於西藏以外地區廣泛流行這一不爭的事實。雖然我自己並不是一個專門研究藏傳佛教藝術的藝術史家，但在李巍先生所收藏的這批金銅佛像中，我亦强烈地感受到漢藏兩種佛教藝術傳統互相輝映、完美結合的歷史大趨勢。因爲在這些佛像中，我們既見到了具有典型漢傳佛教藝術風格的諸佛、菩薩像，又見到了明顯屬於藏傳密教系統，呈現出西天梵相的寂静和忿怒本尊、護法像。這種情形正好折射出了這樣的一個歷史事實，即自西夏、元朝以來，藏傳佛教在中原地區的傳播不斷深入，它與漢傳佛教傳統的結合日趨緊密，從此漢傳和藏傳兩種佛學傳統呈現出你中有我，我中有你的趨勢。在李巍先生的收藏品中，我見到了許多尊形制不一的「大黑天」（摩訶葛剌）護法像，這不禁令我回憶起當年我「上窮碧落下黃泉」，苦苦尋找這位被蒙古人奉爲「國之護法」的大黑天神的往事。自西夏時代開始，大黑天神就廣受西夏藏傳佛教徒的尊崇，蒙古人則把大黑天當成無所不能的戰神來崇拜，明清兩代從宮廷到民間敬奉大黑天神的傳統綿延不絶。爲了弄清這段歷史，我曾經花大力氣在浩瀚的文獻資料中查找大黑天神的踪影，也曾在全國各地走訪過多處大黑天崇拜的勝迹，此番在李巍先生這裏再次與故人（神）相見，端的是分外親切。大黑天神及其大黑天崇拜在漢地的流行可以説是藏傳佛教在内地傳播的一個象徵性的標志。

參觀李巍先生收藏的這批金銅佛像給我留下了無比深刻的印象，總是念兹在兹，不敢或忘。不久之後，我又和談錫永上師等幾位學術同行和專家們一起再度造訪了李巍先生的東方瑰寶公司，對這些金銅佛像重新作了仔仔細細的觀摩和品味，並就其中一些佛像的鑄造年代、地點、工藝特徵和造像形制及其象徵意義等問題進行了非常深入和專業的討論，使大家對這批明清金銅佛像的源流和價值有了更進一步的認識。從那時起，我就一直非常迫切地希望這批金銅佛像有朝一日能够通過合適的渠道得到廣泛的展示，使得它們的價值能爲更多熱愛藏傳佛教文化的人們所了解和欣賞。當我聽説李巍先生將與中華書局合作，精選其收藏品中最具代表性的九十九尊佛像結集出版的消息時，我感到十分的歡喜和欣慰。出版這樣一部高質量的漢藏交融的金銅佛像圖録，實在是漢藏佛教藝術研究史上的一大盛事。在國外迄今我所見到的研究藏傳金銅佛像的最權威的著作是瑞士人Ulrich von Schroeder先生的大作《西藏的佛教雕塑》（*Buddhist Sculptures in Tibet*）一書。我衷心希望這部《漢藏交融——金銅佛像集萃》的問世，能爲研究藏傳金銅佛像的藝術史家們提供極其豐富和寶貴的一手資料，使得這個研究領域的進步有所依托。這部集子的出版又恰逢國慶六十周年這一大好日子，它無疑是獻給國慶六十周年的一份厚禮。我們的國家是由五十六個民族組成的一個多民族、多元文化的統一的國家，不管是漢族，還是藏族，我們都只是中華民族的一個組成部分，不管是漢人，還是藏人，我們都是中國人。就像我們很難將一尊明清鑄造的金銅佛像明確地劃歸漢藏佛教藝術或者藏漢佛教藝術這兩個不同的範疇内一樣，漢藏兩個民族不管在政治上、經濟上，還是在文化上、宗教上早已緊密相連，不可分割。出版這部明清金銅佛像圖集，展示漢藏、藏漢佛教藝術特點，不但對於我們重温漢藏佛教互相交流和融合的歷史，建立漢藏兩個民族間文化和情感上的親和關係大有助益，而且對於我們今天構建中華民族這一全中國人民共同的民族認同，樹立起各個民族同爲中國人的民族自豪感同樣具有極其重要的意義。

衷心感謝李巍先生爲我們奉獻了這樣一部展示、研究漢藏佛教藝術精品的傳世之作！李巍先生爲保護中華民族的文化遺産所做的卓越貢獻將與這部著作一起流芳後世！

王堯（中央民族大學資深教授、中央文史研究館館員、著名藏學家、佛學家）

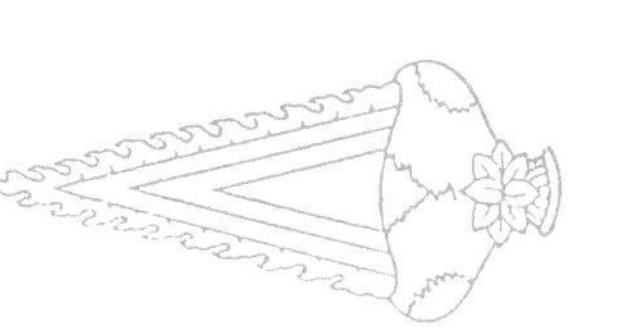

Interactions between Chinese and Tibetan Buddhism and Buddhist Art

Wang Yao

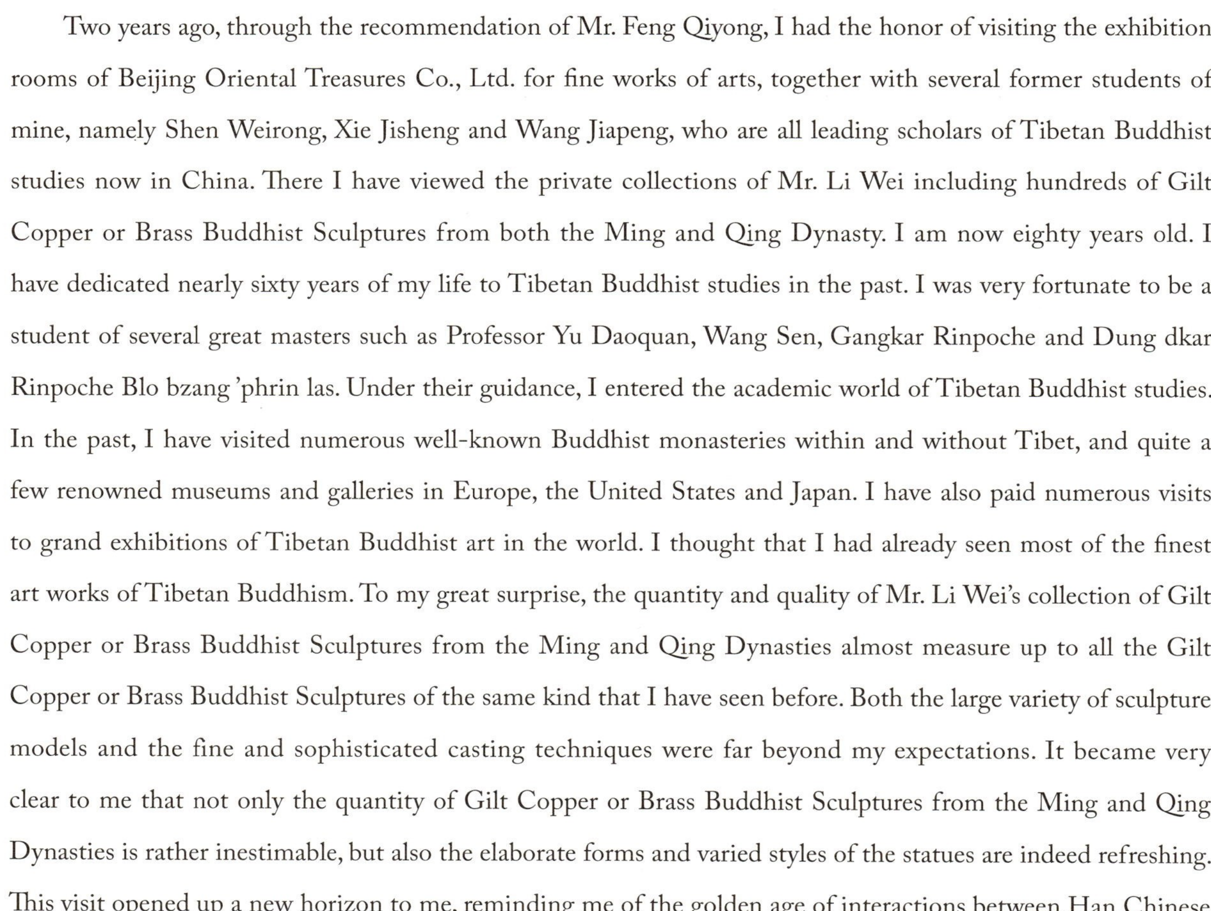

Two years ago, through the recommendation of Mr. Feng Qiyong, I had the honor of visiting the exhibition rooms of Beijing Oriental Treasures Co., Ltd. for fine works of arts, together with several former students of mine, namely Shen Weirong, Xie Jisheng and Wang Jiapeng, who are all leading scholars of Tibetan Buddhist studies now in China. There I have viewed the private collections of Mr. Li Wei including hundreds of Gilt Copper or Brass Buddhist Sculptures from both the Ming and Qing Dynasty. I am now eighty years old. I have dedicated nearly sixty years of my life to Tibetan Buddhist studies in the past. I was very fortunate to be a student of several great masters such as Professor Yu Daoquan, Wang Sen, Gangkar Rinpoche and Dung dkar Rinpoche Blo bzang 'phrin las. Under their guidance, I entered the academic world of Tibetan Buddhist studies. In the past, I have visited numerous well-known Buddhist monasteries within and without Tibet, and quite a few renowned museums and galleries in Europe, the United States and Japan. I have also paid numerous visits to grand exhibitions of Tibetan Buddhist art in the world. I thought that I had already seen most of the finest art works of Tibetan Buddhism. To my great surprise, the quantity and quality of Mr. Li Wei's collection of Gilt Copper or Brass Buddhist Sculptures from the Ming and Qing Dynasties almost measure up to all the Gilt Copper or Brass Buddhist Sculptures of the same kind that I have seen before. Both the large variety of sculpture models and the fine and sophisticated casting techniques were far beyond my expectations. It became very clear to me that not only the quantity of Gilt Copper or Brass Buddhist Sculptures from the Ming and Qing Dynasties is rather inestimable, but also the elaborate forms and varied styles of the statues are indeed refreshing. This visit opened up a new horizon to me, reminding me of the golden age of interactions between Han Chinese and Tibetan Buddhist arts. In the meantime, I deeply appreciate Mr. Li Wei's great enthusiasm and capability of preserving the Buddhist art treasures.

Starting from the end of the 1970s, I had numerous opportunities to teach and do researches at quite a few renowned academic institutions for Tibetan studies in Europe, the United States and Japan. I had engaged in many international academic events in the field of Tibetology often as one single representative of the Chinese Tibetologists. During this period, I had encountered people who, either because of ignorance or ill-intentions, denied the fact that there was close political and religious relationship between Han Chinese and Tibetans during the Ming dynasty. They claimed that the Ming Dynasty was not able to get involved in Tibetan affairs because it lacked of a crushing military force, unlike its predecessors, the Mongolians. This is evidently an arrogant fallacy attributed to their lack of basic knowledge on the history of ancient China, particularly that of the relationship between Han Chinese and Tibetans during the Ming time. As a matter of fact, the centenary rule of Mongol Yuan over Tibet had enhanced the close relationship between Tibet and China Proper. Since then, Tibet was inseparably connected with China Proper in aspects of politics, economy and culture. The administrative system established by the central government of the Mongol Yuan dynasty over Tibet remained intact even after the Yuan dynasty was overthrown and replaced by the Ming Dynasty. Only a slight change was made, namely that the three Pacification Commissions in Tibetan Area of the Yuan Dynasty were changed into three Provincial Military Commissions at the early years of the Ming Dynasty. Even though being inferior to the Yuan Dynasty in terms of military strength, the Ming Dynasty was actually far more superior to the previous dynasty in terms of religious and cultural interactions between China Proper and Tibet. Han Chinese and Tibetans used to live peacefully together under the ruling of the Ming Dynasty. There was absolutely no reason for the central government of the Ming to take military action against Tibet.

The Ming rulers adopted the "divide and rule" policy. In the history of Sino-Tibetan relations during the Ming time, there were eight well-known Dharma kings or religious kings. Countless representatives of Tibetan Buddhist schools and monasteries were invited to the imperial court to make tribute to the Ming and spread Tibetan Buddhism at the same time. Some of these representatives were conferred the tile of a Dharma king or a religious king by the emperors of the Ming. These representatives often brought gifts to the court and were bestowed lavish presents by the court in return. Among others a Gilt Copper or Brass Buddhist Sculpture was a regular item in the long list of the gifts. The Gilt Copper or Brass Buddhist Sculptures of the Ming Dynasty in Mr. Li Wei's collection, were often inscribed in Chinese with the six-character Yongle or Xuande reign marks "Da Ming Yongle nian shi" (bestowed in the years of the Yongle reign of the grand Ming dynasty) or "Da Ming Xuede nian shi" (bestowed in the years of the Xuande reign of in the grand Ming dynasty). These statues demonstrate strongly the close relation between Han Chinese and Tibetan Buddhist arts in this period. As a usual practice, lamas who came to the imperial court would bring Gilt Copper Sculptures from Tibet and offered them to the Court as tributes. In return, the emperors would bestow Gilt Copper Sculptures made under the supervision of the court in China Proper to the lamas. The exchanges of Gilt Copper or Brass Sculptures between Han Chinese and Tibetans was exactly the symbol of the close relationship between the two nationalities both politically and religiously.

For quite a long time, many oversea specialists and scholars of Buddhist studies have always focused on the connections between Indian Buddhism and Tibetan Buddhism, laying a particular emphasis on the studies of Indo-Tibetan Buddhism. Since they do not have profound knowledge on the history of the interactions between Chinese and Tibetan Buddhism, the historical link and close relation between Chinese and Tibetan Buddhism was usually ignored. Fortunately, outstanding achievements are made by Chinese scholars in the field of comparative studies of Sino-Tibetan Buddhism in recent years, and gradually the true face of the history of Sino-Tibetan Buddhist interactions is revealed. Many precious objects of Tibetan Buddhism from the Palace Museum were exhibited. Numerous Chinese texts concerning Tibetan tantric Buddhism were newly discovered and published. Especially a great number of Chinese texts and other artefacts of Chinese and Tibetan Buddhism were discovered from both the Dunhuang and Khara Khoto collections. Recent researches on these newly discovered texts and artefacts show evidently that Chinese Buddhism used to be one of the two major sources of Tibetan Buddhism, and even Chinese Ch'an Buddhism had achieved great popularity among followers of Tibetan Buddhism during the period of the first diffusion of Buddhism in Tibet, and left its imprints in the doctrines and teachings of various Tibetan Buddhist schools in the period of the second diffusion of Buddhism in Tibet, especially the rNying ma pa and the bKa' brgyud pa tradtions.

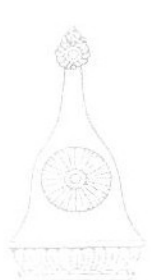

On the other hand, from the Tangut kingdom of Xia, through the Mongol Yuan, Ming and Qing dynasties as well as the Republic of China, Tibetan Buddhism surged into the Han Chinese regions and spread widely. The influences of Tibetan Buddhism were not only visible within the imperial courts but all over the country. The fact that Tibetan Buddhism had penetrated deeply into Chinese cultural and religious life could be well testified by Mr. Li Wei's collection of Gilt Copper or Brass Sculptures. We all know well that our country has suffered a severe cultural disaster during the 10-year period of the Cultural Revolution. A great number of our cultural relics were lost during that period. However, that Mr. Li Wei was still able to save and collect such a large

number of Gilt Copper or Brass Buddhist Sculpture from the Ming and Qing Dynasties all over the country shows that the original number of these sculptures was truly gigantic and that Tibetan Buddhism enjoyed a great popularity all over the country. Although I am not an art historian specialized in the studies of the Tibetan Buddhist art, I am very much impressed by the perfect combination of Chinese and Tibetan Buddhist arts which adds radiance and beauty to each other. Among these Buddhist statues, I have seen both images of Buddha and Bodhisattvas in typical Chinese Buddhist art styles, and those of terrifying and wrathful deities, which obviously originated from Tibetan Esoteric Buddhism. It illustrates the historical truth that since the time of the Tangut kingdom of Xia and the Mongol Yuan Dynasty, the spread of Tibetan tantric Buddhism in China Proper had gradually intensified, and Tibetan tantric Buddhism had been closely integrated into Chinese Buddhist traditions. Thereafter, these two Buddhist systems became inseperable. In Mr. Li Wei's collection, I saw many statues of the Great Black One, Mahākāla, in different forms. These statues remind me of the days when I was searching high and low for Mahākāla. It is well-known that Mahākāla had been worshiped as the "protecting deity of the country" by the Mongols during the Mongol Yuan dynasty and Mongols regarded Mahākāla as the omnipotent Deity of Wars. In fact, Mahākāla had been worshiped by the Tibetan Buddhists since the beginning of the Tangut kingdom of Xia. In both the Ming and Qing Dynasties, the tradition of worshiping Mahākāla never ceased either at imperial court or among ordinary people. I used to exert all my efforts to hunt for the traces of Mahākāla amidst a large sea of literary sources, and also visited many spots all over the country where the Mahākāla cult left its imprint. This time, I was really happy to once again meet an old friend/deity at Mr. Li Wei's. The popularity of the Mahākāla cult is a token of Tibetan Buddhism's spreading in China Proper.

After having seen Mr. Li Wei's collection, I was deeply impressed by all these Gilt Copper or Brass Buddhist Sculptures, which were always at the back of my mind. Shortly after, I revisited Oriental Treasure Co., Ltd. of Mr. Li Wei together with Master Tam Shek-wing and several academic peers. At this time we carefully examined and appreciated these Gilt Copper or Brass Buddhist Sculptures once again, and made profound discussions on issues such as their original years and places, technical features, the physical forms of the statues and their symbolic meanings, so that the sources and values of these statues of the Ming and Qing Dynasties will be understood in a deeper sense. From then on, I have cherished the wish that these Gilt Copper or Brass Buddhist Sculptures should be shown to a much larger audience via appropriate channels some day in the future, so that more lovers of the culture of Tibetan Buddhism can come to learn and appreciate them. I was really rejoiced and gratified at the news that Mr. Li Wei is going to cooperate with the most prestigious Chinese press Zhonghua Shuju to publish a picture collection of ninety-nine Buddhist statues which were carefully selected from his collection. It is no doubt a truly grand event in the history of Sino-Tibetan Buddhist art studies to publish a high quality picture collection of Gilt Copper and Brass Buddhist Sculptures that shows the interaction between Han Chinese and Tibetan cultures. The most authoritative book in the subject of Tibetan Gilt Copper Sculpture that I have seen abroad is *the Buddhist Sculptures in Tibet* written by a Swiss scholar Mr. Ulrich von Schroeder. I sincerely look forward to the publication of the Interaction of Chinese and Tibetan Buddhist Art – a Collection of Gilt Copper Buddhist Sculptures, which will provide notably rich and precious first-hand materials for the art historians in the area of Tibetan Gilt Copper and Brass Buddhist Sculptures, and hence establish a foundation for them to make progress in this field. Also, since the date of publishing this book coincides with the great day of the 60th anniversary of the founding of the People's Republic of China, this book is evidently a bounteous gift for this anniversary. We are living in a nation of multiple nationalities and a diversified culture that unites 56 nationalities. Regardless of Han Chinese or Tibetan nationality, we are all parts of the great nation of Zhonghua minzu, we are all Chinese people, just like it is hard for us to clearly distinct a gilt copper Buddhist statue made in the Ming and Qing dynasties from either of the two different categories, i.e., Sino-Tibetan and Tibet-Chinese style of Buddhist arts. The two nationalities, both Han Chinese and Tibetan, have long been closely and inseparably linked to each other both in terms of politics and economy and in aspects of culture and religion. The publication of the picture collection of Gilt Copper Buddhist Sculptures in the Ming and Qing dynasties will present the characteristics of Sino-Tibetan/Tibeto-Chinese Buddhist arts, and it will help us not only to review the history of the interaction and integration between Han Chinese and Tibetan Buddhism and establish the cultural and affinitive relationship between the two ethnic groups, but also to build up the common national identity and the national self esteem of the entire country as a unified Chinese nation.

I would take this opportunity to express my profound gratitude to Mr. Li Wei who contributed such an amazing work showcasing the fine art works of Sino-Tibetan Buddhism, which also bears high values for the research works in this area. Along with the publication of this book, the eminent contributions of Mr. Li Wei for the preservation of Chinese cultural heritage will be remembered by generations to come!

Wang Yao, Honorary President of the Institute of Tibetan Studies, Minzu Univesity of China

專論

漢藏佛學交流與漢藏佛教藝術研究

རྒྱ་བོད་ནང་བསྟན་ཆོས་ལུགས་བརྗེ་རེས་དང་རྒྱ་བོད་ནང་བསྟན་ཆོས་ལུགས་ཀྱི་སྒྱུ་རྩལ་ཞིབ་འཇུག

沈衛榮

李巍先生懷抱一顆熱愛祖國的赤子之心，幾十年間以一己之力，收集、珍藏了數以千計的中國古代青銅佛像。這是李巍先生在我們的民族和國家遭受文化劫難的非常時期，有膽識、有遠見地完成的一項義舉、壯舉，他爲保存漢藏佛教藝術珍品做出的艱苦卓絕的努力、他爲保護中華民族文化遺産做出的極爲特殊的貢獻，值得世人敬重、稱揚。

李巍先生收藏品中的大多數是源出於漢藏交界之甘、青安多藏區的藏傳佛教藝術作品，這些彌足珍貴的歷史文物不但見證了漢、藏兩種佛教傳統千餘年來互相交流、相互融合的歷史，而且亦爲研究漢、藏佛教藝術交相輝映的歷史提供了極其寶貴的歷史資料。爲了更好、更清楚地認識李巍先生所收藏的這批青銅佛像的價值，我們有必要對漢藏佛教交流的歷史作一番回顧，特別是對元、明、清三個時代漢藏佛教藝術交流的歷史作一番介紹。

一

印度佛教於公元一世紀經中亞傳到中國內地，復從中國傳到韓國和日本，形成漢傳佛教傳統；而藏傳佛教則是分別於公元七世紀和公元十世紀後（即藏傳佛教史上的前弘期和後弘期）先後兩次從印度、中亞和中國內地等地區傳入西藏的佛教，其後亦成爲蒙古族人民的普遍信仰。漢傳佛教和藏傳佛教既是大乘佛教的兩大宗派，也是當今佛教的兩個最重要的、並且還在繼續發展中的偉大傳統。

與十分漢化了的漢傳佛教相比，藏傳佛教與印度佛教的關聯更深，亦更加包羅萬象。正如英國著名印藏佛教學者 David Snellgrove 指出的那樣，藏傳佛教包羅了印度佛教的所有傳統，印度佛教中有的，藏傳佛教中全有，印度佛教中已經失傳了的，藏傳佛教中亦保存了下來，還得到了發展[1]。例如藏傳佛教中的密教傳統，它來源於印度，但其發展則遠遠超出了印度原有的傳統。西藏歷史上出現了一大批傑出的佛教學者，他們對佛教義理的闡釋，特別是對印度的中觀、唯識、如來藏等哲學思想的闡發有獨特的創見，他們對以公元七世紀印度佛學大師法稱爲代表的佛教因明學的繼承和發揚，以及藏傳佛教覺囊派主張的「他空見」思想等，都極大地豐富了印度佛教哲學思想。此外，藏傳佛教對印度佛教密教傳統的接受、繼承和發展，不僅使西藏的文化和社會深深地打上了被人類學家稱爲「薩滿」的烙印，而且亦使密教成爲藏傳佛教本身的一個標志性特徵。藏傳佛教中的那些極爲複雜的帶有明顯的薩滿性質的密教修行，是西藏人爲豐富世界人文精神做出的最大貢獻[2]。

由於藏傳佛教和印度佛教之間的這種緊密聯繫，長期以來人們形成了這樣的一個錯覺，以爲藏傳佛教遵循的完全是印度佛教的傳統，與十分漢化了的漢傳佛教關聯不大。特別是藏傳佛教史學傳統中對八世紀末年發生在印度上師蓮花戒和漢地禪宗和尚摩訶衍之間的一場宗教辯論，即所謂「吐蕃僧諍」之歷史的重構和解釋，更大大加深了人們的這一錯覺。按照西藏後弘期史家的說法，在八世紀末的吐蕃，漢地的禪宗佛教，特別是其推崇的頓悟思想，在吐蕃信衆中間深得人心，引起了遵循印度傳統，信奉漸悟思想的另一派佛教僧衆的反對，進而引發了激烈的衝突。爲了辨明是非，吐蕃贊普主持了一場在印度和漢地佛教大師之間進行的宗教辯論。結果來自漢地的禪師和尚摩訶衍在辯論中敗北，於是贊普宣布今後吐蕃佛教遵從印度上師蓮花戒主張的中觀漸悟說，禁止漢傳禪宗佛教繼續在吐蕃流傳。今天我們借助敦煌漢、藏文文獻和藏傳佛教前弘期遺存藏文文獻——《禪定目炬》(*bSam gtan mig sgron*)中的相關記載，不難發現西藏史學傳統中對「吐蕃僧諍」的說法基本上是一種「創造出來的傳統」，與歷史事實並不符合[3]。

漢藏兩個民族間的文化交流源遠流長，漢藏佛教之間你中有我，我中有你。首先，藏傳佛教的來源其實並不祇是印度佛教一個途徑，漢傳佛教對於藏傳佛教傳統的形成同樣有過巨大的影響和貢獻。佛教是在吐蕃贊普松贊干布時期分別通過其迎娶的尼婆羅尺尊公主和大唐文成公主兩位妃子傳入吐蕃的。文成公主入藏時將佛教的種子帶進了吐蕃，據傳現供奉於拉薩大昭寺，被藏人視爲最神聖的、稱爲「Jo bo」的釋迦牟尼佛像，就是文成公主入藏時帶進去的。而拉薩的小昭寺亦是在她主持下建造的。文成公主居藏時期，既有大唐派往印度的使臣或求法途經吐蕃的漢僧往還，亦有常住吐蕃的漢族和尚在此傳法、譯經、教授弟子。如果我們相信佛教確實是在松贊干布在位時開始傳入吐蕃，並進而在吐蕃生根、發芽的話，那麼文成公主及其隨行的漢地和尚們爲此而做出的貢獻是無論如何不應該被磨滅的。

公元八世紀下半葉既是吐蕃王國的全盛時期，也是佛教在吐蕃得到迅速發展的時期，同時它還是漢藏佛教交流的黃金時期。特別是在吐蕃占領敦煌等中國西北地區，並在中亞建立起了一個僅次於大唐帝國的强盛的吐蕃帝國時期，漢藏佛教之間的交流達到了一個後人難以企及的高度。當時曾出現過像[吴]法成（'Gos Chos grub）這樣兼通藏、漢的大譯師，他不但曾將爲數甚多的漢文佛經翻譯成了藏文，而且亦將一些佛經從藏文譯成了漢文。其中他親手翻譯有《般若波羅蜜多心經》、《諸心母陀羅尼經》、《薩婆多宗五事論》、《菩薩律儀二十頌》、《八轉聲頌》和《釋迦牟尼如來像法滅盡之記》等，經他手集成的有《大

[1] David Snellgrove, *Indo-Tibetan Buddhism: Indian Buddhists and Their Tibetan Successors*, Boston: Shambhala Publication, 2003, p.118.

[2] Geoffrey Samuel, *Civilized Shamans: Buddhism in Tibetan Societies*, Washington and London: Smithsonian Institute Press, 1993, p.8.

[3] 沈衛榮，《西藏文文獻中的和尚摩訶衍及其教法：一個創造出來的傳統》，《新史學》，卷16，第1號，臺北，2005年，頁1～50。

乘四法經論及廣釋開決記》、《六門陀羅尼經論並廣釋開決記》、《因緣心釋論開決記》、《大乘稻葉經隨聽手鏡記》和《嘆諸佛如來無染着德贊》等，還有講義録《瑜伽論手記》和《瑜伽論分門記》等[4]。法成漢譯的這些佛教文獻中有些有漢文的異譯本，有些則是僅有的漢譯本，即使是擁有多種漢文異譯本，其中還有出自鳩摩羅什和玄奘之手的《般若波羅蜜多心經》，法成的這個譯本從内容到質量依然是獨樹一幟[5]。

一個值得注意的現象是，許多屬於純粹漢傳佛教的東西，甚至包括漢傳的僞經都曾經被翻譯成藏文。例如著名漢傳僞經《首楞嚴經》，曾先後被兩次翻譯成藏文。第一次是在吐蕃王朝時期，於九世紀初吐蕃厘定譯語之前。這個譯本曾經在吐蕃及中亞地區普遍流行，敦煌出土的藏文佛教文獻中多有對這部漢傳佛經的引述，而這部經之第九、十兩品的藏文譯本今仍見於藏文大藏經中。到了清乾隆年間，此經又在乾隆皇帝和其上師章嘉活佛的主持下重新從漢文翻譯成藏、滿、蒙等多種文字[6]。此外，像唐代義净翻譯的《金光明最勝王經》曾於吐蕃王朝期間被多次翻譯成藏文。還有像《佛説盂蘭盆經》這樣深受漢傳佛教徒喜愛、帶有明顯漢傳佛教印記的漢文佛經亦被翻譯成了藏文。類似的例子還有《七曜經》[7]。尤其值得稱道的是，幾乎所有重要的早期漢傳禪宗經典都曾被譯成藏文。從敦煌出土的古藏文文獻中，我們見到了幾乎所有重要的早期禪宗文獻的藏文譯本，例如菩提達磨的《二入四行論》以及《七祖法寶記》（《歷代法寶記》）、《頓悟大乘正理決》、《楞伽師資記》、《頓悟真宗金剛般若修行達彼岸法門要決》等等。由此可見，早期漢傳禪宗佛教確實已經在藏傳佛教中得到很廣泛的傳播，並留下了很深的影響[8]。不幸的是，隨着八世紀末「吐蕃僧諍」的發生、九世紀中朗達磨的滅佛，以及後弘期藏族史家對「吐蕃僧諍」這一事件之歷史傳統的建構，漢藏佛教之間的交流趨於停頓，儘管「和尚」的影子事實上從没有在藏傳佛教中消失。藏文史著中提到，和尚離開吐蕃時曾像菩提達磨當年離開中原時一樣有意留下了一隻鞋子，預示他所傳播的禪法雖然遭受磨難，但日後一定將在吐蕃廣爲弘揚。所以，不管是在寧瑪派的大圓滿法，還是在噶舉派的大手印法中，漢地禪宗教法的影響從没有被徹底排除。

與漢傳禪宗佛教在吐蕃傳播的歷史撲朔迷離的景象相反，晚近以來隨着對敦煌藏文佛教文獻、黑水城出土漢譯藏傳佛教文獻和其他西夏、元代漢譯藏傳密教文獻的發掘和研究的不斷深入，藏傳佛教於漢地傳播的歷史越來越清晰地爲人們所了解。傳統上人們將吐蕃末代贊普朗達磨滅佛後的一個多世紀稱爲西藏歷史上的「黑暗時期」，然晚近却有西方佛學家將它稱之爲「西藏的文藝復興」時期，其最主要的原因在於組成藏傳佛教之精華及其最典型特徵的密教傳統實際上就是在這段時間内形成的[9]。藏傳佛教後弘期的興起事實上也並不衹是通過「上路弘傳」和「下路弘傳」兩個途徑，即從西部的納里速和東部的朵思麻兩個地區開始的復興。吐蕃占領下的中亞地區，特别是以敦煌爲中心的中國西北地區，在藏傳佛教後弘期的歷史上曾經扮演過極爲重要的角色。在吐蕃的軍事統治被推翻以後，吐蕃佛教文化的影響並没有隨之消失，吐蕃佛僧及其印度上師在這些地區的活動並没有受到吐蕃本土遭受滅佛之劫難的影響，因此藏傳佛教，特别是其側重的密教傳統，於此得到了進一步的傳播和發展[10]。這就是爲何藏傳密教的文獻和藝術品在敦煌早期洞窟中就已經出現的原因所在[11]。

二

十一世紀初，藏傳密教開始在居住於中央歐亞地區的西夏、回鶻和漢人中間傳播，從德藏吐魯番出土的回鶻文佛教文獻和俄藏黑水城出土漢、西夏文佛教文獻中透露出的信息來看，藏傳密教在高昌回鶻王國和西夏王朝内都曾有較大規模的傳播，其流行程度或當超過漢傳佛教。像早先從未曾在漢地流傳的無上瑜伽密本尊喜金剛、勝樂以及大黑天、金剛亥母等本尊禪定，以及像藏傳佛教噶舉派所傳的拙火、中陰、夢幻身等屬於「那若六法」（*Na ro chos drug*）的瑜伽修法和薩思迦派所傳的深道密法「道果」法等，都已經開始在回鶻、西夏及其統治下的漢人中間流傳。這一段歷史長時間被淹没在歷史的迷霧之中，直到晚近我們有機會親眼目睹一個世紀以前被俄國殖民主義者劫掠去的、現藏於俄羅斯科學院東方研究所聖彼得堡分所的黑水城出土西夏、漢文佛教文書，才使得重構十一至十四世紀藏傳佛教於西域和漢地傳播的歷史成爲可能[12]。最近，寧夏地區又陸續出土了大量屬於西夏時代的西夏文、漢文佛教文書，如寧夏考古文物研究所先後在賀蘭山區的拜寺溝方塔和山嘴溝佛教寺院遺址中，發現了不少藏傳密教文獻的西夏文和漢文譯本，其中有西夏文《吉祥遍至口和本續》（即著名的《三菩怛本續》）和漢譯《吉祥勝樂等虚空本續》等最著名的藏傳密教無上瑜伽部續典，還有不少修習密教本尊和相關的各類儀軌文書[13]。從這些文獻和相關的佛教遺址來看，在蒙古興起以前，藏傳密教早已在以中國西北的甘、青、安多和蒙古等地爲主的所謂中央歐亞地區普遍流傳。這一地區在藏傳佛教後弘期的發展史上無疑占有一個重大的位置。

藏傳佛教在回鶻和西夏人中間的普遍流傳爲繼其而起在中央歐亞史上寫下輝煌篇章的世界征服者——蒙古人信仰藏傳佛教打下了深厚的基礎[14]。有元一代，藏傳密教更在蒙古統治者中間深入人心，世界征服者的精神世界顯然没有被受其統治的漢族百姓信奉的孔孟之道所占領，却被來自西藏的喇嘛所傳秘密法所征服，薩思迦款氏家族的上師世襲元朝帝師之高位，與元封「大成至聖文宣王」孔老夫子一樣享受各省設廟祭祀的待遇。藏傳佛教更進一步從甘青地區蔓延，深入到中原腹地，南到杭州、福建等地，都留下了許多元代藏傳佛教遺址。蒙古皇帝曾在宫廷内組織修習以喜金剛法爲主要内容的所謂「秘密大喜樂禪定」，據稱參加修習的既有皇室貴胄，亦有朝廷大臣。他們對修習密法是如此地熱衷，以至於完全忘記了他們肩負的治理朝政的職責，使得堂堂大元竟然不足百年而亡。這種修習藏傳密法的習俗還曾蔓延到宫廷之外的尋常百姓之家，雖然時常遭人詬病但業已成爲一時之尚。元廷邀請了大量西藏高僧來中原傳法，史載當時藏族喇嘛絡繹道途，以致官設驛道傳舍容納不下。除了大量的薩

[4] 上山大峻，《敦煌佛教の研究》，京都：法藏館，1990年，頁170～246。

[5] 沈衛榮，《漢、藏譯〈心經〉對勘》，談錫永、邵頌雄等著譯，《心經内義與究竟義》，臺北：全佛，2005年，頁273～321。

[6] 沈衛榮，《藏譯首楞嚴經對勘導論》，《元史及民族與邊疆研究集刊》，第十八集，上海：上海古籍出版社，2006年，頁81～89。

[7] Matthew Kapstein, "The Tibetan Yulanpen jing佛说盂蘭盆经", *Contributions to the Cultural History of Early Tibet*, edited by Matthew T.Kapstein and Brandon Dotson, Leiden, Boston: Brill, 2007, pp. 211～238; Takashi Matsukawa, "Some Uighur Elements surviving in the Mongolian Buddhist Sūtra of the Great Bear", *Turfan Revisited The First Century of Research into the Arts and Culture of the Silk Road*, Edited by Desmond Durkin-Meisterernst etc., Berlin: Dietrich Reimer Verlag, 2004, pp.203～207.

[8] 參見木村隆德，《敦煌語禪文獻目録初稿》，《東京大學文化交流研究施設研究紀要》第4號，1980年，頁93～129; Jeffrey L. Broughton, *The Bodhidharma Anthology, The Earliest Records of Zen*, Berkeley: University of California Press, 1999。

[9] Ronald M. Davidson, *Tibetan Renaissance: Tantric Buddhism in the Rebirth of Tibetan Culture*, New York: Columbia University Press, 2005.

[10] 沈衛榮，《重構十一至十四世紀西域佛教史》，《歷史研究》，北京，2006年第5期，頁23～34。

[11] 田中公明，《敦煌密教と美術》，京都：法藏館，2000年。

[12] 沈衛榮，《序説有關西夏、元朝所傳藏傳密法之漢文文獻——以黑水城所見漢譯藏傳佛教儀軌文書爲中心》，《歐亞學刊》，第7期，北京，2006年。

[13] 寧夏文物考古所，《拜寺溝西夏方塔》，北京：文物出版社，2005年；寧夏文物考古所，《山嘴溝西夏石窟》，北京：文物出版社，2007年。

思迦派喇嘛以外，其他許多各大小教派的著名高僧亦都曾受到元廷的邀請。例如，噶瑪噶舉派的第三、第四世活佛就都曾應邀來到元大都傳法，而當時名重一時的沙魯派高僧卜思端輦真竺（Zhva lu pa Bu ston Rin chen grub，一二九〇～一三六四）和覺囊派掌門朵波巴攝囉監藏（Dol po pa Shes rab rgyal mtshan，一二九二～一三六一）同樣曾受到元廷的邀請，雖然他們並沒有應邀來到中原傳法[15]。而漢人中尊貴如宋代末帝趙顯者，竟然被蒙古大汗送到了後藏的薩思迦寺，孤影青燈苦讀數十年，成了一名能用藏文著書立説的藏傳佛教大師[16]。而也只有在元朝這樣的大一統時代，才能够出現漢、藏、蒙、畏兀兒等各族高僧通力合作，勘同漢、藏法寶（佛經），編撰《至元法寶勘同總録》這樣史無前例的大工程[17]。

出於對蒙古大汗重西藏喇嘛而輕漢地儒士的不滿，以及對藏傳佛教秘密修法的無知，元朝以來的漢族士人習慣於妖魔化或者情色化西藏喇嘛和藏傳佛教。他們常常將藏傳密教貶損爲上不了大雅之堂的方技、巫術和房中術。令人不可思議的是，長期以來藏傳密法雖曾遭人肆意詬病，但却同樣令人着迷，它在漢人信衆中間流傳之廣遠遠超出了我們的想象。在據稱是從元朝宮廷中流傳出去、誤傳爲元朝首任帝師八思巴編集的漢譯藏傳密教文獻集《大乘要道密集》中，一共收録了以薩思迦派所傳「道果法」爲主的八十三篇儀軌文書。其中一大部分是元代翻譯的作品，但亦有相當一部分是西夏時代翻譯的。作爲歷代漢人修習藏傳密法所依據的主要法本，一直到上個世紀六十年代，《大乘要道密集》受到了漢地藏傳佛教徒的普遍重視[18]。近年來更是一次次地重印。顯而易見的是，收録入《大乘要道密集》中的那些藏傳密教文獻，還衹是自西夏至元朝出現的漢譯藏傳密教文獻中的一小部分而已。晚近，我們在中國國家圖書館和臺灣故宮博物院藏善本文獻中都發現了不少西夏和蒙元時代翻譯，並且在明、清兩代宮廷中繼續流傳的漢譯藏傳密教文獻。例如被視爲臺灣故宮博物院鎮院之寶的題爲《吉祥喜金剛集輪甘露泉》和《如來頂髻尊勝佛母現證儀》兩種藏傳佛教長篇儀軌，分別由「持咒沙門莎南屹啰集譯」和「大元帝師發[八]思巴述，持咒沙門莎南屹囉譯」，顯然與見於《大乘要道密集》中的元譯藏傳密教文獻屬同一類型[19]。這兩部儀軌，從數量上看其長度已遠遠超過了見於《大乘要道密集》中的八思巴帝師所造四部儀軌的總和。它們的發現充分表明《大乘要道密集》中的八十三種儀軌並不是當時翻譯成漢文的藏傳密教儀軌的全部。而在北京國家圖書館古籍善本書目中，我們又發現了多種西夏、元代漢譯藏傳密教儀軌，它們是：一、《端必瓦成就同生要一卷》；二、《因得囉菩提手印道要一卷》；三、《大手印無字要一卷》；四、《密哩斡巴上師道果卷第十》；五、《喜金剛中圍内自受灌頂儀一卷》；六、《新譯吉祥飲血壬集輪無比修習母一切中最勝上樂集本續顯釋記一卷》；七、《吉祥喜金剛本續王後分注疏不分卷》；八、《修習法門卷》[20]。以上所列八種儀軌中有好幾種同樣標明爲「元釋發[八]思巴集，元釋莎南屹囉譯」，明顯與見於《大乘要道密集》中的元譯藏傳密教儀軌屬於同一種類型。而其中的《密哩斡巴上師道果卷第十》與見於《大乘要道密集》中的同名儀軌上卷完全一致，這再次説明元代漢譯藏傳密教儀軌確實遠不止見於《大乘要道密集》的那些，僅《密哩斡巴上師道果卷》就至少曾刊印過十卷，而《大乘要道密集》中僅保存了其中的兩卷。這些文書既有明抄本亦有清抄本，説明它們於元、明、清三代的宮廷，乃至民間的流傳可謂不絶如縷[21]。值得一提的是，在北京故宮博物院内曾發現一部明代寫經《各佛施食好事經》（*gTor ma'i cho ga la sogs bzhusho, gTor ma byin rlabs*），該經藏漢文對音，泥金寫本，護經封版爲象牙所製，雕刻着精美的佛像，並刻有清晰的明成化款識。其主要內容即是施食供養諸密宗主尊及護法神，如本尊大持金剛上師、喜佛、上樂輪、啞蠻答葛、大輪金剛、多聞天王、六臂護法、二臂護法、四臂護法、葛剌嚕巴、一切空行等。此外還有向其他各神祇，如根本上師、一切護神、一切居士波羅門天仙、多聞天王咎巴剌擁財佛母、南瞻部洲一切土主並當方地祇等的施食儀軌[22]。這部施食儀軌或亦當與在臺灣故宫博物院內發現的兩部藏傳佛教儀軌屬於同類的作品，譯成於元朝，而於明初重刻。相信這類作品今後還將繼續有所發現。

三

西藏喇嘛（西番僧）因在元末宫廷中傳播「秘密大喜樂法」而聲名狼藉，甚至被認爲是導致元朝驟亡的罪魁禍首。取元而代之的明朝皇帝們曾口口聲聲説要引此爲前車之鑒，可他們説的是一套，做的却又是另外一套。他們不但没有將番僧視爲洪水猛獸，拒其於千里之外，相反却開門招納，來者不拒，明代入朝和於內地活動的西藏喇嘛在數量上遠甚於前朝。《明史》中説：「初，太祖招徠番僧，本藉以化愚俗，弭邊患，授國師、大國師者不過四五人。至成祖兼崇其教，自闡化等五王及二法王外，授西天佛子者二，灌頂大國師者九，灌頂國師者十有八，其他禪師、僧官不可悉數。其徒交錯於道，外擾郵傳，內耗大官，公私騷然，帝不恤也。然至者猶即遣還。乃宣宗時則久留京師，耗費益甚。」[23]實際的情形恐怕有過之而無不及。

與元朝的蒙古大汗們一樣，明代皇帝多半對藏傳密教情有獨鍾，其中又以明成祖永樂皇帝最爲突出。明封八大教王，即大寶、大乘、大慈三大法王和闡化、闡教、輔教、贊善、護教等五位教王，其中除了大慈法王是宣德年間授封的以外，其餘七位教王都受封於永樂年間（一四〇三～一四二四）。永樂皇帝曾召請五世哈立麻活佛大寶法王在南京爲其父母舉辦了盛况空前的超薦大法會[24]，而且還主持刻印了第一部藏文「甘珠爾」經[25]。永樂皇帝對藏傳佛教的熱衷常被人解釋爲是出於政治利用這一目的，而從《清涼山志》中保存有三通明成祖致繼大寶法王之後來京朝貢，後居五臺山的另一位著名番僧大慈法王釋迦也失的詔書中，我們或可以看出他對大慈法王的關心實際上超出了一般皇帝對於來華入朝之遠夷的熱情，其中一定有個人信仰的因素在起作用[26]。

由元入明，宫廷內修習藏傳密教的傳統顯然没有中斷。雖然迄今爲止我們尚未發現有明代新譯藏傳密教文獻傳世，但明以前翻譯的那些密教文獻顯然繼續在明代得到重視和利用。前述現藏於臺北故宫博物院的《吉祥喜金剛集輪甘露泉》和《如來頂

[14] 沈衛榮，《論蒙古信仰藏傳佛教的西夏背景》，《西域歷史語言研究集刊》，北京：科學出版社，2007年，頁273～286。

[15] David S.Ruegg, *The Life of Bu ston Rin chen grub*, Rome, 1966; Ngag dbang blo gros grags pa. *Jo nang chos 'byung zla ba'i sgron me*, Beijing: Krung go bod kyi shes rig dpe skrun khang, 1992, p. 28.

[16] 馬麗華，《風化成典——西藏文史故事十五講》，北京：中國藏學出版社，2009年。

[17] 黄明信，《漢藏大藏經目録異同研究——〈至元法寶勘同總録〉及其藏譯本箋證》，北京：中國藏學出版社，2003年。

[18] 沈衛榮，《〈大乘要道密集〉與西夏、元朝所傳藏傳密法——〈大乘要道密集〉系列研究導論》，《中華佛學學報》，No. 20，臺北：中華佛學研究所，2007年；Beckwith, Christopher, "A Hitherto Unnoticed Yuan-Period Collection Attributed to 'Phags pa", *Tibetan and Buddhist Studies commemorating the 200th Anniversary of the Birth of Alexander Csoma de Crös*, edited by Louis Ligeti, I. Budapest: Akadémiai Kiadó, 1984, pp. 9～16.

[19] 臺灣國立故宫博物院，《佛經附圖：藏漢藝術小品》(*Convergence of Radiance: Tibeto-Chinese Buddhist Scripture Illustrations from the Collection of the National Palace Museum*，臺北，2003年。

[20] 《北京圖書館古籍善本書目》，北京：書目文獻出版社，1987年，頁1604、1620。

[21] 國家圖書館所藏八種藏傳密教文獻中的前三種，即《端必瓦成就同生要一卷》、《因得啰菩提手印道要一卷》和《大手印無字要一卷》，源出於清代江蘇常熟著名藏書樓——述古堂，爲著名藏書家錢曾所藏。而錢曾則得之於其叔父錢謙益所藏，據傳錢謙益和柳如是曾合修藏傳密法，並將它們作爲修法的秘本。參見陳寅恪，《柳如是别傳》，北京：生活·讀書·新知三聯書店，2001年，頁811。[清]錢曾著，管庭芬、章鈺校證，《讀書敏求記校證》，上海：上海古籍出版社，2007年，頁340。

髻尊勝佛母現證儀》這兩部儀軌均爲明「正統四年正月十五日」御製寫印，製作十分精良，至今保存完好。這說明明初的皇帝並没有因爲番僧肇禍導致元朝失國而摒弃藏傳佛教，相反依然重視藏傳密教儀軌的修習。明朝宮廷內作藏傳佛事已司空見慣，當時宮內有「番經廠，習念西方番唄經咒。宮中英華殿所供西番佛像，皆陳設近侍，司其香火。其隆德殿、欽安殿香火，亦各有司也。凡做好事，則懸挂旛榜。惟此廠仍立監齋神於門傍。本廠內官皆戴番僧帽，穿紅袍，黄領黄護腰，一永日或三晝夜圓滿。萬曆時（一五七三~一六一九），每遇八月中旬神廟萬壽聖節，番經廠雖在英華殿，然地方狹小，須於隆德殿大門之內跳步叱。而執經頌念梵唄者十餘人，妝韋馱像，合掌捧杵，向北立者一人，御馬監等衙門捧活牛黑犬圍侍者十餘人。而學番經、跳步叱者數十人，各戴方頂笠，穿五色大袖袍，身披瓔珞。一人在前吹大法螺，一人在後執大鑼，餘皆左持有柄圓鼓，右執彎槌，齊擊之。緩急疏密，各有節奏。按五色方位，魚貫而進，視五色傘蓋下誦經者以進退若舞焉。跳三四個時辰方畢。」[27]

明成化以後，藏傳佛教在漢地的影響越來越大，北京僅大慈恩、大能仁、大隆善護國三座寺院內就有七位法王，其中大慈恩寺內就有法王三位，加上西天佛子、灌頂大國師、國師等職四百三十七人及喇嘛人等共七百八十九人。據統計，上述三座寺院內共有西藏喇嘛上千人，而當時京內與西藏喇嘛有關的寺院有二十餘座之多。而從烏思藏來京城朝貢的喇嘛則更是絡繹不絕，致使朝廷賞賜不貲，而後來者又不可量。按慣例，烏思藏番王進貢定期三年一次，定數僧人不過一百五十人。但西藏受封爲法王者常常違反成例，連續差僧人四五百人，甚至一千五百餘人進京入朝。與元朝一樣，西藏喇嘛在明代宮廷中十分活躍，他們常被邀請入大內誦經，習念番唄經咒，設壇作慶贊事，跳步叱舞。藏傳佛像亦充斥各大寺院，例如曾經盛極一時的大慈恩寺於世宗滅佛時竟被毀於一旦，寺內歡喜佛等所謂「夷鬼淫像」先遭毁弃。後來整座寺院「詔所司毁之，驅置番僧於他所」。當時宮廷「禁內舊有大善佛殿，中有金銀佛像，並金銀函貯佛骨佛牙等物。世宗欲撤其殿建皇太后宮，命侯郭勛、大學士李時、尚書夏言入視基址。言請勅有司以佛骨瘞之中野，以杜愚惑。世宗曰：朕思此物，智者曰邪穢，必不欲觀，愚者以爲奇異，必欲尊奉。今雖埋之，將來豈無竊發？乃燔之於通衢，毁金銀佛像凡一百六十九座，頭牙骨凡萬三千餘斤」[28]。可見，明代流傳的金銀佛像的數量是相當巨大的。

上行下效，宮廷中對藏傳密教的熱衷顯然也影響到民間，明代普通百姓信仰藏傳佛教的風氣當亦很盛行。來自西藏的活佛多被人神化，遭人追捧，其神通被吹得神乎其神，連冒牌的喇嘛都很受歡迎，史載：「有番僧，短髮，衣虎皮，自稱西天活佛弟子，京城男女拜禮者盈衢。」[29]因信仰藏傳密教的人數衆多，使得販賣藏傳佛教法寶、法器成爲一項十分盈利的買賣，據明野史《典故紀聞》的記載，當時「京城外有軍民葉玘、靳鸞等發人墓，取髑髏及頂骨以爲葛巴剌碗並數珠，假以爲西番所産，乘時市利，愚民競趨之，所發墓甚衆」[30]。元末流行的「秘密大喜樂禪定」修法看起來在明代並没有完全消除，民間修這種秘密法者，恐怕也不祇是個別的現象，其情形或與元朝基本類似。例如《留青日札》中記載，明時「有淫婦潑妻又拜僧道爲師爲父，自稱曰弟子，晝夜奸宿淫樂。其丈夫子孫亦有奉佛入伙，不以爲耻。大家婦女雖不出家，而持齋把素，袖藏念珠，口誦佛號，裝供神像，儼然寺院。婦人無子，誘云某僧能干，可度一佛種。如磨臍過氣之法，即元之所謂大布施，以身布施之流也，可勝誅邪！亦有引誘少年師尼，與丈夫淫樂者，誠所謂歡喜佛矣」[31]。

與藏傳佛教於民間廣泛流傳的事實相應，明代的藏傳佛像，如「歡喜佛像」等，同樣不僅成批地出現於宮廷，而且亦開始流向民間。《萬曆野獲編》中有記載說：「予見内廷有歡喜佛，云自外國進者，又有云故元所遺者。兩佛各瓔珞嚴妝，互相抱持，兩根湊合，有機可動，凡見數處。大璫云：每帝王大婚，時必先導入此殿，禮拜畢，令撫揣隱處，默會交接之法，然後行合巹，蓋慮睿稟之純樸也。今外間市骨董人，亦閑有之，製作精巧，價亦不貲，但比内廷殊小耳。京師敕建諸寺，亦有自内賜出此佛者，僧多不肯輕示人。此外有琢玉者，多舊制。有綉織者，新舊俱有之。閩人以象牙雕成，紅潤如生，幾遍天下。」[32]於明末清初江南的藝術市場上，從宮廷内府傳出的鍍金烏思藏佛像亦已成爲書畫骨董收藏家們所注意的目標[33]。由此看來，明代金銅佛像數量大、流通廣，本是由來已久的事情。

值得一提的是，明代甘、青藏族地區與中央的關係日益緊密，成爲藏傳佛教東向於内地傳播的根據地。明封八大法王中有兩位來自烏思藏以外的朵甘思地區，一個是安多靈藏的贊善王，另一位是康區館覺的護教王，而身爲新興格魯派教主宗喀巴大師弟子的大慈法王釋迦也失也在甘青地區有極大的影響。在應邀來朝之前，釋迦也失原本在烏思藏地區默默無聞，然而他代師出使的朝貢之旅却完全改變了他的命運。他不但憑借其明封大慈法王這一響當當的名頭的影響和在朝廷所得賞賜等賦予的强大的經濟力量，於拉薩建立起了格魯派的第二座大寺院——色拉寺，而且還在北京經營了當時最重要的藏傳佛教寺院——大慈恩寺。這座寺院往後一直由其弟子經營，成爲藏傳佛僧和藏傳佛教於北京發展的一個重要據點。此外，大慈法王的弟子還在安多的河州建立和經營一座藏傳佛寺——弘化寺，將格魯派的影響擴展到了安多地區，並使之成爲該地區最重要的一個政治、宗教乃至軍事中心[34]。

四

清朝與西藏地方的政治、經濟和軍事關係較明代更加緊密，藏傳佛教在清代中國的傳播也更加廣泛、深入，它在滿、漢、蒙古等民族中都有廣泛的信衆，更成爲蒙古民族的普遍信仰。早在滿清問鼎中原以前，滿人已開始接觸和修習藏傳佛教。大家知道，滿人本來信仰的是通靈、通天的薩滿、巫師，但清代薩滿巫師常常將喇嘛視爲同類。起先，薩滿教士們常從藏傳佛教中吸

[22] 王家鵬，《明成化藏漢對音寫經淺探》，《故宮博物院院刊》，1987年第4期。

[23] 《明史》卷三三一《西域傳》三。

[24] 参見商傳，《永樂皇帝》，北京：北京出版社，1989年，頁234～239；Patricia Berger, "Miracles in Nanjing: An Imperial Record of the Fifth Karmapa's Visit to the Chinese Capital", *Cultural Intersections on Later Chinese Buddhism*, edited by Marsha Weidner, Honolulu: University of Hawai'i Press, 2001, pp. 145～169.

[25] Jonathan A. Silk, "Notes on the History of the Yongle Kanjur", *Suhrllekhāḥ: Festgabe für Helmut Eimer*, hrsg. von Michael Hahn, Jens-Uwe Hartmann and Roland Steiner, Swisttal-Odendorf: Indica-et-Tibetica-Verl., 1996, pp. 153～200.

[26] 釋鎮澄原纂，釋印光重修，《清涼山志》，中國名山勝迹志叢刊，王雲龍主编，臺北：文海出版社，卷5，頁211～212。

[27] 劉若愚，《酌中志》，北京：北京古籍出版社，1994年，卷16，頁118～119。

[28] 《典故紀聞》卷十七，頁310；相同的記載亦見於《明實録》七九，《世宗實録》卷一八七，葉五（頁3957）；《留青日札》卷二七，佛牙，頁510；《萬曆野獲编》，卷4，廢佛氏，頁916。

[29] 《明實録》三七，《英宗實録》卷二九九，葉二（頁6350）。

[30] 《典故紀聞》卷15，頁278～279。

[31] 《留青日札》卷27，念佛婆，頁511。

[32] 《萬曆野獲编》卷27，頁659。

[33] 参見井上充幸，《徽州商人と明末清初の藝術市——其貞〈書畫記〉を中心に》，《史林》八十七卷四號，2004年7月，頁42，注5。

[34] 参見Otosaka Tomoko乙阪智子，"A Study of Hong-hua-si Temple regarding the relationship between the dGe lugs-pa and the Ming dynasty", *Memoirs of the*

收養分，甚至將喇嘛們時時念誦的「六字真言」作爲他們自己行法時所用的咒語，並將藏傳佛教密法中的一些儀軌整合到薩滿教的儀軌之中。後來，隨着藏傳佛教的影響力越來越大，薩滿們開始感受到自身的權威受到藏傳佛教喇嘛們的威脅，於是便將喇嘛們當作自己的競争對手，不斷向他們挑戰，要與喇嘛們比試身手，一決高下，以便從喇嘛手中奪回原來屬於他們的信衆。但藏傳佛教在滿人中間的影響顯然已經不可挽回。

早在清朝初年，滿人對摩訶葛剌，即大黑天神的崇拜就已經相當普遍，這顯然是繼承了蒙古人留下的傳統。清太宗皇太極曾在盛京建蓮花浄土實勝寺（俗稱黃寺或皇寺），專門奉祀摩訶葛剌神。實勝寺內供奉的主尊神像據説就是元世祖忽必烈時八思巴帝師用千金於五臺山鑄成的蒙古舊物，可見滿人信仰藏傳佛教與蒙古人對他們的影響有很大的關聯[35]。已與蒙古和碩特部親王固始汗結成了政治同盟的五世達賴喇嘛，也在清入主中原以前就曾派人往瀋陽與清太宗皇太極取得聯繫。一六四二年，五世達賴又親往北京入朝，受到順治皇帝的隆重歡迎，被受封爲「西天大善自在佛所領天下釋教普通瓦赤喇怛喇達賴喇嘛」，擔當起了天下釋教領袖的職責[36]。清代前期的皇帝，特別是康熙和乾隆皇帝等，都與藏傳佛教有很深的淵源，都曾拜章嘉呼圖克圖爲師，熱情地支持藏傳佛教於內地的傳播，主持過漢、藏、滿、蒙佛經的翻譯和刻印工程。清代藏傳佛教的盛行，與清朝皇帝對藏傳佛教的推崇有很大的關係[37]。

號稱「十全老人」的乾隆皇帝晚年儘管曾經在其著名的《喇嘛説》一文中，公開地將他對藏傳佛教的熱情支持歸結爲統治西藏、蒙古的便宜措施，還用相當激烈的言辭對藏傳佛教所奉行的活佛轉世制度冷嘲熱諷。但他在《喇嘛説》中所説的那些冠冕堂皇的言辭並不見得一定是他發自內心的真心話，而多少有點像是他爲其過分信仰藏傳佛教之行爲作辯護的政治説辭，像是他爲樹立和維護自己作爲一位漢文化傳統中的聖武皇帝的光輝形象而使出的善巧方便。相同的例子也發生在康熙的第十七子果親王允禮身上。允禮曾經寫下過名喚《七筆勾》的打油詩，從漢族儒家文化的視角出發，評判和貶損西藏和藏傳佛教文化，用嘲諷、挖苦的筆調將釋教風流一筆筆地勾畫了去。讓人吃驚的是，允禮原本却是一位精通藏傳佛學，特別是寧瑪派教法的藏傳佛教徒，他不但收藏了大量藏文和蒙文的藏傳佛教經典，而且自己亦能直接用藏文著作，闡發藏傳佛教密意[38]。受個人身份的限制，他們在對待藏傳佛教的態度上明顯地言行不一。

乾隆無疑曾是一位虔誠的藏傳佛教徒。他被藏族僧衆捧爲文殊菩薩轉世，自己亦以菩薩自居。他不但專寵三世章嘉呼圖克圖，尊其爲國師，對他言聽計從，而且也十分優禮六世班禪喇嘛，竟然欽命在熱河（承德）和北京香山，分別建造了以班禪祖廟扎什倫布寺爲模樣的須彌福壽廟和宗境大昭廟，將它們作爲班禪的行宮[39]。爲了便於他自己隨時修習藏傳密法，乾隆皇帝還在宮內建造了多座藏式佛殿作爲他的私人佛堂，紫禁城寧壽宮內的梵華樓就是其中的一座[40]。更加難能可貴的是，乾隆皇帝對藏傳佛教的興趣不僅僅衹是密宗修法，他也非常推崇十分重視佛教戒律和義理的黃教，即宗喀巴創立的格魯派。他還曾讓章嘉活佛組織譯師，將《西藏文大藏經》中闕譯的著名的漢傳佛教疑僞經《首楞嚴經》譯成藏、蒙、滿等多種文字，用心於藏傳佛教的發展及其與漢傳佛教的溝通[41]。若論對藏傳佛教義理了解之深刻，中國歷代皇帝中恐無出乾隆之右者。

當然，清人對藏傳佛教的信仰同樣亦離不開密宗修習，他們所修習的密宗修法不少直接繼承自蒙古人。與此相應，喇嘛的神通也常爲清人所津津樂道。清代來華的高麗燕行客朴趾源在他的《熱河日記》中，記録下了不少他從漢族士人那裏道聽途説來的神話故事，如説活佛有神通法術，能洞見人之臟腑，具照見忠奸禍福的五色鏡等。元朝時因發掘宋皇陵寢而臭名昭著、並遭漢族士人痛恨的河西僧楊璉真伽，到了清代竟亦已轉世爲神通廣大的活佛，説其「有秘術有開山寶劍，念咒一擊，雖南山石椁，下錮三泉，無不立開，金凫玉魚，托地自跳，珠襦玉匣，狼藉開剥，甚至懸尸瀝汞，批頰探珠」[42]。極爲有趣的是，乾隆皇帝本人亦因信奉藏傳佛教而被描繪成一個神通廣大的術士。《清稗類鈔》中記載了這樣的一個故事：「高宗（乾隆帝）訓政稱上皇。一日早朝已罷，傳召和珅入對。珅至，則上皇南面坐，仁宗（嘉慶帝）西向坐一小杌。珅跪良久，上皇閉目若熟寐然，口中喃喃有所語。久之忽啓目曰：『其人姓名爲何？』珅應聲對曰：『高天德、苟文明。』上復閉目，誦不輟。移時揮出，不更問。仁宗大愕。越翌日，密詔珅問曰：『汝前日召對，上皇云何？汝所對作何解？』珅曰：『上皇所誦爲西域秘密咒。誦之，則所惡之人，雖在千里外，亦當無疾而死，或有奇禍。奴才聞上皇持此咒，知所欲咒者必爲教匪悍酋，故以此二人名對也。』」[43]

清代民間修藏傳密法者當也不乏其人，大名鼎鼎的遺老錢謙益或也有可能曾和其寵妾柳如是合修過藏傳密法，這個事實是陳寅恪先生尋繹、索隱而揭示出來的。在錢謙益侄子錢曾的藏書樓——述古堂中藏有《端必瓦成就同生要一卷》、《因得囉菩提手印道要一卷》和《大手印無字要一卷》三種被歸入「攝生類」的秘籍。錢曾在《讀書敏求記》中注解説：「此爲庚申帝演媟兒法。張光弼《輦下曲》『守内番僧日念吽，御厨酒肉按時供。組鈴扇鼓諸天樂，知在龍宫第幾重？』『描寫掖庭秘戲，與是書所云』『長緩提稱吽字，以之爲大手印要』殆可互相證明。凡偈頌文句，悉揣摩天竺古先生之話言，閲之不禁笑來。其紙是搗麻所成，光潤炫目。裝潢乃元朝内府名手匠，今無能之者，亦一奇物也。」[44]

陳寅恪先生認爲，「遵王[錢曾]所藏此種由天竺房中術轉譯之書，當是從牧齋處得來。所附諸語，應出牧齋之手，遵王未必若是淹博。牧齋平生佛教著述中，有《楞嚴經蒙鈔》之巨制。——故牧齋雖著此書，原與其密宗信仰無關。但牧齋好蓄異書，兼通元代故實，既藏有演揲兒法多種，其與河東君作『洞房清夜秋燈裏，共簡莊周説劍篇』之事，亦非絶不可能。果爾，則牧齋『因愛生病』之語，殆有言外之意。」[45]事實上，述古堂所藏這三部秘籍並非什麼「天竺房中術轉譯之書」，而是藏傳

Research Department of the Toyo Bunko (the Oriental Library), No.52, Tokyo: The Toyo Bunko, 1994, pp.69～101.

[35] 事見《蓮花净土實勝寺碑記》，見Martin Gimm, "Zum mongolischen Mahākāla-Kult und zum Beginn der Qing-Dynastie—— die Inschrift Shisheng beiji von 1638——," OE 42 (2000/01), pp. 69-103.

[36] 馬麗華，《風化成典——西藏文史故事十五講》，北京：中國藏學出版社，2009年，頁262～266。

[37] Samuel M.Grupper, "Manchu Patronage and Tibetan Buddhism during the First Half of the Ch'ing Dynasty: A Review Article", *The Journal of the Tibet Society*, pp. 47～75；賴惠敏、張淑雅，《清乾隆時代的雍和宫——一個經濟文化層面的觀察》，《故宫學術季刊》第23卷第4期，頁131～164。

[38] Vladimir L.Uspensky, *Prince Yunli (1697～1738): Manchu Statesman and Tibetan Buddhist*. Tokyo: Institute for the Study of language and Cultures of Asia and Africa, 1987.

[39] Ruth W.Dunnell and James A.Millward eds., *New Qing Imperial History: The Making of the Inner Asia Empire at Qing Chengde*, RoutledgeCurzon, New edition, 2004.

[40] 王家鵬，《故宫六品佛樓梵華樓考——清代宫廷佛堂典型模式》，《明清論叢》（第一輯），1999年。

[41] 參見沈衛榮，《藏譯首楞嚴經對勘導論》，《元史及民族與邊疆研究集刊》，第十八集，上海：上海古籍出版社，2006年，頁81～89。

[42] 朴趾源，《熱河日記》，頁166、170。

[43] 徐珂，《清稗類鈔》(北京：中華書局，1984～1986)，《方伎類》。

[44] 錢曾著，管庭芬、章鈺校證，《讀書敏求記校證》，上海：上海古籍出版社，2007年，頁340。這三部漢譯藏傳密法今藏北京國家圖書館古籍善本書分館内。

[45] 陳寅恪，《陳寅恪集——柳如是别傳》，北京：生活·讀書·新知三聯書店，2001年，頁811。

佛教薩思迦派所傳「道果法」的八部輔助秘修寶籍中的三部[46]，它們都應該是在元朝末年譯成，以後復從宮廷流向民間的。這三部秘法中所涉及雙修等内容，也確實與元代宮廷中所傳的「秘密大喜樂禪定」，或曰「演揲兒法」等「雙修」或「多修」修法有直接的關聯。不管錢謙益和柳如是二人是否真的曾經一同修習過這類藏傳秘法，但這類元譯秘籍在清宮廷外的流傳即充分表明自西夏時代就開始在中央歐亞和漢地傳播的、以薩思迦所傳「道果法」爲主要内容的藏傳密法同樣曾在清代民間流傳過。

自清入民國，直到近現代，藏傳佛教在漢人中間的傳播從來就没有停止過，民國時期來漢地弘法，並留下很深影響的藏地喇嘛則更是不勝枚舉。引進藏傳佛教，推動漢藏佛教的交流和融合曾是近代漢傳佛教試圖現代化的一項重要舉措。這段時間又出現了漢譯藏傳佛教文獻的高潮，像著名的法尊法師，其譯經的功德實在可與玄奘、法成等大師媲美，以其一己之力，就把以宗喀巴大師之論著爲主的格魯派的主要佛學著作翻譯成了漢文。當時爲了滿足漢地信衆修習密法的需要，不但重新刻印了《大乘要道密集》這樣的舊譯儀軌，而且大量由藏傳密教上師新傳的各種密法儀軌也被其各自的弟子譯成漢語流通。現存民國時期翻譯的藏傳密教文獻之數量 相當可觀，至今已被整理出版的還衹是其中很小的一部分[47]。許多著名的漢族知識分子，如人稱「最後的儒家」的梁漱溟等，竟然也都曾皈依藏族佛教上師，嘗試過修習《恒河大手印》等藏傳密法，以求性靈的超越[48]。總而言之，自元朝以來，藏傳佛教一直是漢傳佛教中一個醒目的外來成分，是中華文化的一個組成部分。漢、藏兩種佛教傳統間有着千絲萬縷的聯繫，這兩種佛教傳統相輔相存、相得益彰，共同爲豐富我們多民族文化寶庫做出了傑出的貢獻。

五

與上述漢藏佛教互相交流、互相滲透的歷史相應，漢、藏佛教藝術間的交流和融合更是昭然若揭，彼此難分你我。以前西方藝術史家們通常把明代出現的佛教藝術品，特別是金銅佛像，貼上「漢藏佛教藝術」(Sino-Tibetan Buddhist Art) 的標簽，細究起來「漢藏藝術」這個名稱實際上包含着深受漢地影響的藏傳佛教藝術和深受西藏影響的漢傳佛教藝術兩個傳統[49]。所以晚近有學者建議分別用「漢藏」(Sino-Tibetan) 和「藏漢」(Tibeto-Chinese) 兩個不同的名稱來表徵漢藏佛教藝術交流的兩個不同方向。其中「漢藏佛教藝術」指的是那些在西藏生產，其圖像學特徵明顯是藏式的，但却反映出明顯的漢傳佛教藝術風格的繪畫和雕塑。而「藏漢佛教藝術」則指那些在漢地生產，但其圖像特徵和藝術風格帶有明顯的藏式影響的佛教藝術作品[50]。一般説來，「藏漢佛教藝術」傳統事關圖像學和藝術風格兩個方面的融合，而「漢藏佛教藝術」傳統則主要是藝術風格的合流。當然要明確區分出這兩個傳統的佛教藝術品並不是一件十分容易的事情，在漢地製作的藏傳佛像與在西藏、甚至尼泊爾等地製作的藏傳佛像形制十分相似，即使是專業的佛教藝術史家也很難僅僅依靠對傳統藝術風格的把握而將這兩種傳統的藝術作品精確地區分開來。人們往往還必須借助刻在這些佛像上的銘文，或者根據其底座的裝飾才能把它們正確地區分開來」[51]。特別是在明代(一三六八~一六四四)早期，藏傳佛教藝術風格對漢地佛教金銅造像的影響十分顯著而藏傳和漢傳兩種藝術風格的逐漸融合使得後來漢地的佛像製作雖然繼續以藏傳佛教圖像爲基礎，但其風格則純粹采用漢式。而到了清代（一六四四~一九一一），漢地生產的藏傳佛像顯示出來的這種傾向則更加明顯，現藏於紫禁城中寶相樓的，清乾隆年間（一七三六～一七九五）製作的近八百尊金銅佛像就是其中最明顯的例證[52]。

漢藏或藏漢佛教藝術之間的雙向交流源遠流長，且滲透到各種佛教藝術品類之中，茲僅就漢藏兩個傳統在金[青]銅佛像藝術方面的交流略述其大概。藏傳佛教造像在其千餘年的發展歷程中受到了各種不同的佛教藝術傳統的影響，其中有來自印度、尼泊爾、克什米爾等地的南亞傳統，有來自于闐、敦煌等地的中央歐亞傳統，更有來自漢地的東亞傳統，其中尤以與漢地佛教造像藝術的交互影響最爲突出。中原地區所造金銅佛像在很早就被傳到吐蕃地區，目前在西藏發現的最早的漢地造金銅佛像源出於北魏時期（三八六～五三四），其中最早的一尊是造於四六二至四六三年的彌勒佛坐像，另外還有一尊釋迦牟尼像和一尊釋迦牟尼立像分別造於四七三年和四八四年。除了這三尊有具體紀年的漢式金銅佛像外，還有近十尊明顯屬於北魏——隋唐時代流行的中原風格的金銅佛像。這些佛像有些應當是在漢地生產而被帶到吐蕃的作品，而有些則可能是吐蕃藝術家仿造漢地風格而在吐蕃本地生產的[53]。值得一提的是，被認爲是西藏最神聖的一尊金銅佛像，即現在供奉在拉薩大昭寺內的被稱爲「Jo bo」的釋迦牟尼佛十二歲身量像也是漢地產品，傳說是在文成公主於六四一年入藏時被帶到吐蕃的。這尊佛像曾歷經劫難，最終被安奉在大昭寺內，成爲藏傳佛教徒平生最希望親往頂禮膜拜的至聖至寶，在其臉上涯粉貼金成爲歷代有名望的藏傳佛僧和有財勢的施主們常常做的一件有大功德的好事。

漢藏佛教藝術的交流於元時進入了一個新的歷史階段，漢藏金銅佛像鑄造藝術的互相交流和融合是當時西藏金銅佛像鑄造藝術發展的一個重要特徵。有元一代，隨着藏傳佛教在蒙古宮廷和內地的傳播不斷深入，藏傳佛教造像藝術亦在元朝的大都（今北京）、上都和江南的杭州等地留下了許多傑出的作品。元代皇室曾在歷任帝師的指導下在大都廣建藏傳佛教寺院，設置專門的政府機構，負責澆鑄藏傳金銅佛像。元朝首任帝師八思巴於一二六二年進京時携其弟子、尼泊爾工匠阿尼哥入朝，後者深得元世祖忽必烈賞識和器重，於至元十年（一二七三）被授予「諸色人匠總管」；至元十五年（一二七八）又被擢升爲光祿大夫、大司徒，領將作院事。據稱阿尼哥「長善畫塑及鑄金爲像」——他長年在朝廷設置的宮廷造像機構「梵像提舉司」內鑄造佛像，據稱「凡兩都寺觀之像，多出其手」[54]。阿尼哥於一三〇六年在大都逝世後，他的兒子阿僧哥和弟子劉元繼其衣鉢，對藏傳佛教造像藝術在內地的傳播做出了卓越的貢獻。《元代畫塑記》中對自一二九五到一三三〇年間「諸色人匠總管府」承做

[46] 這幾部書直到近代一直被漢族士人歸入「房中術」一類，參見施蟄存，《文藝百話》，上海：華東師範大學出版社，1994年。關於這幾部書對於薩思迦所傳「道果法」的意義，參見Ronald Davidson, *Tibetan Renaissance: Tantric Buddhism in the Rebirth of Tibetan Culture*, p.194～204.

[47] 這批民國時代漢譯藏傳密教文獻中的一部分收録於近年出版的《中國藏密寶典》，1～6册，北京：民族出版社。

[48] 陳來，《梁漱溟和密宗修習》，中國人民大學哲學家講壇，2009年4月22日。

[49] Heather Karmay, *Early Sino-Tibetan Art*, 1975, p. 1.

[50] Heather Stoddard, *Early Sino-Tibetan Art*, Second Edition, Bangkok: Orchid Press, 2008, Preface to the Second Edition, p. xxii; Ulrich von Schroeder, *Buddhist Sculptures in Tibet*, Volume Two: Tibet & China, Hong Kong: Visual Dharma Publications Ltd., 2001, p. 1244.

[51] P. H. Pott, *Introduction to the Tibetan Collection of the National Museum of Ethnology*, Leiden, p. 36.

[52] *Von Schroeder, Buddhist Sculptures in Tibet*, p. 1244～1245.

[53] Von Schroeder, *Buddhist Sculptures in Tibet*, p.1222～1236；黄春和，《藏傳佛像藝術鑒賞》，北京：華文出版社，2004年，頁18～21。

[54] 《元史》卷203，《阿尼哥傳》。

佛像有非常詳細的記載，從中可知當時造像數目之巨大。例如，「仁宗皇帝皇慶二年八月十六日，敕院使也納，大聖壽萬安寺內，五間殿八角樓四座，令阿僧哥提調其佛像，計並稟搠思哥斡節兒八哈失塑之，省部給所用物。塑造大小佛像一百四十尊；東北角樓尊聖佛七尊；西北趓樓餒山子二座，大小龕子六十二，內菩薩六十四尊；西北角樓朵兒只南磚一十一尊，各帶蓮花座光焰等；西南角樓馬哈哥剌等一十五尊；九曜殿星官九尊；五方佛殿五方佛五尊；五部陀羅尼殿佛五尊；天王殿九尊；東南角樓四臂馬哈哥剌等一十五尊。」[55]可見元朝宮廷藏傳佛教造像活動確曾非常之盛。阿尼哥及其弟子們將西番碌、西番砂、西番顏色、西番火鍍砑金等藏傳佛教藝術的製作技術和材料帶到了元朝宮廷內，並將它們廣泛地運用於元朝宮廷藏傳佛教藝術創作中。元朝宮廷製作的藏傳佛像等藝術品，在藏傳佛教圖像形制的基礎上，融合中原和尼泊爾佛教藝術風格，形成了一種新的、獨特的藝術風格，即在元代文獻中被稱爲「西天梵相」，或者「西番佛像」的宮廷藏傳佛教藝術流派[56]。這一流派又反過來對同時期烏思藏本土藏傳佛教藝術的創作產生了巨大的影響，在現存薩思迦寺和夏魯寺的部分金銅佛像中，我們可以明顯看到這種「西天梵相」的影子。

到了明朝，宮廷造像的風氣更甚於前朝。明廷亦曾設專事造像的機構，稱「佛作」，隸屬「御用監」，專門製作藏式佛像。明代製作藏式金銅佛像於永樂和宣德年間達到鼎盛時期，形成了著名的永樂金銅佛像風格，藏文稱之爲「永樂琍瑪佛像」。永、宣年間明代宮廷生產的這類佛像，乃十五世紀初受西藏和尼泊爾藝術影響在西藏中部和南部地區發展起來的一種新的藝術風格，與元朝的「西天梵相」形成不同的形制和風格。明代兩京曾建造了衆多的藏傳佛教寺院，需要大量的金銅佛像。金銅佛像常常用作朝廷賜予番僧貢使的禮品，而來中原朝貢的番僧絡繹道途，這同樣需要大量的金銅佛像。所以，在西藏寺院的收藏品中，我們見到了大量刻有「大明永樂年施」字樣的明代金銅佛像[57]。永樂、宣德年造金銅佛像傳入西藏後，對西藏本土同時期金銅佛像生產也產生了極大的影響，這一時期西藏最著名的造像藝術家勒烏瓊巴（Sle'u chung pa）所造佛像即具有明顯的永樂年間漢地造藏傳佛像特徵。此外，從漢地佛教藝術風格對西藏佛教造像藝術的影響而言，它主要反映在附帶有四大天王像和十六羅漢像的釋迦牟尼佛像身上。據傳早在藏傳佛教後弘期開始時，魯梅措稱（Klu mes Tshul khrims 十~十一世紀時人）曾將一套帶有四大天王像和十六羅漢像的釋迦牟尼佛畫像帶到吐蕃，藏於葉兒巴寺中，從此成爲藏傳佛教藝術家複製、參照的對象。明封大慈法王釋迦也失也曾將一套十六羅漢像帶回吐蕃，放置在他創建的色拉寺中。漢藏傳統的金銅四大天王像最早於明初出現在噶舉派的登薩替寺（gDan sa mthil）中，它們看起來像是尼泊爾藝人仿製漢式天王像類的作品。這類作品在大昭寺、江孜白居寺等寺院中出現的明代造像中爲數不少，當然它們更多地出現在臨近漢地的朵甘思（康）和朵思麻（安多）地區[58]。

清代是藏傳佛教藝術創作的又一高峰時期，其規模、地域和現存作品數量等都遠遠超過了前代。藏傳佛教在漢地的傳播不僅局限於朝廷，而是無遠弗屆，且深入到民間。除北京外，山西五臺山、河北承德、東北瀋陽、蒙古察哈爾等地均成爲藏傳佛教及其藝術品東傳的重要中心。清代的金銅佛像以精雕細琢、矯飾、典雅和華麗著稱，糅合漢藏兩種藝術風格。特別值得一提的是，清代在蒙古和東北地區，出現了一系列金銅佛像澆鑄中心，其中最爲著名的是由哲布尊丹巴活佛扎納巴扎爾開創的蒙古藏傳佛教金銅佛像藝術，其作品基於蒙古族傳統藝術審美文化，融合西藏和漢地佛教藝術風格，自成一體[59]。

六

綜上所述，漢藏兩種佛教傳統經歷了上下一千四百餘年互相交流、滲透和融合的歷史，早已是你中有我、我中有你。對這段歷史的回顧和研究不但對於佛教研究這一學科的進步大有裨益，而且無疑也對增進漢藏兩個民族之間的相互理解，培養漢藏兩個民族在文化上和感情上的親和力有重要的意義。李巍先生收藏的這批金銅佛像，見證了漢藏佛教交流和融合的歷史，爲漢藏、藏漢佛教藝術研究的深入提供了極爲豐富的新材料；而李巍先生爲收藏這批金銅佛像所作的種種努力本身對增進漢藏兩個民族的團結和共同進步具有表率意義。這部金銅佛像圖集的出版不但是對李巍先生個人收藏漢藏佛教藝術精品之功德的表彰，而且更是對漢藏兩個民族互相交融的佛教文化的表彰。

沈衛榮（中國人民大學國學院教授、副院長，漢藏佛學研究中心主任）

[55] 《元代畫塑記》，北京：人民美術出版社，1964年，頁56。

[56] 參見熊文彬，《元朝宮廷的“西天梵相”及其藝術作品》，《中國藏學》，2000年第2、3期。

[57] 參見熊文彬，《藏傳金銅造像風格的發展》，中國藏學研究中心、中國社會科學院民族學與人類學研究所编，《中國社會科學院民族學與人類學研究所藏藏族文物》，北京：中國藏學出版社，2008年，頁11–12；Stoddard, Early Sino-Tibetan Art, Second Edition, pp. 65–97；von Schroeder, Buddhist Sculptures in Tibet, Volume Two：Tibet & China, p. 1246.

[58] von Schroeder, Buddhist Sculptures in Tibet, Volume Two, p. 1245.

[59] 熊文彬，《藏傳金銅造像風格的發展》，頁12–13。

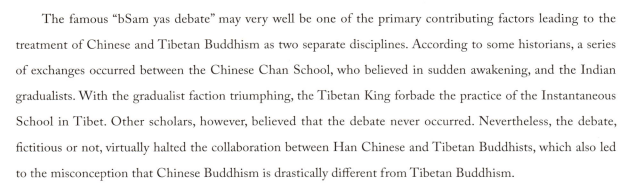

On the Interaction of Sino-Tibetan Buddhist Traditions

Shen Weirong

Mr. Li Wei's collection of gilt copper Buddhist statues is a convincing witness of the close relationship between Chinese and Tibetan Buddhist traditions. In order to gain a better understanding of the value of these Sino-Tibetan or Tibeto-Chinese artworks, I would like to provide a short history of the interaction of Chinese and Tibetan Buddhist traditions and a brief discussion on the significance of the comparative studies of Chinese and Tibetan Buddhist traditions.

I

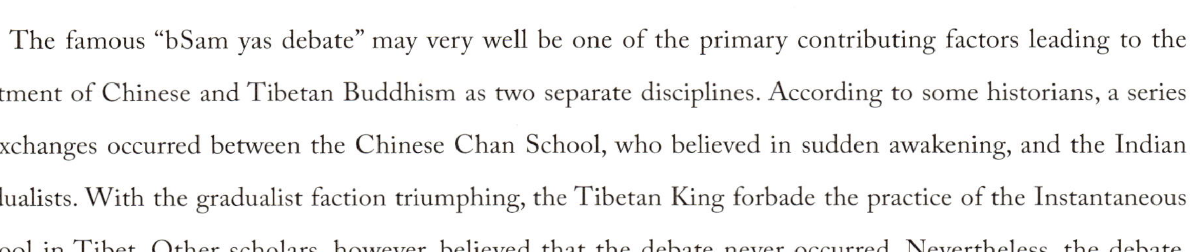

The famous "bSam yas debate" may very well be one of the primary contributing factors leading to the treatment of Chinese and Tibetan Buddhism as two separate disciplines. According to some historians, a series of exchanges occurred between the Chinese Chan School, who believed in sudden awakening, and the Indian gradualists. With the gradualist faction triumphing, the Tibetan King forbade the practice of the Instantaneous School in Tibet. Other scholars, however, believed that the debate never occurred. Nevertheless, the debate, fictitious or not, virtually halted the collaboration between Han Chinese and Tibetan Buddhists, which also led to the misconception that Chinese Buddhism is drastically different from Tibetan Buddhism.

Historically, Han Chinese and the Tibetans share a long and rich history culturally. According to Tibet's own historical tradition, Buddhism was transmitted to Tibet when King Srong btsan sgam po married two Buddhist wives, one princess from Nepal, another from Tang China. It was suggested that the *Jo bo* Buddhist statue, currently housed at the Jokhang Temple in Lhasa, was brought to Tibet as part of Princess Wencheng's dowry. When the Chinese princess was residing in Tibet, Chinese monks stopped by Tibet along their way to India for their Buddhist training. Many monks, who went to Tibet, also helped with the translation of Buddhist texts. Assuming that Buddhism was transmitted during the lifetime of King Srong btsan sgam po, then one cannot deny the influence of the Chinese Buddhism on Tibetan Buddhism.

The latter half of the eighth century is considered the golden age of the united Tibetan kingdom, which is also the golden age for the exchange between Chinese and Tibetan Buddhism. There were translators such as 'Gos Chos grub who excelled in both Chinese and Tibetan. He alone translated numerous texts from Tibetan into Chinese. His translation is considered unique in terms of its high quality in content and in style. Many texts that are considered the hallmark of Chinese Buddhism were translated into Tibetan. One such example is *Śūramgama-sūtra*. This Sūtra alone was translated twice, once during the time of the Tibetan kingdom, and once during the Qing dynasty. Similarly, other scriptures that were popular in China, such as *the Golden Light Sūtra,* and *the Ullambana Sūtra*, as well as many Chinese Chan classical texts discovered in the Dunhuang cave, were also translated into Tibetan. In spite of the "bSam yas debate" in the late eighth century, and the persecution of Buddhism by King Glang dar ma in the century after, the shadow of the Chinese monk has never entirely disappeared from Tibetan Buddhism. Whether it is the rNying ma pa's "Great Perfection" (rdzogs chen) or the bKa' brgyud pa's "Great Seal"(phyag chen), Chinese Buddhism has definitely left a strong imprint on Tibetan Buddhism.

Despite King Glang dar ma's Buddhist persecution, Tibetan Buddhism and the tantric practice in particular, flourished in the century after his reign. This period is considered by the Western scholars as Tibet's renaissance and the beginning of the second dissemination of Buddhism in Tibet. During this time, China's Northwestern regions centered in Dunhuang played an important role in re-transmitting Buddhism in Tibet. Many Tibetan monks and their Indian gurus appeared to be unaffected by the persecution, evident in the tantric texts and arts uncovered in the Dunhuang grotto caves. Furthermore, since the 11th century, Tibetan Buddhism has been transmitted to the Chinese in Central Eurasia, via Tangut and Uighur. As indicated by the Khara Khoto collection of Buddhist texts in Chinese and Tangut, as well as *Turfan Uigurica* and other texts newly found in Ning Xia province, Anuttarayoga practices such as Hevajra, Cakrasaṃvara, Mahākāla and Vajravārāhī were widely practiced throughout the Tangut and the Uighur kingdom. By the Yuan dynasty, Tibetan Buddhism reached China Proper. The Mongolian emperors were documented to be practicing Tibetan Buddhism. Projects were launched in which the high-ranking monks of Chinese, Tibetan, Mongolian and other backgrounds collaborated in the comparative study of the Buddhist scriptures written in different languages. Similarly, in the Ming and Qing dynasties, the emperors were also interested in Tibetan Buddhism. For example, Emperor Yongle invited the fifth Karma pa lama to perform ceremonies for the emperor's parents and sponsored the engraving of the first copy of *bKa' 'gyur*. The early Qing emperors were equally supportive of the translation and dissemination effort. During the Republic Period, Tibetan Buddhism was quite popular again in China. To import Tibetan Buddhism into China proper was considered as one important measure to modernize Buddhism. Until now, though Tibetan Buddhism is sometimes still considered by Han Chinese foreign to the indigenous Chinese Buddhism, there are efforts to harmonize the two traditions in Modern China.

II

The study of Indo-Tibetan Buddhism has become one of the most well-developed and successful areas in the modern world of Buddhist studies. Unfortunately, it has overshadowed an equally important area – Sino-Tibetan Buddhist Studies. In the Western academic tradition, Indian studies seems inseparable with Tibetan and Mongolian studies, but is rarely connected with Chinese studies. The history of Buddhist conquest of China seems equal to the history of Buddhist sinization. Scholars have largely approached the study of Chinese Buddhism as the study of Chinese philosophy and the study of Chinese cultural and social history. The study of Chinese Buddhism is mostly kept apart from Indo-Tibetan Buddhist studies. In terms of methodology, the study of Chinese Buddhism emphasizes philosophic-historical discussion of Buddhist doctrine and its interaction and integration with Confucian and Daoist thoughts and other Chinese traditional ideas. Chinese Buddhist studies became a part of the studies of Chinese philosophical and intellectual history. Contrary to the study of Chinese Buddhism, Indo-Tibetan Buddhist studies, especially in the European tradition, place the emphasis on the philological and textual study. Given the difference in approach, the gap between the two branches is unsurprisingly too wide to be integrated.

In the 1920s and 30s, under the support of Cai Yuanpei, Liang Qichao, Hu Shi and other well-known Chinese scholars, Baron Alexander von Staël-Holstein from Estonia established a Sino-Indian Research Institute in Beijing. The baron took an innovative approach to reconstructing the Mahāyāna Buddhist tradition. Multilingual scholars were gathered around him to study scriptures written in languages such as Tibetan,

Sanskrit, Chinese and Mongolian. There were also attempts to record the verbally transmitted teachings known to the Buddhist monks from Tibet and Mongolia living in Beijing at the time. Both the baron and his Chinese colleagues had left works of comparative studies of Sanskrit, Tibetan, and Chinese Buddhist scriptures.

Unfortunately, their efforts and initiative did not receive much timely attention in the West and within China, and few had continued their pursuit. The language barrier, and the perceived methodological differences between the areas has largely contributed to the lack of interest in Sino-Tibetan Buddhism. Among scholars of Indo-Tibetan Buddhist studies, there are only a few who are able to read and consult Chinese Buddhist texts. Even fewer recognize the importance and necessity of the comparative studies of Chinese Buddhism with Indo-Tibetan Buddhism to the better understanding of the Mahāyāna Buddhist tradition both in India and in Tibet. Similarly, scholars of Chinese Buddhist studies or East Asian Buddhist studies mostly concentrate only on Chinese Buddhist texts and rarely pay attention to the close relation of Chinese Buddhism to Indo-Tibetan Buddhism as the baron did. In stark contrast to Indo-Tibetan Buddhist studies, Sino-Tibetan Buddhist studies is yet to be recognized as an independent discipline.

Obviously, to separate Chinese Buddhist studies from Indo-Tibetan Buddhist studies is a mistake. Chinese Buddhist texts and Chinese Buddhist studies are highly beneficial to the progress of Indo-Tibetan Buddhist studies. First of all, Chinese translations of Buddhist scriptures are invaluable resource not only for Chinese philology, but also for studies of the formation and development of Buddhist canon and the Mahāyāna Buddhist tradition. As suggested by the Japanese scholar Seishi Karashima, "If one reads them closely, these translations, which greatly predate most of our extant Sanskrit and Tibetan manuscripts of Buddhist texts, may provide substantial clues to the origination and development of Buddhist scriptures. Particularly, early Chinese translations, ranging from the second to the fourth century of the Common Era, are primary sources for the study of the formation of Mahāyāna Buddhism." Furthermore, by the seventh century, the major project of translating Indian texts into Chinese virtually ended with the works of Xuanzang (595-664), by whose time much of the Mahāyāna texts had already been translated into Chinese numerous times and major East Asian Buddhist schools were well formed. Contrary to that, the transmission of Buddhism in Tibet had only begun. Clearly, the Chinese Canon is critical in the understanding of Mahāyāna Buddhism, regardless of the research perspective, Indian, Tibetan and Chinese alike.

As the Chinese Canon and the Tibetan Canon preserve the translations of the majority of the original Sanskrit texts of which a substantial part are unfortunately lost in the past, a comparative study of the two Canons is important to the study of Buddhism, especially Mahāyāna Buddhism. Thus, a critical comparison of Chinese and Tibetan versions makes one of the most relevant works of Sino-Tibetan Buddhist studies. To compare the two canons, the Chinese Canon contains only 2920 texts, many of which are different versions of the same text, whereas the Tibetan version contains 4569 texts. The Chinese Tripiṭaka contains more texts of earlier periods, while the Tibetan canon contains more of later periods. The two Canons are complementary in terms of coverage and content. For example, the Chinese translations of the *Prajñaparamitā Sūtra*, *Mahāratnakūta-sūtra*, *Avatamsaka-sūtra*, *the Lotus Sūtra*, and *the Mahāsamnipata-sūtra* appeared as early as the second century. In comparison, the translation project of the Tibetan Canon did not appear until the seventh century. The translation effort climaxed in the end of the eighth and the beginning of the ninth century for the

first time. Not only texts of Sanskrit origin, but also Chinese texts were translated into Tibetan. With prolific translators such as 'Gos Chos grub, the Tibetans translated over hundreds of volumes of scriptures from Chinese to Tibetan. Despite that, some of the early Hīnayāna and Mahāyāna texts are nowhere to be found in the Tibetan Canon.

Although there is yet an accurate count of the texts found in one canon but not in the other, it is obvious that the texts in the Tibetan Canon far outnumbers those in the Chinese one. To illustrate, within the Khara Khoto collection, a series of Buddhist scriptures translated during the period of Tangut kingdom of Xia were recently discovered. While no Chinese version of these texts exists in extant editions of the Chinese canon, one can find the corresponding texts within the Tibetan Canon. In further examination, the majority of the texts missing in the Chinese Canon are tantras, and ritual texts (cho ga) and *śastras* related to these tantras. While the tantric practice became popular in the eighth century India, the translation effort in China had long passed its prime – most Chinese schools had been formed and stabilized. The tantras that were transmitted to China Proper during the Tang period were only these of Krīya, Caryā and Yoga practices centred around the Mahāvaironcana Tantra and Vajrasekhara Sūtra. Texts of Anuttarayoga practices such as Guhyasamāja, Hevajra, Cakrasaṃvara and Kālacakra tantras never became popular in China Proper before Tibetan Buddhism was disseminated in China Proper during the Mongol-Yuan dynasty. Although there were a number of Anuttarayoga tantras translated by Dānapāla, Dharmarakṣa and others in the Song dynasty, the quality of the translations is extremely poor – content related to the actual practice was often omitted, making the texts difficult to understand. Moreover, the practice of tantra was discouraged by Song emperors, making the overall impact of the translations of these tantric texts on the Chinese society was minimal.

Unlike the situation in China Proper, the Anuttarayoga practice became the mainstream during the second dissemination in Tibet. The Anuttarayoga tantras and their related ritual texts are essentially the content for *gSang sngags gsar ma* (The New Secret Mantras). As a result, unlike the Tripiṭaka classification within the Chinese Canon, the Tibetan Canon is categorized into *bKa' 'gyur* (texts ascribed to the historical Buddha and other Buddhas) and *bsTan 'gyur* (exegetical treatises). And within *bKa' 'gyur*, the number of texts under *bka' sde snod gsum* (Tripiṭaka) and *rgyud sde bzhi* (four sections of tantra) far exceed the number of Chinese texts under the Vinaya and Sūtra categories, in particular, most texts in *rgyud sde bzhi* cannot be found in the Chinese Canon. Undoubtedly, the Tibetan Canon is our only key to understanding the Anuttarayoga practice.

Similarly, the Madhyamaka philosophy and other Indian Buddhist philosophy proliferated rapidly in the seventh century and after never gained wide currency in China Proper or East Asia but were highly influential in Tibet. Works by such figures as the Middle Way philosophers Candrakīrti (c. 600-650) and Śāntideva (early eighth century) and the logician Dharmakīrti (seventh century), who flourished when the Chinese Buddhist schools had already developed, were rarely translated into Chinese. In contrast, the works by these and other authors became the basis of the scholastic tradition in Tibet. Buddhist philosophical teachings such as Madhyamaka were widely transmitted in Tibet by Śāntrakṣita and Kamalaśīla during the time of the first dissemination, and Atiśa of the second, which were subsequently incorporated into Tibetan Buddhism by scholars such as Sa skya paṇḍita Kun dga' rgyal mtshan and Tsong kha pa Blo bzang grags pa etc.. Considering the Madhyamaka section of *bsTan 'gyur*, there are a total of 156 commentaries in the section, but 131 of them lack a corresponding Chinese version, which includes half of Nagarjuna's writings and all of Candrakīrti's writings on Madhyamaka. Similarly, on Indian logic or Hetuvidyā, only three of the 70 texts were translated into Chinese. In short, for historical reasons, much of the teachings in Tibetan Buddhism are missing in Chinese Buddhism.

Clarifying the similarities and differences of Chinese and Tibetan Buddhist Canons or Chinese and Tibetan Buddhism at large makes the first step of Sino-Tibetan Buddhist studies. Unfortunately, only effort in comparing the two canons was made seven hundred years ago with the support of the Yuan dynasty in Chinese history. The result is an index of the two canons, *Zhiyuan fabao kantong zonglu*. Published in 1287, it is indeed an important milestone in systematizing the study of Sino-Tibetan Buddhism. Unfortunately, the index is not without flaws. Comparing the index with the content of the Tibetan Canon reveals that it contains many mistakes. Even with the aid of computational and linguistic methods, arriving at an accurate index is only one of the initial stages in understanding the complex relations between Chinese and Tibetan Buddhism.

Sino-Tibetan Buddhist studies enjoyed a golden period during the latter half of the last century. This was due to the discovery of the classical Chinese and Tibetan texts in the Dunhuang cave library. Paul Demiéville's 1952 work, *Le Concile de Lhasa*, has been praised by academics both in the East and the West, inspiring much study of the transmission of Chinese Chan Buddhism in Tibet. During the 1970s and 1980s, a number of Japanese scholars, most notably Ueyama Daishun, conducted careful comparative studies of a great number of Chan texts found in Dunhuang, clarifying the history of the transmission of Chinese Chan Buddhism in Tibet. Other Tibetologists and Buddhologists such as Giuseppi Tucci, David Seyfort Ruegg, Luis O. Gómez and Samten G. Karmay also paid considerable attention to the historicity of "bSam yas debate". However, this trend did not persist into the 1990s. Since then, Chinese Buddhism and Tibetan Buddhism have again been seen as two separate disciplines, even though the study of Dunhuang manuscripts was still at its early stages. Similarly, discoveries of classical Tibetan texts in other areas also require further detailed scholarly treatment, such as those found in Tabo are similar to their Dunhuang counterparts. Classical text, like *bSam gtan mig sgron*, which systematically outlines the view, meditation, conduct, and fruit of the Gradual School, Instantaneous School, Mahāyoga and Atiyoga, are awaiting further examination. Moreover, the study of the history of the transmission of Tibetan Buddhism in Central Eurasia and China, especially during the 11th to 14th centuries, has yet to be seriously researched, due to the fact that the Khara Khoto collection has only become widely available recently. Likewise, the imperial records of the Ming and Qing dynasties will also shed light on the historical context of Tibetan Buddhism in China. In short, with the amount of rich resources available, Sino-Tibetan Buddhism as a discipline has just as much to offer as Indo-Tibetan Buddhism.

Shen Weirong, Renmin University of China

總論

甘青地區民間藏傳佛像新發現

ཀན་སུའུ་དང་མཚོ་སྔོན་ས་ཁུལ་དུ་དམངས་ཁྲོད་བོད་བརྒྱུད་ནང་བསྟན་གྱི་སྐུ་བརྙན་གསར་རྙེད་བྱུང་བ།

王家鵬

金銅佛像是藏傳佛教藝術中的重要組成部分，也是西藏藝術中最具代表性的文物之一。一千三百多年來，藏族藝術家們創造了無數的佛像傑作，取得了令世界矚目的輝煌成就。藏傳佛教藝術發源於青藏高原，其影響範圍廣大，早在十一世紀末十二世紀初就傳入西夏，元代以後隨着西藏地方歸入祖國版圖，藏區與内地聯繫日益緊密，藏傳佛教東向發展傳播内地，促進了藏漢佛教文化藝術的密切交流，藏傳佛教藝術走出青藏高原，深刻影響了内地佛教藝術，創造了大量以漢藏藝術結合爲特徵的佛教藝術作品，如敦煌465窟壁畫、北京居庸關雲臺石刻浮雕佛像、杭州飛來峰石雕佛像等都是膾炙人口的名作。除了這些不可移動的文物遺存外，還有大量的可移動的佛教文物，金銅佛像就是其中的重要一項。但是由於自然災害、兵燹戰亂，佛教文物能够躲過災難留存至今的萬不存一，今天國内的藏傳佛教金銅佛像主要收藏在西藏布達拉宫、西藏博物館等國家文物部門和各寺院中。内地博物館、寺廟也有部分收藏，精華主要在北京故宫博物院。相比而言，私人收藏佛像數量稀少，高品質的佛像更是鳳毛麟角。本書收入的金銅佛像全部爲李巍先生的個人收藏。三十多年來，他滿懷着珍愛中華文物的赤子之心，風風雨雨，集腋成裘，投入了個人全部財力與心血，爲保護祖國文物遺産做出了可貴貢獻。

這是一批深藏民間尚未公布的藏傳佛教造像的新資料，除了李先生的收藏外，在近幾年的文物考察中，筆者在青海地區民間還見到數量不少的珍貴佛像，收集了大量的資料，説明這些佛像不是李先生一人的孤立收藏，是在「文革」等非常時期，甘肅、青海一帶藏漢群衆，冒險密藏下來的[1]，是一批與甘青歷史緊密相關，有重要研究價值的文物。總體觀察，這批佛像造型風格與我們比較常見的衛藏地區佛像，明清時期内地佛像大多相同或相似，但也有部分佛像不僅造型稀見，而且還刻有未見發表過的藏文、漢文、梵文款識印記，其藴含的豐富歷史文化信息，對研究元代以來甘青地區以及相連的四川、雲南等地區的藏傳

[1] 湯惠生著《經歷原始——青海游牧地區文物調查隨筆》109頁記載，玉樹囊謙縣嘎丁寺初建於明代中期，原來寺院規模很大，香火旺盛，收藏有很多早期的唐卡和銅佛像，在1958年均毁於一旦，好在陳林根恰活佛在劫難之餘搶救了一部分並且深深地埋在地下。20世紀80年代宗教政策開放之後，這些文物又重見天日，陳林根恰活佛説："這些都是我親手埋到地下的，又親手把它們挖出來。"廣西人民出版社，2004年出版。

"文革"期間還有大批金屬文物包括佛像被當作廢銅爛鐵送進煉銅廠，幸有文物工作者及時發現，文物部門組織專業人員從廢銅爛鐵中揀選搶救回大量的文物，成爲博物館的重要藏品。一些群衆千方百計從廠裏把部分佛像買回家中密藏，使這些珍貴的藏傳佛教佛像得以躲過劫難，爲保護祖國歷史文化遺産做出了貢獻。

佛教文化藝術發展，以及西北地區漢藏佛教文化交流提供了寶貴的實物資料，開闊了我們研究的視野，同時也提出了大量新的研究課題。藏傳佛教金銅佛像，基本爲傳世品，一旦離開它的起源地，就難以找到可靠的考古學依據，研究極爲困難。本文僅就初步的觀察研究，談談對這些佛像的認識。許多問題的解決還有待今後深入發掘藏漢文史料，有待甘、青、川、滇地區佛教考古工作的廣泛開展。

一　多元藝術風格

元、明、清以來藏傳佛教在朝廷的大力扶持下，在甘青地區發展繁榮，寺院星羅棋布，每座寺院都要繪畫塑造造像，推動了佛教藝術的發展。每座寺院都有豐富的文物，壁畫、佛像、唐卡，尤其是歷史悠久的大寺院，其文物數量規模之宏大可以想見，可惜由於歷史的原因多已不存了[2]。甘青地區民間收藏的佛像是劫後餘燼，彌足珍貴。本書收入的佛像反映了這一地區佛教文化藝術的特點。佛像雖來源不同，風格各異，但從造型特點、藝術風格、工藝技法多方面研究，可見不同佛像産地、時代的聯繫，對於了解西藏與甘青地區漢藏佛像藝術交流的歷史大有裨益。

首先給觀者留下深刻印象的是這批佛像多姿多彩的造型與藝術風格，既有較常見的衛藏地區佛像，也有藏西地區佛像，還有漢地風格顯著的内地所造佛像。佛像題材廣泛，諸佛菩薩，金剛護法，顯宗密宗造像都有。佛像的時代大約從十一至十三世紀西藏佛教後弘初期到元、明、清，主要爲清代佛像。佛像多徵集於今青海地區，按照藏族居住區域來説爲安多、康區的文物遺存。

文物是歷史的載體，某類文物的出現必然是與當地的歷史環境緊密相關的，這批佛像能在青海保存下來既有偶然性，更有歷史淵源。青海地處青藏高原東隅邊緣，緊連河西走廊，是連接西藏、甘川藏區、新疆與祖國内地的紐帶，歷史上一直是内地通往西藏的主要通道和絲綢之路的南路幹綫，今天青海的區域是我國藏族居住區中的安多大部分和康區的一部分[3]。安多、康區位於整個藏區的北東兩面，歷史上它是藏族地方同歷代中央王朝政治、經濟、文化交往的必經之地[4]，歷來是漢藏文化密切交匯之地。青海地理位置特殊，藏傳佛教在這裏歷史久遠，基礎深厚，在藏傳佛教文化的形成、發展、傳播過程中，一直起着重要的作用。

藏傳佛像藝術的發展是與佛教歷史進程息息相關的，藏傳佛教起源於西藏，七世紀中松贊干布統一西藏各部，建立吐蕃王朝，佛教也於此時從唐朝、于闐、印度、尼泊爾傳入吐蕃。隨着吐蕃的强盛，勢力東漸，擊敗吐谷渾，青海大部地區納入吐蕃轄地，佛教亦從内地和吐蕃傳入青海。九世紀中葉，吐蕃贊普朗達磨禁佛，佛教遭到毁滅性打擊，吐蕃王朝也隨之崩潰，群雄四起，各霸一方，戰亂頻仍，社會動蕩，吐蕃時期傳入的漢印佛教文化藝術被摧毁蕩盡。佛教沉寂了近百年。經過百年擾攘，殆十世紀中才逐漸安定下來，適應西藏社會發展的需求，佛教獲得重生的機會，先從藏西古格和青海地區開始了復興之路。當朗達磨滅佛時期，寺院封閉，僧人逃散。有三位僧人鑰格迥、藏饒賽、馬爾釋迦牟尼避難到青海，收徒公巴饒賽，公巴饒賽招收弟子，弘揚佛法，河湟地區逐漸發展成爲藏傳佛教的一個中心，對佛教在西藏的復興起了重要作用，被稱爲「下路弘法」。

青海成爲西藏佛教後弘期的發祥地。以敦煌爲中心的西北地區對後弘期藏傳佛教發展影響至深。藏傳佛教的復興與西北地區有極大的關聯。從德藏吐魯番出土的回鶻佛教文獻和俄藏黑水城出土的漢文西夏文佛教文獻，寧夏地區出土的西夏文漢文佛教文書，文物以及佛教遺址研究中，可見在十一世紀初，藏傳佛教已在西夏、回鶻、漢人中傳播，在甘、青、安多和內蒙等西北地區普遍流傳[5]。西夏的佛教藝術亦對西藏產生過重要影響。

十一世紀後，藏傳佛教寧瑪、噶當、薩迦、噶舉諸派相繼形成，進入空前的活躍期，青藏高原大量寺院的建立，推動着佛教造像藝術的勃興。本書圖1金剛薩埵，三角形冠葉，下托彎月，兩股長辮垂挂肩後，辮髮雕成扁片的飄帶形，帽冠髮辮，是十一世紀藏西地區克什米爾風格佛像上的獨特式樣，與西藏阿里地區札達縣熱尼拉康和有明確紀年的拉達克塔布寺十一世紀彩塑像風格式樣相似。插圖1爲塔布寺泥塑佛像[6]，插圖2爲熱尼拉康寺泥塑佛像[7]。圖1金剛薩埵彎眉大眼，眼瞳扁寬嵌銀，細巧嘴唇嵌紅銅，露出淡淡的神秘微笑。胸肌發達，刻出生硬的肌肉輪廓綫，腰胯細瘦，身體比例不協調，具有十一至十二世紀藏西地區佛像鮮明特徵。圖3六臂觀音菩薩，冠葉刻珠寶下托彎月，近似克什米爾佛冠，辮髮雕成扁片的飄帶形，大眼睛嵌銀，耳環鑲嵌銀，紅銅。在頸部用紅銅鑲嵌一道裝飾圈，手戴戒指。佛像保留了波羅造像因素，具有藏西佛像的特點[8]，與藏西古格托林寺內四塔中的東北塔壁畫，十一世紀六臂觀音形象十分接近，但不及畫像輕鬆自如，姿態略僵硬，有趣的是裙面上陰綫淺刻方孔銅錢紋、雲卷紋，顯露了漢文化的影響。

圖2彌勒菩薩立像，身材壯碩，高鼻、深目、厚唇，一道長聖綫從左肩垂下盤繞右側身後，吸收東北印度波羅佛像藝術的因

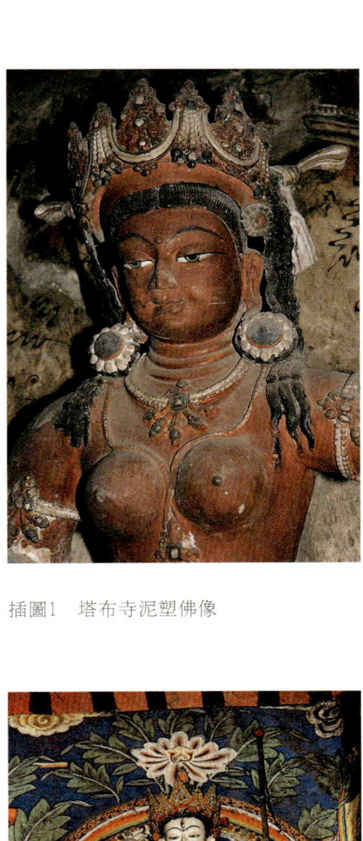

插圖1　塔布寺泥塑佛像

插圖2　熱尼拉康泥塑佛像

[2] 全國解放前夕，青海省境內較正規的藏傳佛教寺院有650座，加上日朝（静房）、參康（修行處）、拉康（佛堂）、噶爾卡（活佛住地）、貢扎（修行院）等不下千座；甘肅省境內約有藏傳佛教寺院300多座。1958年後，全省共保留藏傳佛教寺院11座，1962年西北民族工作會議後，開放137座。"文革"期間除塔爾寺和瞿曇寺外，餘皆關閉，多數拆毁。見蒲文成主編《甘青藏傳佛教寺院》4頁，青海人民出版社1990年版。

[3] 安多（Amdo）、康（Khams）這兩個地名與烏思藏（dBus gtsang，即衛藏）是藏族傳统上的一種地理概念，並非行政區劃，没有非常明確的區分界限，大致有一個地界劃分，安多指今青海巴顏喀喇山以東，包括青海藏區（除玉樹州）、甘肅藏區及四川阿坝在內的地區，所操方言是藏語安多方言；康區包括今西藏昌都地區、四川甘孜、青海玉樹和雲南迪慶州，所操方言是藏語康方言。

[4] 元朝爲加强對全國藏區的管理，由總制院下先後設置了三個宣慰使司都元帥府。一、吐蕃等處宣慰使司都元帥府治所在河州（今甘肅臨夏），轄境包括今青海除玉樹以外的廣大藏區、甘肅南部、四川阿坝等地，通稱"多麥"，古譯"朵思麻"，故又稱朵思麻宣慰司；二、吐蕃等路宣慰使司都元帥府治所在今四川甘孜一帶，轄境包括今四川甘孜藏族自治州，西藏昌都地區及青海玉樹地區，通稱"多朵"，古譯"朵甘思"，故又稱朵甘思宣慰司。三、烏思藏納里速古魯孫等三路宣慰使司都元帥府，管轄烏思（前藏）、藏（後藏）、納里速古魯孫（阿里三圍）三地區，大致即今西藏自治區範圍，簡稱烏思藏宣慰司。參見蒲文成著《青海佛史》117頁，青海人民出版社2001年版。

[5] 參見本書沈衛榮論文《漢藏佛學交流與漢藏佛教藝術研究》。

[6] 引自奥地利德波拉·克林伯格－沙爾特著《王國明燈塔布寺早期西喜馬拉雅地區的印藏佛教藝術》107頁圖102。Deborah E.Klimburg-Salter，*TABO–a lamp for the kingdom: Early Indo-Tibetan Buddhist Art in the Western Himalaya*，Printed and bound in Italy in October

素較多，具有十一至十二世紀尼泊爾佛像特點[9]。但身體已略顯僵直，時代較晚。

本書收入的幾尊佛像保留了較多的印度波羅、克什米爾、尼泊爾藝術因素，與西藏地區十一到十三世紀後弘初期佛像藝術風格接近。這一時期的藏傳佛教造像藝術仍處於吸收和借鑒階段，各種風格並存，既有克什米爾因素，也有波羅藝術的影響，同時還有內地于闐、敦煌等藝術因素，從地域上各種域外風格已經按照藏人的審美趣向融合在一起，相互吸收形成新的風格。阿里地區造像有較濃郁的克什米爾風格，而西藏腹地的後藏和拉薩地區，波羅藝術和于闐敦煌傳統則占有較大比重，從現存作品看主要流行於後藏和山南地區，扎塘寺、葉瑪寺、夏魯寺都是其中典型代表[10]。

這幾尊佛徵集於玉樹地區[11]，十一至十二世紀初時在青海河湟地區，建立了以藏族爲主體的唃厮囉地方政權，首府在今西寧一帶的青唐城。唃厮囉統治者利用絲綢之路北道爲西夏控制後，許多商人改走青海道，大力發展經濟貿易，增强了國力，唃厮囉政權與宋、西夏、遼，以及回鶻、西域都有交往。與宋朝關係尤爲密切。國主宗奉佛教，李遠在《青唐録》卷三十五中記述了青唐城佛教鼎盛的情形：

城之西，有青唐水，注宗哥，水西平原，建佛祠，廣五六里，繞以周垣，屋至千餘盈。爲大像，以黄金塗其身，又爲浮屠十三級以護之……吐蕃重僧，有大事必集僧決之……城中之屋，佛舍居半。惟國主殿及佛舍以瓦，餘雖主之官室亦土覆之。[12]

可見佛教盛行、佛寺衆多的情況，但留存下來的文物已見不到了。這幾尊佛像可能爲瞭解這一時期青海地區的佛像藝術提供了寶貴綫索。

這些佛像約爲十二到十五世紀左右安多、康區流傳的佛像，是本地工匠所作，還是外來匠師的作品，或者是傳自西藏還需深入研究。青海是西藏與內地聯繫的大通道，與西藏、內地佛教藝術的交往緊密，寺院中收藏來自西藏、內地、印度尼泊爾佛像，西藏尼泊爾工匠來青海製作佛像，是很自然的事情，如《安多政教史》記載清代西藏尼泊爾等外來工匠情況：

廣惠寺敏珠爾活佛從西藏帶來秘書、畫師、雕刻師、鐵匠、浮雕匠、尼泊爾金匠等，他們都具備各種技藝，四年之內向各地扎倉配備了所需之物。

瑪爾娘强巴林寺原是一座古寺……衛地商人前來貿易者多，因而寺內有無數的印度、西藏方面所造身、語、意的經、像、塔等重要依止聖物以及供器、用具等……佛堂中供有以印度、尼泊爾的無數青銅佛像爲內藏的彌勒大像……兩處青銅佛殿中有從印度、內地、尼泊爾及西藏請來的大小青銅佛像二百餘尊。[13]

圖18緑救度佛母立像雕刻細膩，精美華麗，女性化特點鮮明。西藏拉薩羅布林卡收藏有相同式樣緑救度佛母像。圖37金剛亥母

舞立姿態，寬寬的飄帶從髮髻後蜿蜒曲折垂下，鑲嵌松石珊瑚，工藝精湛，設計別具匠心。布達拉宮收藏相同式樣金剛亥母立像，尺寸不同但出自同一模本（見插圖3[14]）。圖8四臂菩薩，鏤空背光，造型獨特，門字形框架，左右立柱內側兩條圖案簡潔的纏枝，横梁兩端爲摩羯龍，龍尾翹起聯結翻卷的卷草，正中銜接金翅鳥頭和兩隻手握的飄帶，頂端雕摩尼寶。背光的優美樣式汲取了十四世紀前後的西藏壁畫、唐卡的設計元素。西藏博物館收藏有相同背光佛像（見插圖4[15]）。可見青海與西藏佛像藝術的緊密關係，一些佛像正如《安多政教史》記載的那樣直接來自西藏。

二　佛像題材與工藝

佛像題材多樣，有格魯派供奉的諸佛菩薩祖師造像，也有寧瑪、噶舉、薩迦派供奉諸佛像。圖6唐東杰布身披僧袍，全跏趺坐於三層卡墊上，卡墊下承凸字形方臺座，座前面雕雙獅、法輪，體量高大，工藝精細，形象生動。唐東杰布約與宗喀巴同時代人，香巴噶舉派僧人，是西藏家喻户曉的人物，一生雲游四海，熱心公益，在西藏各地修建寺院，建造鐵橋很多，人稱「鐵

插圖3　西藏布達拉宮藏金剛亥母像

插圖4　西藏博物館藏彌勒佛像

1997.

[7] 引自金維諾主編《中國藏傳佛教雕塑全集·彩塑》圖41，北京美術攝影出版社2001年版。

[8] 參見西藏自治區文物管理局編《托林寺》120頁，中國大百科全書出版社2001年版。

[9] 參見瑞士馮施羅德《西藏佛教雕塑》516頁圖169A彌勒菩薩。Ulrich von Schroedr, *Buddhist Sculptures in Tibet*, Hong Kong: Visual Dharma Publication Ltd., 2001。

[10] 參見熊文彬主編《中國藏傳佛教雕塑全集3·金銅佛下》論文"藏傳金銅佛造像風格综述"，北京美術攝影出版社2001年版。

[11] 這幾尊外來風格鮮明的佛像據李先生講出自玉樹地區某寺院密藏佛像的山洞中，喇嘛爲修復寺院籌集資金，把佛像由李先生請去，並開具了書面證明。

[12] 涵芬樓排印《説郛》卷三五所收的節録本。

[13] 《安多政教史》104、607、622頁。

[14] 引自上海博物館編《雪域藏珍——西藏文物精華》，圖25金剛亥母鎏金銅像，高41.5厘米。布達拉宮管理處收藏。上海書畫出版社2001年版。

[15] 引自西藏博物館編《西藏博物館》94頁，圖4合金銅彌勒佛，13世紀，高23.6厘米、寬12厘米。中國大百科全書出版社2001年版。

橋活佛」，被工匠奉爲祖師。傳説他還是藏戲的創始人。此像爲噶舉派寺院所供奉。

圖33護法神騎在鵬鳥身上，與遍入天形象近似，但面相、所持法器與遍入天不同。圖8四臂菩薩，四臂分上下排列，形象罕見，身份待考。這兩尊佛像是薩迦寺院供奉佛像。圖39喇呼拉護法，又稱毗紐天、羅睺星。上身人形，下身龍身，九頭四臂，頭分三層排列，頂層髮髻上雕鳥頭，是寧瑪派主供佛像。這些佛像十分少見，爲我們提供了圖像學的新材料。

各派供奉的諸神多有出現，反映出青海地區藏傳佛教各教派並存發展的情況。明末清初，格魯派在青海地區廣泛傳播，重點在河湟地區；在玉樹、果洛等邊遠地區，格魯派寺院發展相對緩慢。在果洛寧瑪派寺院一直占據絶對優勢；在玉樹，噶舉派和薩迦派寺院大部分保存下來，占有重要地位。據民國八年（一九一九）金陵大學社會歷史調查組《玉樹調查記》中所統計，當時玉樹地區有寺院96座，其中噶舉派53座，占55.2%；薩迦派和寧瑪派24座，占25%；格魯派19座，占19.8%[16]。這反映出青海藏傳佛教並非格魯派一家獨秀的格局特點。

蒙古各部對格魯派的支持，對格魯派的發展壯大起了重要作用。永樂年間宗喀巴創立格魯派，格魯派以青海爲基地，創立發展，並迅速傳播到廣大蒙古、土族地區。明萬曆年間三世達賴喇嘛兩次來青海活動，使該派迅速在青海傳播。格魯派從青海起步，次第傳入漠南、漠北、漠西蒙古。明末和碩特蒙古首領固始汗從新疆率部入據青海，以青海爲基地，擊敗康藏格魯派的對立勢力，平定川康，支持格魯派取得宗教上的統治地位。

圖46咱雅班智達像是有關蒙古各部與格魯派關係的歷史文物。這是一尊生動寫實的高僧肖像，此像没有刻寫題記，比對北京故宫博物院收藏的咱雅班智達像，兩像形象完全一致。插圖5爲北京故宫咱雅班智達像[17]，銅鎏金，高34厘米，根據佛像底版托忒文題記及《咱雅班智達傳》記載，是他圓寂後由五世達賴批準，請尼泊爾工匠在拉薩所造。此像是新發現的又一尊咱雅班智達像。咱雅班智達（一五九九～一六六二）出身於衛拉特和碩特部蒙古貴族，原名納木海嘉木措，是明末清初衛拉特蒙古和碩特部著名高僧，青年時期在西藏格魯派寺院長期學佛，取得了拉然巴格西學位，擔任過哲蚌寺阿巴扎倉講經師等高級僧職。五世達賴喇嘛受戒時任九名業座中的比丘之一。他與五世達賴喇嘛和占據青海的衛拉特部固始汗都有特殊關係。後奉五世達賴之命回到衛拉特，一生致力於藏傳佛教在西部蒙古的傳播，往返於西藏與蒙古之間，在衛拉特蒙古軍事力量支持格魯派取得在西藏的統治地位的鬥争中，發揮過重要作用。他創制了托忒蒙古文，用托忒文翻譯《金光明經》《金剛經》《四部醫典》等藏文典籍。在溝通蒙藏文化，保留衛拉特民族歷史文獻方面做出了重大貢獻[18]。咱雅班智達的家鄉就在今青海格爾木市的烏圖美仁鄉。咱雅班智達像的流傳與他在青海的活動，與藏傳佛教格魯派在衛拉特蒙古中的重要影響以及與青海蒙古族藏傳寺院有緊密關聯。

在工藝方面，許多佛像特點鮮明，如圖6、圖7、圖10，採用紅銅或銅合金鑄造，不鎏金。眼睛嵌紅銅，眼瞳再嵌銀，嘴唇嵌紅銅。項鏈、臂釧、手鐲、脚鐲嵌銀聯珠綫，薄衣貼體，不刻衣紋，只在裙裾、袈裟袍邊鑲嵌銀或紅銅飾條。飾條表面綫刻卷草纏枝等精美的花紋，工藝難度大，不僅是鑄造技藝，還需鏨刻、花絲鑲嵌等多種綜合技藝才能完成。這種工藝在西藏傳統佛像分類中稱爲「桑唐利瑪」佛像，插圖6北京故宫藏十三至十四世紀西藏桑唐利瑪彌勒佛坐像，上拴清代黄紙條，墨書漢滿兩種文字，漢文：

大利益桑唐利瑪彌勒佛，五十一年十一月初六日收堪布大歲本……（殘斷）[19]

這是乾隆五十一年（一七八六）西藏進貢的一尊桑唐利瑪佛像，具有金屬鑲嵌工藝特點的銅佛像。在北京故宮所藏早期藏西地區克什米爾風格佛像上多見，藏西是桑唐利瑪佛像的主要產地。也有一些波羅風格佛像也用這種工藝。主要特點是黃銅鑄造（也有青銅），局部用紅銅、白銀鑲嵌裝飾，是西藏西部地區約十二至十五世紀比較流行的一種精緻造佛工藝。在十五世紀以後的西藏佛像上已很少見[20]。本書中多尊明清時代佛像，如圖14、17、46、47、86均採用了精湛的金屬鑲嵌工藝，這是明清時期安多康區佛像中流行的一種造佛工藝。採用鑲嵌工藝製造的青銅器叫做青銅錯金銀器。可分爲鑲嵌金屬和非金屬兩類，早在春秋時期的青銅器上已出現，是中國古代青銅文化的重要特色。將這種古老的工藝運用於佛像製作，需先依紋飾圖案在佛像表面鑄

插圖5　北京故宮咱雅班智達像

插圖6　北京故宮桑唐利瑪佛像

[16] 參見浦文成著《青海佛史》265頁，青海人民出版社2001年版。

[17] 見楊新、王家鵬主編《中國藏傳佛教雕塑全集·金銅佛上》圖221，北京美術攝影出版社2002年版。

[18] 參見中國社會科學院中國邊疆史地研究中心編《中國邊疆史地資料叢刊·清代蒙古高僧傳譯輯》成崇德譯《咱雅班智達傳》，全國圖書館文獻縮微複製中心1998年版。

陳慶英文《明末清初格魯派蒙古高僧咱雅班智達之事迹新探》，刊載於《海峽兩岸蒙古學藏學學術討論會論文集》1995年。

[19] 王家鵬主編《故宮文物珍品全集——藏傳佛教造像》圖138彌勒佛坐像。商務印書館（香港）有限公司2003年版。

[20] 詳見王家鵬《藏傳金銅佛像傳統分類例證——故宮藏傳佛像題記解讀》刊於《故宮學刊》2004年第一輯。

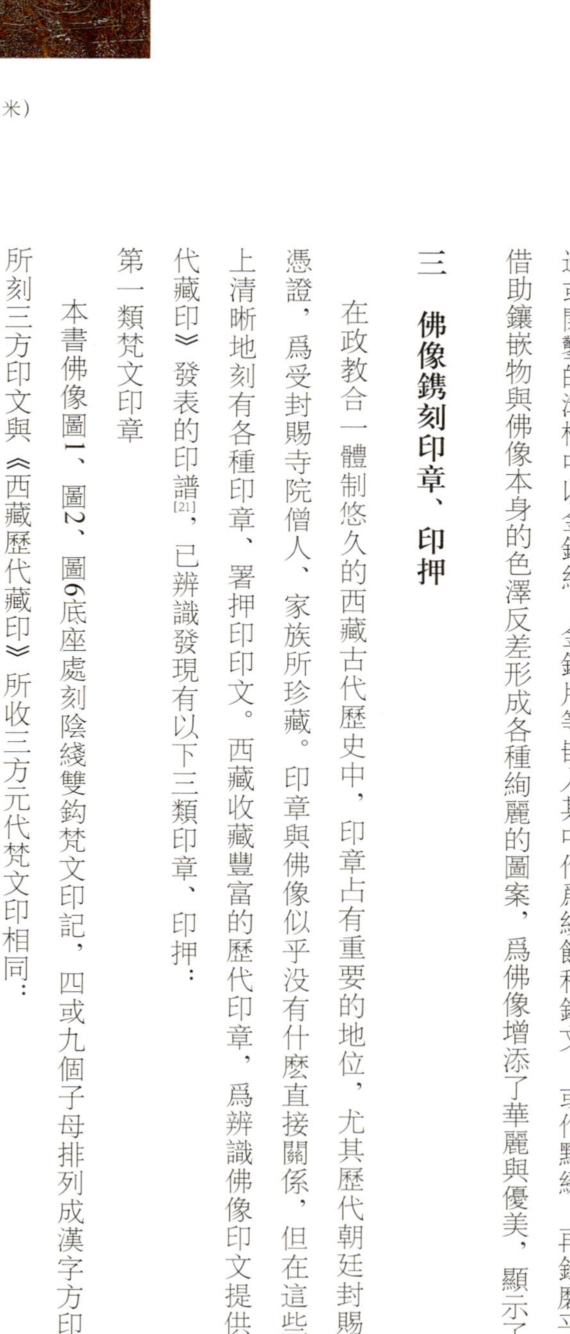

造或開鑿的溝槽中以金銀絲、金銀片等嵌入其中作爲紋飾和銘文，或作點綴，再銼磨平滑，或保留自然凸起形狀，借助鑲嵌物與佛像本身的色澤反差形成各種絢麗的圖案，爲佛像增添了華麗與優美，顯示了造佛匠師的高超技藝。

三　佛像鐫刻印章、印押

在政教合一體制悠久的西藏古代歷史中，印章占有重要的地位，尤其歷代朝廷封賜的官印是權力地位的象徵與憑證，爲受封賜寺院僧人、家族所珍藏。印章與佛像似乎沒有什麼直接關係，但在這些佛像中，我們發現多尊佛像上清晰地刻有各種印章、署押印印文。西藏收藏豐富的歷代印章，爲辨識佛像印文提供了重要依據，對照《西藏歷代藏印》發表的印譜[21]，已辨識發現有以下三類印章、印押：

第一類梵文印章

本書佛像圖1、圖2、圖6底座處刻陰綫雙鉤梵文印記，四或九個子母排列成漢字方印式樣，印文字意待考。佛像所刻三方印文與《西藏歷代藏印》所收三方元代梵文印相同：

圖1金剛薩埵像底座刻梵文印，外框邊長5厘米，插圖7A爲金剛薩埵像刻梵文印。西藏文管會藏元代玉印，火珠紐，高3.5厘米，印面正方，邊長4.5厘米，插圖7B爲梵文玉印印譜。此印印文內容、印的用途不明，有待考證。

圖2彌勒菩薩像底座刻梵文印，外框邊長4.5厘米，插圖8A爲彌勒菩薩像刻梵文印。西藏文管會藏元代象牙印，法輪紐，高6.3厘米，印面正方，邊長4.8厘米，插圖8B爲梵文象牙印印譜。此印印文內容、印的用途不明，有待考證。

圖6唐東杰布像底座刻梵文印，外框邊長5.2厘米，見插圖9A。西藏布達拉宮藏元代玉印，螭紐，高6厘米，方，邊長6.9厘米，據原印所拴布條上的說明，該印是薩迦和帕竹之間統治南部地區的長官之印。插圖9B爲梵文玉印印譜[22]。

插圖7A　金剛薩埵像刻梵文印（邊長5厘米）
插圖7B　梵文玉印印譜（邊長4.5厘米）

插圖8A　彌勒菩薩像刻梵文印（邊長4.5厘米）
插圖8B　梵文象牙印印譜（邊長4.8厘米）

插圖9A　唐東杰布像刻梵文印（邊長5.2厘米）
插圖9B　梵文玉印印譜（邊長11厘米）

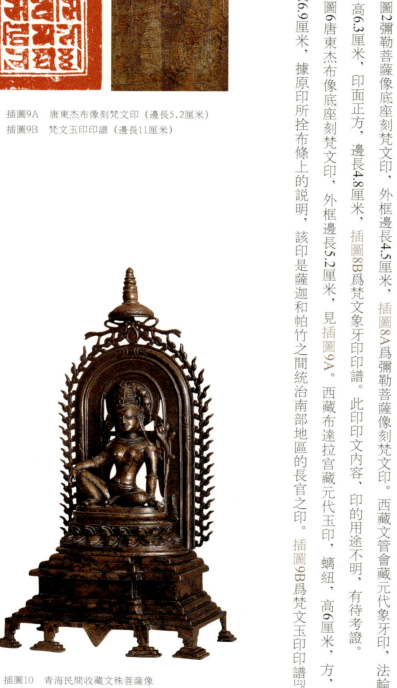

插圖10　青海民間收藏文殊菩薩像

總之，西藏文管會、布達拉宮藏的三方印時代均爲元代，與本書圖2佛像時代十一至十三世紀是基本吻合的。圖6唐東杰布像時代爲明初，比玉印時代稍晚，從原印布條記載「薩迦和帕竹之間統治南部地區的長官之印」看，此印在明初完全可能仍在使用，在唐東杰布像上刻印，時代並不矛盾。唐東杰布是香巴噶舉派名僧，這位長官可能是噶舉派某位領袖人物。

第二類朝廷頒發官印

「統領釋教大元國師」印。插圖10文殊菩薩銅像，原青海個人收藏，全高52.7厘米，青銅鑄造，佛座、佛身、背光分三部分組合而成，從文殊菩薩的形象、佛座、背光的式樣及細部特徵看，具有十一、十二世紀左右東北印度波羅佛像典型風格。與西藏和北京故宮的同類藏品相近。插圖11北京故宮十世紀東印度自在觀音像[23]，佛像的底座後背刻有一方八思巴文印章圖記，印文陰綫刻，外框五點五厘米見方，印文爲「統領釋教大元國師」八個漢字的八思巴文音譯[24]。西藏博物館現存兩方「統領釋教大元國師」玉印，佛像所刻印文與其中一方玉印印文完全一致[25]。插圖12A爲文殊菩薩像刻印，插圖12B爲玉印印譜。插圖13爲西藏博物館藏「統領釋教大元國師」龍紐玉印。顯然是工匠照玉

插圖11　北京故宮十世紀東印度自在觀音像

插圖12A　文殊菩薩像刻印（邊長4厘米）
插圖12B　玉印印譜（邊長11厘米）

插圖13　西藏博物館藏“統領釋教大元國師”龍紐玉印

[21] 歐朝貴、其美編著《西藏歷代藏印》1991年西藏人民出版社出版，是國內第一部用漢文寫的有關西藏印章的研究著作。全書收集印章161枚，有元朝至民國的各類印章的印譜，爲研究藏印提供了豐富可考的珍貴資料。此前還有兩部涉及印章的專著，其一德國學者迪特·舒（Dieter Schuh）的《西藏印章學》（*Grundlagen Tibetischer Siegelkunde*）（1981年）收集印章印文約130種（有重復）。其二恰白·次旦平措及瑪仲·米多吉編《西藏重要歷史資料選編》收印文91種。參見黄顥文《讀〈西藏歷代藏印〉》，《中國西藏》1993年秋季號。

[22] 西藏收藏的三方梵文印印譜及説明引自歐朝貴、其美編著《西藏歷代藏印》17頁，西藏人民出版社1991年版。

[23] 見楊新、王家鵬主編《中國藏傳佛教雕塑全集·金銅佛上》圖三三。北京美術攝影出版社2002年版。

[24] 感謝照那斯圖先生幫助釋讀出印文内容。

[25] 見《西藏歷代藏印》8、9頁。

印印文仿刻在佛像上的，元朝廷封授西藏僧人的國師、帝師印代表朝廷賦予的崇高權力地位，只在重要的文告上鈐蓋，在佛像上刻上國師印，説明了此印的一種特殊用途，增加了我們對元代國師印使用領域的認識。元代所封國師、帝師非薩迦僧人莫屬，佛像所刻國師印表明此像曾爲薩迦派寺中供奉的珍貴佛像。本書圖22與此像尺度形象一樣，是同一模本[26]。

「夾實監藏」四字漢文雙鈎印文，據查此印爲明宮廷賜印，現存兩方同樣文字印，一象牙印，一青玉印，現藏拉薩羅布林卡。象牙印刻款識，右上：「永樂十三年五月日」；左上：「賜思裸般領葛刺」[27]。「思裸般領葛刺」是何人待考。插圖14A佛像刻「夾實監藏」印與插圖14B「夾實監藏」印譜。「夾實監藏」今天譯寫爲「扎什監贊」，有趣的是此印刻於一高僧像（圖45）後背，這是一位佛法精深的高僧形象，從其着裝看可能是一位漢僧。他與「夾實監藏」、「思裸般領葛刺」是何關係，還是個謎。

清朝廷封賜五世達賴喇嘛印。本書圖80四臂觀音像，須彌座後面刻印文一方，自左向右排列漢、滿、藏三種文字[28]。漢文篆書：「西天大善自在佛所領天下釋教普通瓦赤喇呾喇達賴喇嘛之印」。此印文與拉薩羅布林卡所藏一方木紐鐵印文字刻法一致。爲順治九年五世達賴入京朝覲，清朝廷所賜金印的複製印。從佛像造型分析爲內地宮廷所造佛像（詳見下文）。

第三類大喇嘛、第司私印、印押

五世達賴喇嘛私章。圖32白勇保護法，座面左角刻一方八思巴文印，據查爲五世達賴私章。原印爲羅布林卡所藏，木紐鐵印，寶珠紐，高9厘米，方邊長4.3厘米，原印繫有布條説明爲五世達賴喇嘛的印章，原爲金的，收藏後新製，內容待考[29]。

第司桑結嘉措的「壽」字印。圖43蓮花生像、圖75釋迦牟尼佛、圖76無量壽佛、佛像底座與背光刻八思巴文印一方，據查爲第司桑結嘉措的「壽」字印。印藏布達拉宮，銅印，獅紐，高4.7厘米，方，邊長3厘米，一面刻漢字款識「壽」，八思巴字印文字義待考，該印是他的私章[30]。插圖19爲青海民間收藏彌勒佛像，此像黃銅鑄造，高51.3厘米。佛像方座前面刻同樣兩方印與插圖15B相同，佛像眼睛嵌銀，嘴唇嵌紅銅，裙面減底陽刻精美的八寶圖案。佛身採用銀絲銀片鑲嵌雲紋、花朵、瓔珞珠綫，工藝精湛，造型講究，是十七世紀佛像中少見的佳作。第司桑結嘉措（一六五三～一七

插圖14A　佛像刻"夾實監藏"印（邊長5.2厘米）
插圖14B　"夾實監藏"印印譜（邊長5.1厘米）

插圖15A　佛像刻清朝廷封賜五世達賴喇嘛印（邊長11厘米）
插圖15B　五世達賴喇嘛木紐鐵印印譜（邊長11.2厘米）

插圖16　西藏博物館藏五世達賴喇嘛木紐鐵印

〇五）爲著名藏族學者、政治家。清康熙十八年（一六七九）任五世達賴喇嘛第司，主持管理西藏地方政務歷時達二十五年，是十七世紀西藏政治舞臺上重要人物，在任期間主持擴建布達拉宮紅宮，爲格魯派的發展建樹頗多。從幼年起就得到五世達賴的培養，精通五明，博學多才，整理、編纂和修訂了醫藥、天文、曆算、文學、歷史、宗教等大量經典，著述豐富。一六八二年五世達賴圓寂，桑結嘉措爲鞏固自己權位，秘不發喪十五年，並要結噶爾丹，以鉗制達賴汗。一六九四年復以五世達賴名義奏請清廷賜給他王爵，康熙帝封他爲王，並賜金印，印文曰：「掌瓦赤喇呾喇達賴喇嘛教弘宣佛法王布忒達阿白迪之印。」一六九六年，清軍大破噶爾丹後，康熙帝瞭解了事情真相，降旨詰責他秘喪不報，並唆助噶爾丹之罪，桑結嘉措卑辭請恕。其一生經歷跌宕起伏，康熙四十四年（一七〇五）在與統治西藏的蒙古拉藏汗爭奪權利的鬥爭中失敗身亡[31]。這幾尊佛像爲什麼刻有他本人印章？佛像與他有什麼關係？圖75釋迦牟尼佛、圖76無量壽佛爲何具有內地清宮廷風格？是否與他受封「弘宣佛法王」有關，還需我們深入探究。

丹吉林庫房印章。圖37金剛亥母，刻印一方，印文不是文字，而是一特殊符號，爲署押印，經查爲丹吉林庫房印章。《西藏

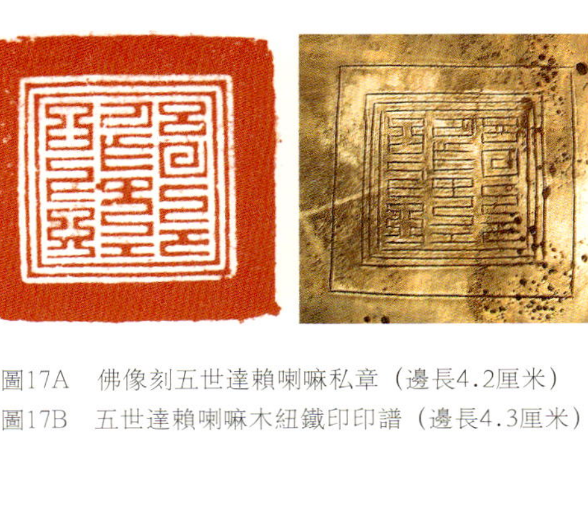

插圖17A　佛像刻五世達賴喇嘛私章（邊長4.2厘米）
插圖17B　五世達賴喇嘛木紐鐵印印譜（邊長4.3厘米）

插圖18A　佛像刻第司桑結嘉措的"壽"字印（邊長3厘米）
插圖18B　第司桑結嘉措銅印印譜（邊長3厘米）

插圖19　青海民間收藏彌勒佛像

[26] 此像原型無疑爲元代佛像，不排除元代以後照樣翻製的可能，何時翻製難以確定，但不會晚於清代。
[27] 見《西藏歷代藏印》44頁。
[28] 見《西藏歷代藏印》60頁。
[29] 見《西藏歷代藏印》66頁。
[30] 見《西藏歷代藏印》70頁。
[31] 參見王森《西藏佛教發展史略》183頁至197頁，中國社會科學出版社1987。

歷代藏印》記載丹吉林是清代西藏拉薩第穆活佛拉讓（府邸），位於大昭寺西北里許。第穆活佛曾三次擔任攝政（掌辦商上事務），在西藏僧俗人民中很有威望，他的拉讓丹吉林具有相當規模，庫房很多，現存庫房印章就有十三枚，書中選印六枚，佛像所刻爲其中一枚[32]。

待辨識八思巴文印。佛像圖31、33上刻的八思巴文印，插圖21係待辨識佛像刻印。插圖22釋迦牟尼佛像，青海民間收藏，十五世紀作品，通高46.8厘米，黃銅鑄造，佛像比例準確，佛面相豐滿，神態慈祥，佛像後背用銀絲鑲嵌出八思巴文印一方，內容待考。插圖23八思巴文印，印文左右採用銀絲鑲嵌，勾勒出六位各執樂器的供養天女，舞姿翩翩，造型優美。

這些佛像鐫刻印文，其功用是什麼呢？如果印文判斷不錯的話，它起碼説明了印主與佛像之間的關係，刻朝廷封賜官印，可能表明佛像與朝廷所賜有關；刻私印表示佛像爲印主所有，或印主贈給某寺院、某人，但在尚未找到確鑿的文獻證明與可考的參照文物之前，對佛像與印主的關係都衹能是推斷。一些轉世活佛的印長期使用，它的時間上限較易確定，而下限就難説，都需要綜合考證。這些首次面世的刻有印記的佛像，涉及到大元國師、五世達賴喇嘛、第司桑結嘉措、第穆活佛等著名歷史人物，有關元、明、清中央朝廷與西藏宗教領袖的關係，各教派大喇嘛收藏佛像的情況，包含了豐富的歷史文化信息，已成爲歷史的證物，其所涉及的歷史研究內容已遠遠超出佛像藝術研究的範疇。

四　明代宮廷永樂、宣德佛樣式及其流風

明代永樂、宣德時期，宮廷製作了大量精美的藏傳佛像，賞賜西藏來朝貢的各派宗教領袖，以永樂時期造像爲主，少量宣德佛像，以其漢藏合璧的造型，精湛的工藝，卓越藝術成就受到文物界、收藏界的推重。本書佛像中有多尊明宮廷所製佛像，造型優美，工藝精湛，題材豐富，品相完好，啓發我們認識永樂、宣德佛像的藝術成就，以及它在明清佛教雕塑藝術史中的深

插圖20A　佛像刻丹吉林庫房印（直徑1.8厘米）
插圖20B　丹吉林庫房鐵印印譜（直徑1.8厘米）

插圖21　待辨識佛像刻印文（邊長2厘米）

插圖22　青海民間藏釋迦牟尼佛像

遠影響。

漢傳佛教雕塑藝術到唐代達到高峰，如敦煌石窟彩塑，龍門石窟石雕佛像。宋以後隨着佛教的衰落，漢地佛教雕塑藝術也逐漸衰落，元以後幾乎乏善可陳了。而藏傳佛教的東傳，爲中原漢傳佛教藝術注入了新鮮血液，誕生了以漢藏藝術結合爲特徵的居庸關雲臺、杭州飛來峰石雕佛像等佳構。永樂佛像藝術正好接續了這一漢藏交融的藝術潮流，以金銅佛像雕塑爲代表達到了一個高峰，金銅佛像因材質貴重，歷來是戰亂時期盜搶的對象，大佛像尤其難逃劫難，現存文物數量稀少，基本爲十幾厘米的小佛像，使得我們對它的藝術成就估計不足，甚至把它放在賞玩的工藝品雕像一類。本書所收永樂、宣德佛像提高了我們的認識。

一、題材豐富多彩，西藏佛教顯宗、密宗像，西藏佛教各派推崇的各類佛像都有，與元宮廷專崇薩迦，清宮廷獨尊格魯不同，顯示了明宮廷佛教藝術對西藏各教派兼容並蓄的作法。本書有如下諸佛：

旃檀佛、釋迦牟尼佛、無量壽佛、彌勒菩薩、金剛薩埵、大持金剛、觀音菩薩、蓮花手觀音菩薩、自在觀音菩薩、四臂觀音菩薩、文殊菩薩、持世菩薩、吉祥天母、大黑天、四臂大黑天、寶帳怙主、馬頭金剛、紅閻魔敵、大成就者毗瓦巴。

永宣佛像嚴格遵循西藏佛像量度的規矩，佛像樣式模本應來自西藏，早有學者注意到相關的圖像資料，如法國海瑟・噶爾美在《早期漢藏藝術》中介紹了兩種：一、永樂版《甘珠爾》完成於永樂八年（一四一〇），是在北京刊印的第一部木刻版藏文經典。其中有多幅插圖版畫，版畫呈四方形，構圖簡潔，高雅精美，創作嚴謹，人物形象刻畫逼真傳神，似乎是遵從了西藏中部同一時代的藝術風格創作的。二、法國巴黎吉美博物館藏的一部第五世噶瑪派黑帽世系活佛得銀協巴傳承下來的佛經和《諸佛菩薩妙相名號經咒》六十幅諸佛菩薩插圖版畫，這部經籍於宣德六年（一四三一）在北京刊印[33]。北京故宮博物院收藏一部《明內府金藏護心經》是有關永樂佛像圖樣的又一重要材料。此經爲明宮廷永樂九年泥金楷書寫本佛經，經的形式爲經折裝，縱寬7厘米，每折面寬6.5厘米，共計385面，經有

插圖23　釋迦牟尼佛像銀絲鑲嵌八思巴文印

[32] 見《西藏歷代藏印》83頁。

[33] 見[法]海瑟・噶爾美《早期漢藏藝術》著，熊文彬譯，第3、4章，中國藏學出版社1994年版。

藍布描金花封套，上書題名《明内府金藏》。經裝在一紫檀木盒内，盒蓋内面刻「護心經」三字。這不是一部單獨的佛經，而是多部佛經、咒語組合，經前有永樂皇帝御製經序。每部經、咒前畫有金綫白描的佛像插圖，總計30幅[34]。在祇有5厘米見方的小紙面上精緻描繪了諸佛菩薩護法像，因是手繪比前述佛經版圖更細緻靈動，形象完全按照藏傳佛教造像量度刻畫，但服飾背光的細部表現又是漢式的，與永樂銅佛像比較除繪畫的細部稍有不同外，造型完全一致，如插圖24《明内府金藏護心經》吉祥天母像、插圖25《明内府金藏護心經》四臂文殊像，兩像與本書圖59、圖71銅像比較，可見其相同的構圖與細部表現，應與永樂銅佛的樣本有直接關係。經内御製經序記載時間是永樂九年（一四一一）、十年（一四一二），這是一部紀年準確的有關永樂銅佛肖像、藝術風格的重要文獻。

從上述圖像資料可見，永樂佛像造型來源不僅是西藏，直接影響還來自與元以來内地漢藏佛教藝術的發展，如居庸關雲臺雕刻、磧砂藏版畫的影響。永樂佛像的出現並不突然，是元以來藏漢文化藝術長期交流的結果。近來發表永宣佛像材料最豐富的是瑞士馮施羅德先生，他在《西藏佛教雕塑》一書中發表了西藏布達拉宫、羅布林卡、大昭寺、薩迦寺收藏永宣佛像六十四尊[35]。（内有重複），按佛像身份統計種類有三十餘種，李先生個人已收藏二十多種，可以構成清晰的系統，甚爲可觀。其中多尊佛像是罕見的珍品，如吉祥天母，僅見西藏博物館收藏一尊，彌勒菩薩立像尚未見發表。這些品相完好的佛像大大開闊了我們的視野，爲永宣佛像的深入研究提供了寶貴的新材料。

二、漢藏交融的設計之美，永樂佛像慈祥和美、雍容大度，裝飾華麗但自然適度，毫不顯纍贅。在造像量度的束縛之下，其造型設計之美，達到元以來的佛教造像藝術的巔峰。它的雕塑母題是西藏的，但在藝術表現上又與西藏原型不同。如忿怒神像，西藏作品着力表現的是凶惡丑陋恐怖，而永宣像同一身份神像給觀衆的感覺則是威而不凶，降低了它的恐怖感。度母豐乳細腰的女性特徵也不明顯，審美主體是漢族的，如方正的面相，衣裙自然起伏的衣褶，華麗的瓔珞，飄逸的帛帶，其髮髻、帽冠、頭飾、珠寶配飾、瓔珞、披帛、蓮座，每一細部都設計精準，樣式統一，高度程式化，是我們鑒定永樂、宣德佛像的主要依據單元，即所謂「母題零件」。永宣佛像把漢藏藝術因素巧妙結合，水乳交融，形成它獨特的藝術風格特徵，雍容而不失秀逸，渾厚之中又温文嫻雅，而這一風格長期影響了整個明清佛像藝術發展，包括内地與西藏。

精湛的工藝是永宣佛像的突出特點，金屬造像是佛像雕塑藝術中工藝最複雜的，集合了塑模、鑄造、鏨刻、打磨、鑲嵌、染色等十幾道工序。據清代宫廷檔案記録，製造一尊銅鎏金吉祥天母像需各類工匠達十二種之多：大器匠、銼刮匠、合對匠、收摟匠、胎基匠、鏨花匠、攢焊匠、磨匠、鍍金匠、洋金匠、畫匠、撥蠟匠[36]。可見造像工藝之複雜。永宣佛像鑄造鏨刻精細，每一縷髮絲、每一粒圓珠都一絲不苟，鍍金層厚光澤亮麗，工藝之精微縝密無可挑剔，確實是明清佛像中的珍品。

今天我們可見到的永樂佛像多爲十幾二十多厘米的小佛，刻款「大明永樂年施」在蓮座前面，由左向右書寫的小字款，一般認爲這是永宣佛像的主要特徵，本書中有幾尊大尺度佛像，圖52彌勒菩薩立像，高35.2厘米，大明永樂年施款；圖72大黑天，高58.2厘米，大明宣德年施款。圖64時輪金剛，高94厘米；圖60寶帳怙主，高52厘米；圖64、60兩像均爲黄銅鑄造，不鎏金，座前沿刻「大明永樂年施」雙鈎楷書款，字按古漢文書寫規矩由右向左書。佛像尺度高大，比例合度，造型精美，鑄造光潤。這些大尺寸不鎏金的佛像，像上所刻由右向左書的大字款識都是首次發表。永宣佛像款識還有幾種處理方式：無刻款，藏漢文兩種文字款，藏文款。如本書圖53觀音菩薩，永宣佛形式，衹在蓮座下沿刻藏文。

觀察永宣佛像的尺度有幾種常見尺寸：18厘米、26厘米、38厘米、53厘米。從佛像尺度與刻款方面，使我們對永樂佛像的認識更全面。現存多見的永宣宫廷佛像基本是20厘米左右高的小像，多是皇帝親賜禮品，得到賜物者視爲拱璧，世代珍藏，所以能較多地保存下來。而供於廟堂的大像，難以躲過一次次灾難，保存下來不易，其研究價值更高。因此我們對永樂、宣德佛像的認識不能局限在十幾二十厘米的小佛像上，如大體量，不鎏金，大字刻款，更符合古漢字書寫習慣的由右向左書寫等，都是啓發我們應予注意的特點。如插圖26瞿曇寺保藏的大鐘上分明刻着大字「大明宣德年施」鑄款，由右向左書。

這樣一批珍貴的永宣佛像，能在甘青地區保存下來，是有歷史淵源的。明王朝建立後，沿襲元制以支持藏傳佛教爲安藏方略，實行「多封衆建」政策，改變元朝獨尊薩迦一派，薩迦帝師掌管宣政院，擁有管轄衛藏十三萬户職權的作法。明初設立西安行都指揮使司於河州，統轄河州、朵甘、烏斯藏等三衛，後升朵甘、烏斯藏爲行都指揮使司，在甘青川等地設置衛所，建立土司制度，把全國藏區都置於中央政權的統一治理之下。

明王朝重視對甘青一帶藏區的經略，隨着明朝在西北的軍事行動，洪武二年（一三六九）即命陝西行省員外郎許允德詔諭吐蕃，洪武三年（一三七〇）故元陝西行省吐蕃宣慰使何鎖南普來降，鎮西武靖王卜納剌及吐蕃諸部來降[37]。太祖朱元璋本着「惟因其俗尚，用僧徒化導爲善」之策，爲獎勵三羅喇嘛招撫罕東諸衛有功，明洪武二十五年（一三九二）朝廷在樂都敕建瞿曇寺，以爲聯結青海各地和西藏的紐帶。

插圖24　北京故宫藏《明内府金藏護心經》吉祥天母像

插圖25　北京故宫藏《明内府金藏護心經》四臂文殊像

插圖26　瞿曇寺大鐘刻“大明宣德年施”款識

[34] 御製經序五篇：

1.御製金剛般若波羅密經序，永樂九年五月初一日

2.御製觀世音普門品經序，永樂九年五月初一日

3.御製真實名經序，永樂九年七月十五日

4.御製佛頂尊勝總持經咒序，永樂十年五月初六日

5.御製大悲總持經咒序，永樂十年五月初六日

佛經八部：

1.金剛般若波羅密經

2.妙法蓮花經觀世音菩薩普門品

3.般若波羅密多心經

4.聖妙吉祥真實名經

5.佛頂大白傘蓋楞嚴陀羅尼經

6.佛説五十三佛大因緣經

7.佛説三十五佛名經

8.稱揚諸佛功德經

真言、神咒、陀羅尼三十一頌。

泥金白描佛像三十幅（有重複）：釋迦牟尼佛、紅閻王、黑閻王、吉祥天母、大持金剛、韋陀、寶帳怙主、四臂觀音、秘密文殊、無量壽佛、大白傘蓋佛母、尊勝佛母、文殊、四臂觀音、手持金剛三怙主、緑救度佛母、沙斡佛母、摩利支天、大威德熾盛光如來、金剛手菩薩、金剛心菩薩、金剛薩埵、一佛二弟子等像。

[35] ［瑞士］馮施羅德《西藏佛教雕塑》二卷，第20章：中國明朝金屬雕像。Ulrich von Schroedr, *Buddhist Sculptures in Tibet*, Hong Kong: Visual Dharma Publication Ltd., 2001。XX Chinese Metal Sculptures of the Ming Dynasty(1368–1644 AD).

[36] 中國第一歷史檔案館藏乾隆三十七年《内務府奏銷檔》編號311～316。

封三羅喇嘛爲西寧僧綱司都綱，成爲西寧衛的宗教領袖。永樂帝在瞭解了藏區各派宗教領袖的政治作用後採用「多封衆建」策略，各教派領袖人物祇要歸順朝廷，來請封的都賜加封號，朝廷厚與賞賜。永樂四年（一四〇六）迎請藏傳佛教噶瑪巴黑帽系五世活佛哈立麻到南京，爲其父母建「普度大齋」，永樂五年封哈立麻爲大寶法王。先後給西藏各教派領袖封授了大寶法王、大乘法王、闡化王、闡教王、輔教王、贊善王王爵，及西天佛子、大國師、國師、禪師等各級封號。藏區各派佛教領袖紛紛赴京朝貢，朝廷給與册封任命，厚與賞賜。藏區的僧俗領袖以得到朝廷封賜爲榮，擁戴效忠朝廷，收到了治理藏區的效果。

永樂、宣德時期宮廷製作的藏傳佛像，是朝廷賞賜僧俗領袖的貴重禮品，見證了永樂、宣德時期宮廷與藏區的緊密聯繫。值得關注的是在這一歷史過程中，甘青地區的藏族人士發揮了重要橋梁作用，早在永樂元年（一四〇三）朝廷派赴西藏迎請哈立麻的就是時任司禮監少監的洮岷藏族人侯顯，明廷先後三次派他出使西藏以加强朝廷與藏傳佛教各派的聯繫，《明史》列傳中有侯顯傳，評價他「顯有才辯，强力敢任，五使絶域，勞績與鄭和亞」。晚年告老還鄉，在家鄉洮州修建了侯家寺[38]，侯氏家族世襲該寺僧綱。《安多政教史》記載：

> 敦請大慈法王的太監侯顯把許多財物交給他的侄子漢官侯文，讓他在祖先貢瑪的舊寺遺址上修建了這座寺……這座寺院，供有以黄金製成的大明洪武東空皇帝的牌位，石築的太監侯顯靈塔。[39]

永樂、宣德時期還有班丹嘉措、班丹札失、釋迦巴藏卜三位出身於甘青洮岷地區的藏族高僧，忠誠效力於明王朝，深受皇帝信任，亦爲溝通中央與西藏地方的聯繫，爲穩定明朝的西北邊疆發揮了獨特的作用，在漢藏佛教文化交流方面作出重要貢獻。其中班丹札失成就最大，十五歲時從叔叔仲欽·班丹嘉措出家爲僧，二十八歲時隨叔叔到南京覲見永樂帝，得到皇帝的賞識，永樂三年（一四〇五）被朝廷派赴西藏迎接哈立麻，任命爲哈立麻的翻譯。多次奉聖旨赴衛藏，先後朝禮並求法於宗喀巴、大寶法王、大乘法王等佛教大師。曾長期在北京主持海淵寺，弘揚佛法。永樂十九年（一四二一）被任命爲僧録司右闡教，以番僧身份在中央政府任要職。永樂二十一年（一四二三）又奉命赴西藏審驗大寶法王哈立麻的呼畢勒罕，這是明中央政府首次審驗敕封大喇嘛轉世。宣德元年（一四二六）受封浄覺慈濟大國師。景泰年間，封爲大智法王。

班丹札失精通漢藏語文，翻譯藏文經典，在京師常以漢語演教，受戒弟子中有許多漢族的地方官員及南印度人。他親自給宣德皇帝灌頂傳法，《安多政教史》記載：

> 宣德元年，火馬年（1426年，丙午）……奉皇上的聖旨著《喜金剛修法·甘露海》，及大輪、大威德十三尊、普明、阿彌陀佛九尊等的曼荼羅儀軌，《多聞子修法》、《中有介紹》等，並將這些著作、儀軌等，連同藏文《喜金剛續二品釋》都譯成了漢文……土猴年（1428年，明宣德三年，戊申），於絳芬殿給皇上授大輪灌頂，於便殿授無量壽佛九尊灌頂。[40]

班丹札失在宣德帝的直接支持下，動用了朝廷的大量人力物力，在岷州建成了規模宏偉的大崇教寺，成爲明朝廷在甘青地區敕建的又一重要寺院，深受明帝重視，先後有多名僧人被封爲法王、大國師、國師、禪師。朝廷多次給大崇教寺賜金印、金佛冠、珍珠袈裟、千輻金輪等。其中多有皇家所賜的精美器物，如金製壇城、金燈、銀燈、水晶和瑪瑙的花瓶、銅香爐、傘蓋等[41]。

明清以來，甘青地區除了大崇教寺、瞿曇寺、弘化寺等皇帝敕建寺廟外，還有許多寺廟中都珍藏着明朝皇帝的賜物，成爲寺院的傳世之寶。《安多政教史》中就留下有關永樂佛像的記載：

> 佑寧寺土觀活佛的吉祥宮……從五臺山迎請來的印度青銅鍛製的佛像，永樂皇帝的本尊佛約一箭之高的喜金剛，約一肘高的勝樂、金剛手、大輪菩薩、大威德等金像及許多塑像畫像……
>
> 明永樂皇帝製造的二尺高的三世佛的金像、金剛持金像、彌勒佛金像、觀世音菩薩金像等……
>
> 活佛府中央的佛堂裏，供奉着據稱係永樂皇帝的本尊三世佛金像及寶座、背墊……[42]

這是有關永樂佛像的重要文獻記載，說明了安多地區歷史上的確有各種尺度永樂佛像，二尺高、一箭高甚至高達一人的大佛像，質地爲金像（包括鎏金像）、合金銅鑄像。

永樂帝是一位雄才大略的皇帝，從文化層面看，他崇信佛教，熱衷建寺刻經，對藏傳佛教興趣濃厚，禮敬西藏高僧，開明代歷朝皇帝崇奉藏傳佛教之端。永樂八年前後在藏區以外首刻藏文版《甘珠爾》大藏經108函，即著名的永樂版藏文大藏經，爲現存最早的刻本藏文大藏經。

永樂帝氣魄宏大，倡導編修了《永樂大典》。鑄造了世界鐘王「永樂大鐘」，高6.75米，重46.5噸，上面鑄有23萬字（漢文22萬字，梵文4245字）。永樂三年（一四〇五）開始派鄭和率領27000多人，百餘艘戰艦七下西洋，歷時28年，航程萬餘里，創造了世界航海一大奇迹。值得一提的是統帥這一龐大艦隊的穆斯林鄭和，却是一位虔誠的藏傳佛教信徒。據明代天順元年（一四五七）無名氏撰《非幻庵香火聖像記》中記載，鄭和曾自己出資請工匠鑄造了十二尊金銅佛像[43]。

[37] 《明實録》卷四二、卷五五。

[38] 侯家寺在今甘肅省卓尼縣流順鄉。詳見浦文成主編《甘青藏傳佛教寺院》542頁侯家寺條，青海人民出版社1990年版。

[39] 智觀巴・貢却乎丹巴繞吉著，吴均、毛繼祖、馬世林譯《安多政教史》，628、629頁。甘肅民族出版社1989年版。

[40] 智觀巴・貢却乎丹巴繞吉著，吴均、毛繼祖、馬世林譯《安多政教史》，642頁。

[41] 參閱吴均《論明代河洮岷的地位及其三傑》，原載《青海民族學院學報》1989年第4期。

[42] 智觀巴・貢却乎丹巴繞吉著，吴均、毛繼祖、馬世林譯《安多政教史》，75、78、85頁。

從永樂帝對藏傳佛教崇信的態度及個性看，要造佛也絕不會衹造精緻小佛，可以推知永樂時期宮廷造過不少大佛像，例如原瞿曇寺佛像，現藏青海博物館的觀音立像，高145厘米，座沿刻「大明永樂年施」漢、藏、梵三種文字款識，華麗精美，是現存刻有年款體積最高大的永樂銅像。如插圖27是北京雍和宮密宗殿內大威德銅鎏金像，高285厘米，重逾六噸，雖未見款識，造型具有典型的永樂特徵，工藝精湛，氣魄雄偉，無疑是現存體量最大的永樂銅佛。它不是雍和宮舊藏，是從北京其他寺中移來的，原存何處已無考。《帝京景物略》中就曾詳細描述了萬曆年間西域雙林寺供奉的大威德金剛形像[44]。

永樂、宣德佛像繁盛期衹有三十年，表面看起來像一場大戲轟轟烈烈一番就悄然謝幕了，其實不然，永樂、宣德佛像作爲一種流行的宮廷佛像藝術樣式，傳播到藏區民間，深受歡迎，得到很高評價。十六世紀噶舉派僧人白瑪噶波（一五二七～一五九二）著《利瑪佛像鑒賞》一文，對西藏、中原內地、印度、尼泊爾等地的金銅佛像作了評述，就造像材質與風格對藏傳銅佛作了分類説明。白瑪噶波高度評價永樂、宣德佛像：

> 漢地新佛像（明代）澆鑄潔凈，鍍金優美，肌肉豐滿，衣褶精美，面部略扁平，眼睛細長。寶座前後鑄有互爲連接的雙層蓮花，上下兩層略微向外分伸，上下層排列有均勻精細的珍珠。寶座連接牢固，上飾交杵金剛，塗有塗料。另一類爲形體較小、無硃砂交杵金剛和文字的敬事佛像，質地係易識辨之漢地黄銅和淡色黄銅[45]。

永宣佛像輸入藏區，對藏地佛像影響深遠，成爲模仿的樣本，被稱爲「永樂利瑪」。來烏群巴是十五世紀中期西藏拉薩地區的著名工匠。扎雅指出來烏群巴利瑪佛像：「鍍金的鑄像與明永樂利瑪像極爲相似，造型美觀。盤起的雙腿自然放鬆，雙排的蓮花環繞法座形成一個蓮花團，兩排蓮花之間的聯接處嵌入較深，花瓣脉絡清晰。」[46]北京故宮保存四尊來烏群巴題記佛像，特點與文獻記載相符，與永宣佛像有相似之處，如寶冠、蓮座的樣式，長裙起伏自然的衣紋刻畫，吸收了永樂、宣德佛像的若干因素[47]。插圖28北京故宮藏來烏群巴造四臂觀音菩薩，紅銅鎏金，高19厘米，面相莊嚴，眉目之間傳達出一種憂鬱感，表現了觀音悲憫衆生的情懷，吸收了漢地佛教造像手法，工藝精美。像上拴黄條：

> 大利益流崇干琍瑪四臂觀音菩薩，乾隆四十六年十一月二十九日收嘎爾丹西勒圖羅藏丹巴……

「流崇干」是藏文音譯，意爲「來烏群的」，即「來烏群巴琍瑪佛像」。此像是具有可靠記録的「來烏群巴琍瑪佛像」，極爲珍貴。

由此可見，永宣佛像已成爲明代藏區的一種流行佛像樣式，藏區工匠依宮廷原像翻模鑄造，或仿造，一直到明晚期，甚至到清代中期，其影響之深，連日理萬機的康熙帝都知曉，他曾在諭旨中提到永樂利瑪佛像：

烏絲藏舊佛中最重者莫過利嘛，利嘛之原出中國。永樂年間宮中所造者爲弟（第）一。又烏絲藏仿其形象煉其銅體造者，亦是利嘛，頗爲可愛，如今甚少。近世又仿利嘛而十不及一。爾春間所進乃漢人所造，非烏絲藏舊物。念爾久在大內，將烏絲藏仿造利嘛無量壽佛一尊賜去，亦可以爲母祝壽可也。[48]

北京故宮收藏的一尊佛像從造型看是清代西藏佛像，但在蓮座上清晰地刻寫「大明宣德年施」，顯然是清代仿刻，不僅是造型，刻款也成爲模仿的對象[49]，可見康熙所言不虛。本書圖99文殊菩薩像完全爲永樂佛形象，細部比例稍有誤差，工藝精細。蓮座底沿刻藏文，漢文意思是乾隆十六年造。說明永宣式樣在藏區長期流傳，影響久遠。永宣佛像取得的藝術成就是元以來藏傳佛教在內地傳播發展，藏漢藝術交流的碩果。

插圖27　北京雍和宮密宗殿大威德銅像

五　清代宮廷康熙、乾隆佛像樣式及其流風

本書中收入多尊與清代宮廷製造佛像有聯繫的作品。根據主要在兩方面，首先是佛像的樣式與北京故宮所藏清宮廷製造的

插圖28　北京故宮藏來烏群巴題記佛像

[43] 參見林梅村著《松漠之間》第九章“《非幻庵香火聖像記》之鄭和遺囑”。生活·讀書·新知三聯書店2007年版。

[44] 劉侗、于奕正著《《帝京景物略》205頁，北京古籍出版社1982年版。

[45] 《利瑪佛像鑒賞》藏文本見《白瑪噶波文集》印度巴倫普爾影印本，1970年。熊文彬漢譯本見王家鵬《藏傳金銅佛像傳統分類例證——故宮藏傳佛像題記解讀》附録，刊《故宮學刊》第一輯。

[46] 見扎雅著，謝繼勝譯《西藏宗教藝術》143頁，西藏人民出版社1987年版。

[47] 王家鵬主編《故宮文物珍品全集——藏傳佛教造像》圖169四臂觀音菩薩坐像。商務印書館（香港）有限公司2003年版。

[48] 《掌故叢編》第二輯，11頁，故宮博物院1928年編印。

[49] 同注31圖。

佛像一致，出自同一模本，佛像的造型說明了兩者間的密切關係。如本書圖89四臂觀音菩薩高72厘米，座面刻藏文四臂觀音名號，蓮座後面刻三行藏文題記贊頌六字真言的功德。此佛樣式尺度與北京故宮所藏康熙二十五年（一六八六）四臂觀音像即爲同一模本。清代康熙時期宮廷開始製作藏傳佛像，康熙佛像存世很少，帶有紀年的更爲珍稀，北京故宮珍藏的康熙二十五年四臂觀音是最重要的標尺文物[50]。插圖29北京故宮康熙四臂觀音像，原存慈寧宮大佛堂，是康熙帝專爲祖母孝莊文皇后祝壽所造，內地工匠作品，黃銅鎏金，高73厘米。雍容華貴，光彩奪目，基本上還保持着永樂、宣德造像傳統，如豐滿圓潤的面相，起伏自如的衣褶。但永宣佛像特有的寶冠樣式、瓔珞佩飾、蓮座形式已多有變化，是清初宮廷造像的珍品。蓮座大蓮瓣圓鼓，雕刻有華麗的卷雲邊。蓮座下沿用漢滿蒙藏四體文字刻銘文，漢文：

大清昭聖慈壽恭簡安懿章慶敦惠溫莊康和仁宣弘靖太皇太后，虔奉三寶，福庇萬靈。自於康熙二十五年歲次丙寅奉聖諭不日告成，永念聖祖母仁慈垂佑，衆生更賴菩薩感應，聖壽無疆云爾。

細察兩像的尺度，造像樣式，工藝特點，藝術風格基本一致，不難看出二者間的緊密關係。如：精緻華麗的五葉冠，葫蘆形髮髻，髻頂飾蓮座珠寶，U形上卷的繒帶；胸前三圈精美的瓔珞珠寶項鏈，左肩頭披羊皮；在乳頭處雕刻大菱形珠寶飾件，左邊飾件上部刻羊頭，羊口叼珠寶，這些細節之處完全相同，都是康熙佛像的典型作法。圖89四臂觀音菩薩的後背製作簡化，蓮座後部光素沒有蓮瓣，正好留出地方刻寫藏文題記。此像是在甘青地區或是北京所造難以確定，但這二像是同一個模本無疑。

本書圖88四臂觀音菩薩（高61厘米）與北京故宮藏品插圖30四臂觀音金佛（高90厘米，重32210克）[51]也是同一模本，北京故宮像蓮莖下刻「大清乾隆年製」款，背光後背刻漢滿蒙藏四體銘文，漢文曰：

乾隆十三年十二月二十日奉特旨赤金成造供奉利益四臂觀世音　番稱堅賴滋克庫布勒庫舍勒佛齊希　蒙古稱都爾本噶爾圖

兩像都爲樣式相同的獨莖蓮花高座，葫蘆形背光，觀音帽冠與臉形不同，北京故宮像長圓面，鼻綫近三角形，是典型的乾隆宮廷佛面像；圖88四臂觀音菩薩方形童子面相，精緻的鏤空的背光，是康熙時期的特點，說明兩像的年代差異。從以上例舉的佛像，可以發現兩者間出自同一種設計造型，細部有差別，但其母型是一致的，這是我們判斷佛像時代、産地風格的基本要素。

其二，佛像上刻有清晰的漢字款識，已見如下文字：大清康熙年製、大清康熙年施、大清乾隆年施、大清康熙年禮部造、大清乾隆年禮部造、大清康熙年布達拉宮供，幾個佛像上還刻有印章、印押（前文已述）。

清宮廷所造佛像今天絕大部分保存在北京故宮博物院，北京故宮內尚未見到有上述款識的佛像，文獻檔案中也尚未見記載，我們對佛像及其款識自然産生疑問。經過對佛像的造型、工藝、款識多方面研究，發現這些佛像確與清宮廷密切相關。先看「大清康熙年禮部造」、「大清乾隆年禮部造」。清朝立國之初，中央負責有關外交事宜的機構是禮部和理藩院。清朝的禮部是天聰五年（一六三一）所設六部的第三個部，其內部組織結構基本上沿襲明代，負責管理國家祀典慶典、禮儀以及學校、科舉等事務。禮部下設的祠祭清吏司設有專門管理佛道的僧録司、道録司。僧道官之選取升補由內務府辦理，由禮部給札。僧録司、道録司之印信均由禮部鑄印局鑄造，禮部頒給[52]。在明清時期宮廷頒發的官印上往往刻有「禮部造」及編號字樣。清朝對寺廟、佛像的建造管理嚴格，據康熙朝《大清會典》記載：

嚴禁京城內外不許擅造寺廟佛像，如呈報禮部，方許建造。其現在寺廟佛像亦不許私自拆毀。[53]

可知禮部負有監督製造佛像之責，朝廷親賜某寺佛像，由禮部負責造像頒發是完全可能的。康熙三十六年（一六九七）清宮廷設立了專門管理藏傳佛教的機構「中正殿念經處」，主管宮廷內喇嘛念經、辦造佛像。乾隆時期又設立雍和宮管理王大臣一職，專管雍和宮佛教事務。宮廷佛事活動的制度化，說明了藏傳佛教在清宮廷中的重要影響。實際上，在康熙三十六年前宮廷

插圖29　北京故宮藏康熙四臂觀音像

插圖30　北京故宮藏四臂觀音金佛

[50] 發表於王家鵬主編《故宮博物院藏文物珍品全集——藏傳佛教造像》圖226、商務印書館（香港）有限公司2003年出版。

[51] 見徐啓憲主編《故宮博物院藏文物珍品全集——宮廷珍寶》圖185，商務印書館（香港）有限公司2004年出版。

[52] 見《光緒會典》卷三六。

[53] 見《康熙會典》卷七十一。

已開始造佛像，賞賜蒙藏僧俗領袖。《康熙朝滿文硃批奏摺全譯》記載：

> 皇太子胤礽奏爲噶爾丹益加途窮等摺
>
> 康熙三十五年九月二十日：皇太子臣胤礽謹奏：奉諭：沿途蒙古人甚多，養心殿所造之佛像即將賜完，若造畢，多送些來，欽此欽遵。問羌國忠：上圍獵所攜之佛像，模型未定，今模型尚未修整畢，故此未造，今仍用舊模型趕造，急速送之，待新模型成功後，另造急速送往。[54]

這是在康熙三十五年平定準噶爾戰役過程中清廷將宮廷所造的佛像賜予蒙古諸部的記載。《大清會典》記載，甘青地區的寺院大喇嘛早在清初順治時期已開始向清朝廷進貢，繳回明朝所給誥敕印箚懇請清朝換發新誥敕印箚：

> 西番各寺，順治八年河州宏化、顯慶寺各遣番僧貢舍利、銅塔、佛像、番犬，及馬駝、氆氌、豹皮、酥油諸物。十年，西寧瞿曇寺等九寺國師、禪師喇嘛進貢。[55]
>
> 西寧番寺，順治十年西寧瞿曇等九寺進貢，又西納演教寺進貢，貢道具由陝西。順治十年，陝西總督奏稱西寧衛瞿曇等九寺國師禪師喇嘛進貢，繳明所給誥敕印箚，懇請換給，禮部提准瞿曇寺國師公噶丹净封爲灌頂净覺弘濟大國師，給鍍金銀印一顆。
>
> 洮岷番寺，按洮州、岷州有番僧、有番族，順治十七年圓覺寺進貢，康熙二年番僧二十一寺換給敕書，五年又給五寺敕書，共二十六寺。分爲四族，定貢期三年一次，貢道由甘肅。
>
> 附載二十六寺：圓覺寺、大崇教寺、講堂寺、剎藏寺、弘教寺、洪福寺、法藏寺、朝定寺、石崖寺、魯定寺、羊圈寺、永安寺、廣善寺、昭慈寺、洪濟寺、崇隆寺、寶净寺、寫兜朵寺、讚林寺、永寧寺、廣德寺、三竹寺、裕竜寺、藏經寺、荔川寺、工布寺。[56]

清王朝重視與青海藏傳佛教領袖的關係，對來朝進貢的大喇嘛按慣例給以豐厚的回賞。皇帝欽賜寺院匾額、佛器、財物，對青海地區許多著名的喇嘛給以册封，賜給國師、呼圖克圖、諾門汗、班智達、堪布、賽赤、倉等名號。這些題有「禮部造」款識的佛像，很可能是清廷賜給青海寺院和有名號的大喇嘛的。

觀察本書中圖77、96「禮部造」彌勒站像恰與北京故宫金彌勒站像是同一模本。插圖31北京故宫藏彌勒金像，純金鑄造，高54厘米，重19030克，康熙時期宫廷作品。身材壯碩，面相豐滿，下身着雙層長裙，身側蓮枝纏繞蟠升，隨身長帛翻卷垂地，嵌大小珍珠183顆，金光燦爛，造型優雅，精工華美，是清宫佛像的代表作。彌勒頭飾蓮座是藏式，而肥碩的體形顯然來自漢地彌勒傳統形象，與藏傳佛教中王子英俊形像的彌勒不同。這一精美的彌勒佛樣一直傳到乾隆時期，也傳到了藏區。

「大清康熙年施」、「大清乾隆年施」文字内容與永樂、宣德佛像款識一樣，衹是完全按古漢字横寫習慣由右向左書寫。插圖32是青海民間收藏的一尊釋迦牟尼佛像，釋迦佛端坐寬大的長方須彌座，座面刻「大清乾隆年施」漢字款，雙鈎寫法從右向

插圖32　青海民間收藏釋迦牟尼佛像

插圖33　釋迦牟尼佛像“大清乾隆年施”刻款

插圖31　北京故宮藏彌勒金像

左書，字體端正有力。插圖33「大清乾隆年施」刻款，釋迦牟尼佛面帶微笑，祥和可親。身着華麗袈裟，上刻高浮雕千佛，衣褶細密流暢，刀法爽利，佛前左右立兩位托鉢侍從菩薩。橫寬的方型背光，頂部五拱圓形，背光正面高浮雕蓮花纏枝，在花枝間雕多位佛、菩薩像，左右雕兩條行龍。插圖34釋迦牟尼佛像背光墨綫圖設計形式基本是漢式的，繼承了明代廟堂佛像的式樣風格，氣勢宏大，我們在青海瞿曇寺瞿曇殿中還可看到這種形式的明代佛像背光。豪華精美的造型與刻款說明了佛像與清宮廷的關係。更引人注意的是須彌座後背還刻有八思巴文印一方，3.2厘米見方，爲五世達賴喇嘛私章[57]，與本書圖33刻印相同。插圖37釋迦牟尼佛像後背刻印。如此印不錯，很可能此佛像爲乾隆宮廷賞賜達賴喇嘛，達賴喇嘛刻上本人的私章寶藏。顯然這是一尊具有重要歷史、藝術價值的佛像。本書圖93釋迦牟尼佛像與此像樣式尺寸完全一樣，通體鎏金，雖沒有刻款識印章，顯然是同一模本。本書圖94釋迦牟尼佛像臺座背光與圖93造型相同。西藏博物館也收藏一尊同樣背光佛像[58]。插圖38西藏博物館藏四臂觀音像，說明這可能是源自明清宮廷的一種樣式佛像，流傳於西藏與青海藏區。

插圖34　釋迦牟尼佛像背光墨綫圖

插圖35　瞿曇寺隆國殿外景

插圖36　瞿曇寺瞿曇殿佛像及背光

[54] 中國第一歷史檔案館編《康熙朝滿文硃批奏摺全譯》，105頁，中國社會科學出版社1996年版。

[55] 乾隆朝《大清會典則例》卷一四三。

[56] 康熙朝《大清會典》卷七十三。

[57] 印文同前述圖33白勇保護法。

隨着歷史環境的變化，清朝治理蒙藏的政策與明朝不同，但基本的策略是一致的，採取「興黃安蒙」的策略，大力扶持藏傳佛教格魯派，禮遇佛教領袖人物，封授藏傳佛教上層人物，藏區佛教領袖定期朝貢，厚與賞賜，使之效忠朝廷，達到控制西藏，安定蒙藏地區的目的。從朝廷賞賜佛像刻款中「施」字含義看，是佛教中施主與上師的供施關係，實質上是反映着朝廷與受賜者間的政治關係，藏區的宗教頭領無不以朝廷的封賞爲榮，借以提高自身的政教地位，清宮廷在賞賜的佛像上刻「施」款完全可能，北京故宮内沒有帶「施」字款的佛像是因此類佛像已賞出，宮内不留，包括明「永樂宣德年施」款像也是清代西藏地方回獻皇宮的，所以北京故宮收藏的永宣佛像數量不多。「大清康熙年施」、「大清乾隆年施」佛像還需深入研究。這些題記佛像爲研究清宮廷佛像提供了新材料。

清宮廷與甘青寺院關係密切，從康熙年間起設置駐京呼圖克圖，在京供職者十二名，其中青海僧人占七位，有塔爾寺的阿嘉、拉科，佑寧寺的章嘉、土觀，廣惠寺的敏珠爾，德千寺的賽赤，東科爾寺的東科爾，全部爲格魯派喇嘛。其中影響最大的是章嘉國師系統，成爲格魯派在北京、内蒙、山西地區的最高領袖，與達賴、班禪和外蒙古的哲布尊丹巴並列的四大活佛系統。這充分説明了青海格魯派上層在安撫蒙番中的特殊地位，由於歷代中央王朝的重視，册封任用高僧，進一步刺激了藏傳佛教界人士對佛教文化的苦學和研修，安多藏傳佛教界向以名僧輩出享譽海内外[59]。乾隆欽定駐京喇嘛班次時，定章嘉爲左翼頭班，敏珠爾爲右翼頭班，均爲青海大呼圖克圖。乾隆時期以三世章嘉國師爲代表的青海僧人對清宮廷影響至深，長期指導修建宮廷藏傳佛教殿堂，製作佛像、法器。至今北京故宮保留下各類豐富的藏傳佛教文物，以及大量相關的檔案資料。紫禁城内最大的藏傳佛殿雨花閣就是在三世章嘉指導之下修建的[60]。清宮檔案詳細記録乾隆的指示：

插圖38　西藏博物館藏四臂觀音像

插圖39　北京故宮藏三世章嘉若必多吉像

插圖40　北京故宮雨花閣外景

插圖41　北京故宮雨花閣内景

插圖37　釋迦牟尼佛像後背刻印

乾隆十八年……胡世傑呈覽奉旨：壇城木樣交章嘉胡圖克圖細看。欽此。

乾隆四十一年……副都統金將遵旨擬畫得雨花閣上安設無量壽佛寶塔紙樣一張交太監胡世傑呈覽奉旨：照樣準做，成做時其塔上風帶坯片要厚，再歡門交章嘉胡圖克圖畫。有蓮花座喇嘛字先呈樣，塔肚内應裝臓亦着問章嘉胡圖克圖，欽此。

三世章嘉是精通佛教五明的一代大師，親自參與指導宮廷佛像法器製造，如檔案所記：

乾隆三十六年……傳旨着三和金輝同去見章嘉胡土克圖，問造鈴杵如何對用響銅、金子、寶石之法。

乾隆四十四年十月初三……傳旨照佛海觀音菩薩法身着章嘉胡土克圖擬佛一尊畫樣呈覽。

乾隆四十六年十一月二十四日將紫金利瑪釋迦牟尼佛、宗喀巴請至中正殿交章嘉胡土克圖慶贊呈覽。[61]

清宮廷内有藏族匠師長期在宮廷作坊工作，參與宮廷佛教藝術的創作。其中有來自安多、康區的匠師亦完全可能。甘青流傳的佛像造型多有與北京故宮收藏的皇家佛像形制一致情況，決非偶然巧合，以章嘉國師爲代表的青海高僧把安多康區流行的佛像樣式傳入宮廷。原本爲北京地區的佛像式樣，隨着宮廷佛像賞賜甘青寺院，成爲當地佛像製作模仿的樣板。由此可見，清宮廷佛像與甘青地區民間佛像之間相互影響和緊密聯繫。

藝術現象往往會直接或間接地反映出歷史長河中民族文化交流融合的痕迹，觀察佛像造型樣式、工藝特點，更多地採用了漢地佛像藝術的表現手法，漢風爲主，在裝飾細部上吸收西藏佛教藝術的樣式。從佛像款識也反映出漢藏結合的理念，一些佛像是典型的永樂樣式佛像，康熙、乾隆樣式佛像，但祇刻藏文款識。或漢藏兩體文字款識，可見明清宮廷爲代表的佛像藝術深刻影響了甘青地區佛教藝術的發展，漢藏交融是甘青地區明清佛像藝術風格的突出特點，成爲元以來甘青地區佛教藝術的主旋律。

王家鵬（故宮博物院研究館員，藏傳佛教文物研究、鑒定專家，文化部國家非物質文化遺產保護工作專家委員會委員）

[58] 見熊文彬主編《中國藏傳佛教雕塑全集·金銅佛下》圖80四臂觀音，銅鎏金，高約30厘米，明代。北京美術攝影出版社2001年版。

[59] 參見浦文成《青海佛教史》18頁、245頁。

[60] 詳見王家鵬《故宮雨花閣探源》，《故宮博物院院刊》1990年1期。

[61] 中國第一歷史檔案館乾隆十八年、三十六年、四十一年、四十四年、四十六年《清内務府養心殿造辦處各作成做活計清檔》。

New Discoveries of Buddhist Statues in Gansu-Qinghai Area

Wang Jiapeng

The gilt copper Buddhist statue is an important part and one of the most characteristic features of Tibetan Buddhist art. For more than 1,300 years, Tibetan artists have created numerous masterpieces of Buddhist statues, scoring brilliant achievements that have been remarkable in the art history of the world. The Tibetan Buddhist art, originated in the Tibetan Plateau, has been very influential in many other areas outside Tibet. As early as at the turn between the 11th and the 12th century, Tibetan Buddhism was introduced into the Tangut kingdom of Xia. Ever since the Mongol Yuan Dynasty, Tibet has been an integral part of China. The political and cultural relationship was increasingly intensified between Tibet and China Proper. Tibetan Buddhism penetrated deeply eastward into China Proper. Chinese and Tibetan Buddhist arts interacted closely. Having spread out of Tibetan Plateau, Tibetan Buddhist arts had exerted great influences on Chinese Buddhist arts, giving birth to a huge number of works of Buddhist arts that had absorbed features of both Han Chinese and Tibetan Buddhist arts. In addition to immobile cultural relics, there are also numerous movable Buddhist antiques, of which gilt cooper Buddhist statue is an important one. Gilt copper Buddhist statues depicted in this book all belong to the private collection of Mr. Li Wei, who has made a remarkable contribution to the protection of the cultural relics of our motherland.

Mr. Li Wei's collection provides fresh materials on Tibetan Buddhist statues. All these statues have been kept secret among private citizens and never been revealed before. Generally speaking, the style of these statues bears similarity with the ones commonly found in dBus-gTsang area or with those that were manufactured in China Proper during the Ming and Qing dynasty. Yet, there are also statues which are quite unique in style of modeling. As well, the inscribed Tibetan or Han Chinese scripts are rarely seen before. Thus, these newly discovered statues are rich in historical and cultural features and provide an invaluable resources to researchers who study the development of Tibetan Buddhist culture and art in the Gansu-Qinghai area and the neighboring regions of Sichuan and Yunnan Province. They offer a wider scope of insight and propose a great number of new research subjects. This present study is an attempt of providing the historical and artistic contexts of these statues based on my preliminary observations on these statues.

I. Buddhist Statues of Verious Artistic Styles

During the Yuan, Ming and Qing Dynasties, Tibetan Buddhism has developed prosperously in Gansu-Qinghai area due to the promotion of the imperial courts. Temples are scattered everywhere, painting and sculpturing their own statues, thus greatly promoting the development of Buddhist arts. Buddhist statues presented in this book represent the characteristic features of the Buddhist culture and art in this area. Although the statues are collected from different channels and in varied styles, the origin and possible date of these statues can be established through studying their modeling features, artistic styles and craftsmanship, which can offer great help to understanding the interaction between Tibetan and Han Chinese arts of Buddhist statues in Tibet and the Gansu-Qinghai area.

The very first thing that leaves a deep impression on the viewers is the colorful and diverse modeling and artistic styles, which were adopted in the commonly seen statues of dBus-gTsang area, the ones from western Tibet, as well as those made in China Proper with apparent Han Chinese features. A wide scope of subject matters has been adopted. There are statues of various Buddhas, Bodhisattvas, Protective Deities, Buddhist guardians, and figures of both exoteric and esoteric Buddhism. The date of these statues ranges from the 11th -13th century, i.e. the period of the second diffusion of Tibetan Buddhism, to the Yuan, Ming and Qing Dynasties. The majority of these statues must be products of the Qing Dynasty. These statues have been mostly collected from today's Qinghai area, namely in Amdo and Khams regions of Tibet.

Cultural relics serve as the historical vessel, and the excavation of certain cultural relics must be closely related to the local historical environment. That these statues have been preserved in Qinghai is not only a chance happening, but related to certain specific historical factors. Qinghai is located on the eastern edge of the Tibetan Plateau and borders the Hexi Corridor, serving as link of Tibet, Tibetan areas of Gansu and Sichuan, Xinjiang and China Proper. In the history, Qinghai always served as the major road leading to Tibet from China Proper and the southern part of the Silk Road. Modern Qinghai Province includes substantial parts of two major Tibetan regions, namely Amdo and Khams. Amdo and Khams are located on the north and the east of the whole Tibetan area respectively, and have served historically as the bridge between Tibet and China eroper. Amdo and Khams have long been the places where Tibetan and Han Chinese cultures used to converge. This is a place where Tibetan Buddhism is deeply rooted, and has always been playing an important role during the formation, spread and development of the Tibetan Buddhist culture.

Qinghai was the place where the second diffusion of Buddhism took place. The north-west area of China, centering at Dunhuang City, has had deep influence on the development of Tibetan Buddhism in this period. The revival of Tibetan Buddhism had its root in the north-west area of China. According to the German collection of Uighur Buddhist literatures excavated in Turfan, Russian collection of Chinese and Tangut Buddhist literatures excavated in Khara Khoto, and the Tangut and Chinese Buddhist literatures/cultural relics recently excavated in Ningxia, it becomes quite evident that back in early 11th century, Tibetan esoteric Buddhism was already spreading among Tangut, Uighur and Han Chinese people, gaining popularity in north-west areas such as Gansu, Qinghai, Amdo and Inner Mongolia. Tangut Buddhist arts have also had major impact on Tibet.

After the 11th century, various Buddhist sects such as rNyingma pa, bKa'gdams pa, Saskya pa, and bKa'rgyud pa were established in succession. Tibetan Buddhism entered an unprecedented period of rapid development, during which a large number of temples and monasteries were built on the Tibetan Plateau. Tibetan art of statues building was greatly promoted. Picture 1 Bodhisattva Vajrapānī, Picture 2 Standing Statue of Bodhisattva Maitreya, Picture 3, Six-armed Avalokiteśvara in the current volume have all retained the artistic elements of India, Kashmir and Nepal, similar to the artistic style of Buddhist statues of the period of the second diffusion of Buddhism between 11th and 13th century. During this period, the statue-building art was still at the stage of absorbing and learning, resulting in the co-existence of multiple styles, elements seen Kashmir, Pala, Khotan and Dunhuang arts are evident here as well. Following the aesthetic preference of the Tibetans, various non-Tibetan yet exotic styles were fused together to create a fresh new style.

It is uncertain whether these statues circulated in Amdo and Khams around 12th to 15th century were made by local craftsmen or alien craftsmen from other places, or originated from central Tibet. Each assumption is likely, for the Gansu-Qinghai area was a broad pass linking central Tibet and China Proper, having close relationship with Buddhist arts from both sides. Therefore, it is quite natural that temples and monasteries in this area preserved Buddhist statues from Tibet, China Proper, India and Nepal. Also, it was rather usual that craftsmen from central Tibet and Nepal came to Amdo and Khams to erect Buddhist statues. In *Religious History of Amdo* (*mDo smad chos 'byung*), several mentionings are made about craftsmen from central Tibet or Nepal coming to Qinghai during the Qing Dynasty for building Buddhist statues. Judging from these facts, it is clear that Qinghai has a close relationship with the art of Buddhist statues of Central Tibet.

II. Motifs and Craftsmanship of Buddhist Statues

Buddhist statues have various subjects, including all Buddhas, Bodhisattvas and Patriarchs worshiped by dGelugs pa school, as well as those worshiped by rNying ma pa, Saskya pa and bKa'brgyud pa. For instance, Picture 6 displays the Stature of Thangstongrgyalpo worshiped by bKa'brgyud pa monasteries; Picture 8 displays the statue of the four-armed Bodhisattva and Picture 33 depicts a Buddhist guardian riding a legendary bird—both motifs are rare and possibly worshiped by Saskya pa monasteries; Picture 39 depicts Rahula, who is the primary idol of rNying ma pa school. This kind of Buddhist statues provides us fresh new iconographic materials and reflects the fact that various schools of Tibetan Buddhism had once co-existed and developed in Qinghai area. It also shows that dGelugs pa school was not the most dominant Buddhist school in Qinghai during the Qing Dynasty.

Supports from the Mongolian tribes attributed greatly to the growth of dGelugs pa school. Zaya Paṇḍita (1599-1662) was the most proeminent Buddhist monk from the Khoshuud group of the Oyirat Mongol tribe at the end of the Ming Dynasty and the beginning of the Qing Dynasty. Picture 47 is a vivid portrait of him. This portrait is almost identical with the one kept in the Palace Museum, only the inscription is missing. The spread of the portrait had a lot to do with his missionary activities in Qinghai. It also reflects his great influence in Oyirat Mongol tribes and in the dGelugs pa school.

In terms of craftsmanship, quite a lot of Buddhist statues have distinct features; for example, in Picture 6, 7 and 10, the statues are made of copper or copper alloy, with no plated gold. The eyes are embedded with copper, pupils embedded with silver and lips with copper. The necklaces, armlets, bracelets and anklets are all embedded with silver bead threads, while thin clothes fit the body, with on clothes patterns but silver or copper girdles on the edge of dresses or cassocks. On the surface of the girdles, there are delicate patterns such as curly grass or twisted branches, all made with exquisite craftsmanship which requires for not only modeling but also various skills such as carving and inlaying. Among traditional categories of Tibetan Buddhist statues, the ones made with this kind of craftsmanship are called"*Sang Tang Li Ma*" Buddha, and a number of pieces from the 13th-14th century are kept in the National Palace Museum, with Qing-style yellow labels reading"Sang Tang Li Ma Buddha". The major features of such statues are: they are made of brass while copper and sliver are inlaid to decorate certain parts. This craftsmanship of Buddhist-statue-building is very unique and was popular from the 12th to 15th century, and is rarely applied to the Tibetan Buddhist statues after the 15th century. It can be assumed that these are features peculiar to the craftsmanship of Amdo and Khams during the Ming and Qing Dynasty.

III. Seals and Marks Inscribed on Buddhist Statues

Tibet was ruled by a theocratic regime for a long period in history. Seals were given great importance in Tibet, especially the ones conferred by imperial courts. They were cherished by monks or lay people as symbol and proof of power and status. To our surprise, there are numerous seals and other inscription of various kinds inscribed on many Buddhist statues in Mr. Li Wei's collection. Two types of seals have been identified:

First, seals were bestowed to officials by imperial court

1. Seal of the State Preceptor of the Yuan Dynasty is in charge of Buddhist Affair. Picture 22 depicts the copper statue of Bodhisattva Mañjuśrī, whose styles of image, throne and aureole and other subtle features belong to the typical style of the Pala Buddhist statues of north-east India during the 11th to 12th century. Some seals in 'Phagspa scripts are found on the back side of the Buddha throne, square-shaped, bearing the inscription in 'Phagspa scripts of the eight Chinese characters "Tongling shijiao da Yuan Guoshi (State Preceptor of the Grand Yuan who is in charge of Buddhist Affairs). The script is identical with that on the jade seal of the State Preceptor of the Grand Yuan Dynasty in charge of Buddhist Affairs kept in Tibet. The script indicates the peculiar usage of the seal — since the authorization operation is to seal on important notice document and Buddhist statues, the seal was used to authorize power and post to Tibetan monks who served as state preceptor or imperial preceptor. The state preceptor seal mark on this statue just shows that it was an invaluable statue once worshiped in Saskya temples.

2. Chinese characters of "Jia Shi Jian Zang " inscribed on the back of the statue in Picture 45. This seal was granted by the imperial court of the Ming Dynasty. There are two seals with the same inscription preserved in Nor bu gling ka, Lhasa, while one is made of ivory, the other of jade. The inscription of the ivory seal reads: On the May day of the 13th Year of the Yongle reign on the top right corner; "Bestowed to Si Luo Ban Ling Ge la" on the top left corner. The statue depicts an eminent monk with profound Buddhist accomplishments, whose relationship with Jia Shi Jian Zang and Si Luo Ban Ling Ge la is yet to be explored. "Jia Shi Jian Zang" is the Chinese phonetic transcription of Tibetan name bKra shis rgyal mtshan, while Si Luo Ban Ling Ge la might be that of Shes rab rin [chen] grags.

3. Seal of the fifth Dalai Lama granted by the imperial court of the Qing Dynasty. On the back of the Sumeru throne of the four-armed Bodhisattva Avalokiteśvara in Picture 80, there are squarely-arranged inscriptions written in Chinese, Manchu and Tibetan scripts, arranged from left to right in sequence. The seal inscription in Chinese characters read: Seal of Dalai lama who is Vajradharā, the Omniscient, the great Buddha of the goodness of the western heaven who is in charge of Buddhist affairs of the world under heaven. Judging from the modeling style, this is a statue built at the imperial court of the Qing dynasty.

The second category includes private seals and seal marks of Grand Lama.

1. The private seal of the fifth Dalai Lama. Picture 32 depicts the statue of the protective deity *Bai Yong Bao*. On the left corner of the throne, there is a seal in 'Phagspa scripts, which is identical with the private seal of the fifth Dalai Lama. The original seal is kept in Nor bu gling ka, Lhasa.

2.Longevity seal of sDe srid Sangs rgyas rgya mtsho. The statue of Padmasambhava in Picture 43, the statue of Śākyamuni in Picture 75, and the statue of Buddha Amitayus in Picture 76, all have a seal in 'Phagspa scripts on the aureole of the throne, which is identified to be the "Longevity" seal of sDe srid Sangs rgyas rgya mtsho. The seal is now kept in the Potala Palace.

3. Seal of the treasure house of bDe skyid gling. Picture 37 depicts Vajravārāhī, the seal on the statue is not insribed with characters, but a special symbol. It must be a seal signature, i.e., Shu Yayin. It is identified to be the depot seal of bDe skyid gling, which used to be the mansion of the De mo Rinpoche of the Qing Dynasty, located miles away on the northwest of Jokhong, in Lhasa, Tibet.

4. Seals in 'Phags pa scripts to be identified. The meanings of seals in 'Phags pa scripts on the Buddhist statues in Picture 31 and Picture 33 are to be deciphered.

These statues with seals, discovered for the first time, are related to important historical figures including the state preceptor of the Yuan Dynasty, the fifth Dalai Lama, and bDe srid Sangs rgyas rgya mtsho, indicate the close relation between the central imperial governments of the Yuan, Ming and Qing Dynasty and their contemporary religious leaders. They deserve further investigation in the future.

IV. Yongle and Xuande Styles of the Imperial Court of the Ming Dynasty and Their Legacy

During the Yongle and Xuande reign of the Ming Dynasty, a great number of fine Tibetan Buddhist statues were created. Depicted in this book are several Buddhist statues produced by the imperial court of the Ming Dynasty, which claim delicate modeling, exquisite craftsmanship and rich motifs, all with well-preserved appearance. These statues facilitate us to understand the artistic accomplishments of the statue building art during the Yongle and Xuande reign and their profound influence in the art history of the Ming and Qing Dynasty.

I. These statues cover a wide range of motifs. These statues of Ming origin in this collection cover various traditions, both exoteric and esoteric. It is distinct from the fact that the imperial court of the Yuan Dynasty was particularly in favor of Saskya pa, while the Qing court favored dGelugs pas. The Ming court seemed unbiased to all traditions of Tibetan Buddhism. 20 Buddhist statues of Ming origin are included in the book.

Buddhist statues of the Yongle and Xuande reign follow strictly the measuring rules of Tibetan Buddhist iconography, and the models adopted are also assumedly from central Tibet. Scholars have already noticed related iconographic materials before. For instance, Heather Karmay had introduced two kinds of them in her book *Early Sino-Tibetan Arts: I. The Illustrated engraving in Bka'-'gyur* (Yongle edition) produced in the 8th year of the Yongle reign (1410). II. The sixty illustrated engravings of Buddha and Bodhisattvas in *Zhufo posa miaoxiang minghao jingzhou* printed in Beijing in the sixth year of the Xuande reign (1431). One other important reference on Buddhist iconography of the Yongle reign is the *Ming neifu jinzang huxinjing* preserved in the Palace Museum, Beijing. This is a Buddhist scripture written in golden ink at then imperial court during the Yongle reign; it combines several scriptures and mantras with a foreword by the Yongle Emperor. Prior to each scripture or mantra, there is a contour drawing of Buddhist statue painted in golden ink. Altogether there are 30 drawings, delicately depicting the images of Buddhas, Bodhisattvas and protective deities. They had directly influenced the model of gilt copper statues of the Yongle reign. The forewords of the scriptures were written in the 9th and 10th year of the Yongle reign. It is certainly a very importance source regarding the modeling and artistic styles of gilt copper statues of the Yongle reign.

Given the iconographical materials introduced above, it is thus clear that the origin of the modeling of gilt copper statues of the Yongle reign was not only central Tibet. It was also influenced by the interaction and development of Sino-Tibetan Buddhist arts since the Yuan Dynasty. Influences are also from the Cloud Platform of Juyongguan Fortress and Jisha Tripiṭaka engravings. The appearance of the Buddhist statues of the Yongle style was not incidental at all. It was the result of long-term cultural and artistic exchanges between Tibet and China Proper. Several Buddhist statues depicted in this book are unique, thus invaluable masterpieces, such as the statue of Śrī-Devī (dPal ldan lha mo) and the standing statue of Bodhisattva Maitreya, providing valuable fresh new materials for researches on the Yongle and Xuande style of Buddhist statues.

II. The beauty of the statues is fused with both Han Chinese and Tibetan elements. Amiable and peaceful, elegant and generous, Buddhist statues of Yongle style are gorgeously decorated with both grace and delicacy, simplicity and gentility, reaching the summit of the arts of Buddhist statue modeling ever since the Yuan Dynasty. The motif of the copper sculpture is mostly Tibetan, but the artistic presentation is different from the Tibetan archetype, while every subtle part precisely and systematically designed. Buddhist statues of Yongle and Xuande style are of a skillful fusion of both Han Chinese and Tibetan artistic elements. This peculiar artistic style had a long-term influence on the late development of Buddhist statues building both in Tibet and in China Proper during the Ming and Qing Dynasty.

The Buddhist statues of the Yongle and Xuande reign claim exquisite craftsmanship. The craftsmanship of metal sculpture is the most complicated one in the art of Buddhist statues, which requires dozens of procedures including modeling, casting, craving, polishing, inlaying, coloration and gilding. According to an account in the imperial court of the Qing Dynasty, the making process of a gilt copper statue of Śrī-Devī requires 12 procedures. The craftsmanship of the Yongle and Xuande Buddhist statues is so exquisite and impeccable that they are often considered as the best one among gilt copper Buddhist statues of the Ming and Qing Dynasty.

There are several large-sized Buddhist statues depicted in this book: Bodhisattva Maitreya in Picture 52, Mahākāla in Picture 72, and Kālacakra in Picture 64. These statue are large-sized, exquisitely modeled and un-gilt. Both the statues and their engraved seal scripts which are in large characters and written from right to left, are published for the first time. Besides, there are some other types of Buddhist statues of the Yongle and Xuande reign: 1. statues without inscriptions, 2. statues with inscriptions in both Chinese and Tibetan scripts, 3. statues with inscriptions only in Tibetan script. These large-sized statues have facilitated us to better understand Yongle statues in terms of size and seal scripts.

There are certain historical background for these Buddhist statues of the Yongle and Xuande reign to have been preserved in Qinghai. As the Ming was established, it continued to implement the former Yuan strategy to stabilize Tibet through promoting Tibetan Buddhism. However, the Ming, unlike the Yuan, did not particularly favor Sa skya pa sect, and instead implemented the "divid and rule" policy. At the beginning of the Ming Dynasty, *Xian xing du zhihui shisi* was established in Hezhou, ruling the three places of Hezhou, mDo khams and dBus gtsang. Later, both mDo khams and dBus gtsang were upgraded to *Xing duzhihui shisi* respectively. The Ming not only set up military and administrative offices in Gansu, Qinghai and Sichuan, but also promoted aboriginal headmen to be governmental officials. Therefore, the central government of the Ming was able to control the whole Tibetan areas effectively. Religious leaders of various Tibetan districts all went to the Ming capital to pay tribute to the court, and the court in return granted them with official appointment and lavish material rewards. Religious leaders took pride in imperial conferring and rewards and paid their loyalty to the court. In this way, all Tibetan districts kept close ties with the central government of the Ming dynasty. From the cultural perspective, Yongle emperor worshiped Buddhism and was enthusiastic about building temples and engraving scriptures; he had profound interests in Tibetan Buddhism and highly respected famous monks from Tibet, starting the tradition of Ming emperors promoting Tibetan Buddhism in history.

Tibetan Buddhist statues made by the order of imperial court during the Yongle and Xuande reigns were used as valuable presents to religious or lay leaders of Tibet and witnessed the close relationship between the imperial court and Tibet during the Yongle and Xuande years. Temples and monasteries in Qinghai once preserved many items bestowed by Ming emperors, which were cherished by these temples and monasteries as treasures to be handed down from generation to generation. Records about Buddhist statues of the Yongle reign in *mDo smad chos 'byung* provide evidence that these status of various sizes which were kept in Amdo area.

As a popular imperial artistic style, Buddhist statues of the Yongle and Xuande years were circulated and well received among people in Amdo area. Back in the 16th century, Padma dkar po (1527-1592), a well-known bKa' brgyud pa monk wrote the treatise *On Appreciating Buddhist Statues*, which highly appraised Buddhist statues of the Yongle reign. The Yongle and Xuande style of Buddhist statues entered Tibetan areas and became a very popular style of Buddhist statues. Sle'u chung pa was a famous craftsman living in Lhasa, Tibet in mid-15th century, whose beautiful Buddha modeling had absorbed artistic features of the Yongle Buddhist statues of the Ming Dynasty. There are four statues made by Sle'u chung pa preserved in the Palace Museum, Beijing, whose features are similar to what historical documents described. Craftsmen in Tibetan areas copied or imitated the statues made by the imperial court of the Ming dynasty, and the trend didn't stop until late Ming, even mid-Qing. The artistic accomplishments of Buddhist statues of the Yongle and Xuande years were the result of development of Tibetan Buddhism in China Proper and the interaction between Tibetan and Han Chinese arts.

IIV. Kangxi and Qianlong Styles of Buddhist Statues in the Imperial Court of the Qing Dynasty and Their Respective Popularity

In this volume, several works which can be identified with statues made by the order of the imperial court of the Qing Dynasty are included and discussed. The identification are mainly based on two aspects: Firstly, these statues share the same modeling with those made in the imperial court of the Qing Dynasty and were preserved in the Palace Museum; the same model illustrates the close relationship between these two. Take the statue of the four-armed Bodhisattva Avalokiteśvara in Picture 89 as an example, the modeling and size of this statue just share the same model with the statue of the same Bodhisattva preserved in the Palace Museum. The statue of the four-armed Bodhisattva Avalokiteśvara preserved in the Palace Museum is the most standard Buddhist statue of the Kangxi period. By careful examining, it turns out that the size, modeling, craftsmanship, and artistic style of the two statues are almost identical, hence showing the close relations between the two.

The statue of the four-armed Bodhisattva Avalokiteśvara in Picture 88 also share the same model with the

pure-gold statue of the same Bodhisattva preserved in the Palace Museum. The one in Palace Museum has a seal inscription engraved on the lotus stalk of the state, reading *Made in the Qianlong Years of the grand Qing Dynasty,* and inscriptions engraved on the back of the aureole, written in Chinese, Manchu, Tibetan and Mongolian scripts. Both statues have a high single-stalk throne and calabash-shaped aureole.

From above examples, it is thus clear that these two statues were made from the same model. Despite of some subtle differences, the master models are identical.

Secondly, there are clear inscriptions of Chinese characters on the statue; they read as following: "Made in the Kangxi reign of the Grand Qing Dynasty, Bestowed in the Kangxi reign of the Grand Qing Dynasty", Bestowed in the Qianlong reign of the Grand Qing Dynasty, Made in the Kangxi reign of the Grand Qing Dynasty by the Ministry of Rites, Made in the Qianlong reign of the Grand Qing Dynasty by the Ministry of Rites, and Offered by Potala Palace in the Kangxi reign of the Grand Qing Dynasty. There are also other seals and marks on certain statues.

Most Buddhist statues made by the order of the imperial court of the Qing Dynasty are preserved in the Palace Museum. Through careful examination I found out that the above-mentioned inscriptions are found on none of them. There are no mention of it in Qing literary sources either. Therefore, further textual researches on the statues and their inscriptions are very much needed. However, it is quite certain that these statues have a close relation to these made by the order of the Qing imperial court in terms of the modeling, craftsmanship and inscriptions. For example, there are inscriptions reading *Made in the Kangxi Reign of the Grand Qing Dynasty by the Ministry of Rites, Made in the Qianlong Reign of the Grand Qing Dynasty by the Ministry of Rites.* The Ministry of Rites was set up at the very beginning of the Qing dynasty. Among the many responsibilities of the Ministry of Rites, to manage Buddhist and Taoist affairs was one important item. The Qing Dynasty had a set of strict regulations in terms of ruling and controlling the building of temples, monasteries and Buddhist statues. The Ministry of Rites was in charge of supervising the production of Buddhist statues. It was absolutely possible that the Buddhist statues which were bestowed by the imperial court to a certain temple were actually produced and issued by the Ministry of Rites. In the 36th year of the Kangxi reign (1697), the imperial court set up an institution which specialized in administering Tibetan Buddhism: Office of Chanting Sutras in Zhongzheng Palace, whose main responsibility was to administer the chanting events of Lamas in the Forbidden City and the building of Buddhist statues. During the Qinglong reign, the grand minister of Yonghe Palace was appointed to be particularly in charge of administering the Buddhist affairs of the Yonghe Palace. The institutionalization of Buddhist activities in the Forbidden City showed that Tibetan Buddhism had great influence within the imperial court of the Qing Dynasty. In fact, prior to the 36th year of the Kangxi reign, imperial production of Buddhist statues had already begun and the statues had been bestowed to both religious and non-religious leaders in Tibet. According to the Code of the Grand Qing Dynasty, grand Lamas had been paying tributes to the imperial court of the Qing Dynasty as early as in the Shunzhi years, i.e. at the very beginning of the Qing Dynasty. The imperial court of the Qing Dynasty attached great importance to its relationship with Tibetan Buddhist leaders, and regularly bestowed the tribute-paying Lamas with rich rewards in return. Qing emperors had in person bestowed titles on many famous Lamas from Qinghai, such as Hutuktu and Normen Khan. It is quite possible that, these Buddhist statues with the inscriptions of Made by the Ministry of Rites had been

bestowed by the imperial court of the Qing Dynasty to temples and grand lamas in Qinghai.

The standing statues of Bodhisattva Maitreya in Picture 84 and 96 share the same model with the pure-gold statue of Bodhisattva Maitreya preserved in the Palace Museum. Inscriptions of Bestowed in the Kangxi Reign of the Grand Qing Dynasty and Bestowed in the Qianlong Reign of the Grand Qing Dynasty are also identical to that of the Buddhist statues of the Yongle and Xuande periods. The strategy adopted by the Qing Dynasty was basically identical to the Ming strategy, which was to promote Tibetan Buddhism so as to stabilize the Mongolian regions. The imperial court greatly supported the dGe lugs pa sect of Tibetan Buddhism by courteously receiving religious leaders, bestowing titles on the Tibetan Buddhist upper class, and richly rewarding the tribute-paying leaders from Tibetan regions, so as to gain their loyalty towards the imperial court, stabilize Tibetan and Mongolian area. Judging from the Chinese character "shi" (bestow) in the inscription, which literarily indicates the relationship between patrons and monks, reflecting the political relationship between the imperial court and the bestowed. Religious leaders from Tibet took pride in receiving the imperial bestowing without exception. Their religious and political position was greatly enhanced by it. It is quite possible that these statues with the character "shi" inscription were exclusively used to bestow various religious institutions and personalities by imperial court of the Qing Dynasty. It explains the fact that all Qing statues preserved in the imperial palace are without the same inscription.

The imperial court of the Qing Dynasty had close ties with temples and monasteries of Tibetan Buddhism in Gansu and Qinghai. As early as in the Kangxi years, the post of Hutuktu in residence of Beijing was established. Among all 12 lamas who took the post of Hutuktu in residence of Beijing 7 were monks from Qinghai, and all belonged to the dGe lugs pa sect. The reincarnation line of State Preceptor lCang skya Hutuktu was the most influential lama in Beijing and became the fourth greatest reincarnation line only next to that of Dalai lama, Pan chen lama in Tibet and Jebtsundamba Hutuktu in Outer Mongolia. What fully illustrated the peculiar position of the upper-class dGe lugs pa lamas from Qinghai in stabilizing Mongolian tribes in the region was, when Emperor Qianlong authorized the order of Lamas in residence of Beijing, lCang skya lama was appointed as the first of the left wing, while sMin grol lama as the first of the right wing, both were addressed as the Grand Hutuktu of Qinghai. In the Qianlong years, the Qinghai monks, represented by the 3rd lCang skya State Preceptor, had profound influence on the imperial court of the Qing Dynasty. They supervised the building of Tibetan Buddhist temples and monasteries in the imperial palace and production of Buddhist statues and other Buddhist ritual instruments. Today there are various kinds of Tibetan Buddhist relics preserved in the Palace Museum.

The 3rd lCang skya Hutuktu, profound in his Buddhist craftsmanship, participated in person in supervising the building of imperial Buddhist statues and other Buddhist ritual instruments; he also employed Tibetan craftsmen to provide long-term service in the imperial workshop, taking part in the creative work of Buddhist arts. It is possible that some craftsmen were from Amdo area. It is by no means a coincidence that the Buddhist statues circulating in the Gansu-Qinghai areas share the same modeling with the imperial Buddhist statues preserved in the Palace Museum; it was the eminent Qinghai monks, represented by State Preceptor lCang skya Hutuktu, who brought the popular styles of Buddhist statue to the imperial court. Meanwhile, style of Buddhist statue that was popular in Beijing were brought to temples and monasteries in the Gansu-Qinghai areas along with these statues bestowed by the imperial court to these temples and monasteries and became models for local production of Buddhist statues. These facts have all showed the mutual influence and close stylistic similarities between the Buddhist statues made in the Gansu-Qinghai area and these of the imperial court of the Qing Dynasty.

It is not uncommon that artistic styles and fashions often reveal, directly or indirectly, traces of cultural and religious interactions among various ethnic groups in history. By observing the modeling and craftsmanship of Buddhist statues, it becomes evident that the Han Chinese style has dominated the way of artistic expression, while Tibetan factors have been applied to subtle decorative details. The inscriptions on the Buddhist statues have also shown the idea of combining Han Chinese and Tibetan styles: several Buddhist statues, either in typical Yongle style or in Kangxi and Qianlong style, either only carry Tibetan inscriptions or bilingual inscriptions of both Chinese and Tibetan scripts. These facts have shown that, Han Chinese Buddhist arts, which are represented by these from the imperial court of the Ming and Qing Dynasty, have profoundly influenced the development of Tibetan Buddhist arts in the Gansu-Qinghai area. The mix of Han Chinese and Tibetan factors is a distinct feature of the artistic style of the Ming and Qing Buddhist statues in the Gansu-Qinghai areas, and has become the main theme of Buddhist arts in the Gansu-Qinghai areas.

Wang Jiapeng, Research Fellow of the Palace Museum

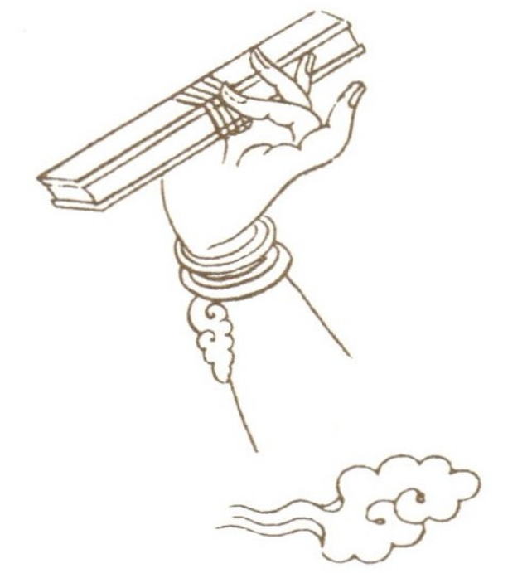

圖版

Plates

多元藝術風格佛像

Buddhist Statues of Diverse Artistic Styles

མིང་ཕོ་བྲང་གི་སྒྱུ་རྩལ་ཁྱད་ཆོས་ཅན་གྱི་སྐུ་བརྙན།

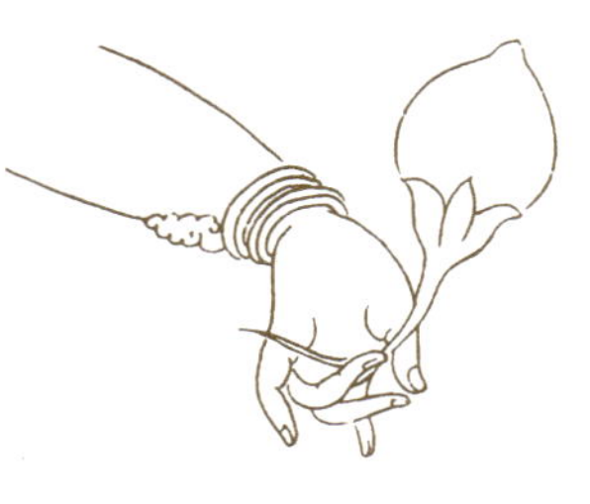

多元藝術風格佛像

甘青地區歷來是漢藏文化密切交匯之地。藏傳佛教在這裏歷史久遠，基礎深厚。在藏傳佛教文化的形成、發展、傳播過程中，這一地區一直起着重要的作用。自元、明、清以來，藏傳佛教在朝廷的大力扶持下，在甘青地區發展繁榮，推動了佛教藝術的發展。本書有西藏佛教後弘期早期佛像和明清時期佛像，產地包括衛藏地區、藏西地區及內地作品。一些佛像上刻有藏文、梵文題記和印章、印押圖記。佛像雖來源不同，風格各異，但從造型特點、藝術風格、工藝技法多方面研究，可見不同佛像產地、時代的聯繫，對于瞭解西藏與甘青地區漢藏佛像藝術交流的歷史大有裨益。

金剛薩埵

རྡོ་རྗེ་སེམས་དཔའ།

黃銅，高129厘米，11～12世紀

Vajrasattva

Brass　Height: 129cm　11th-12th century

金剛薩埵頭戴三葉花冠，三角形冠葉雕珠寶，下托彎月，耳朵戴大圓耳璫，耳上部飾兩朵蓮花，兩股長辮垂挂肩後，辮髮雕成扁片的飄帶形，刻出細細的髮絲和捆扎的髮節，帽冠髮型獨特，是十一世紀藏西地區克什米爾風格佛像上的式樣。彎眉大眼，扁寬的眼瞳嵌銀，細巧嘴唇嵌紅銅，露出淡淡的神秘微笑。胸肌發達，刻出生硬的肌肉輪廓綫，腰胯細瘦，身體比例不協調。右手掌托金剛杵，手指彎曲，自然生動；左手掌上彎，握金剛鈴（已佚）。袒上身，下着印度式的纏腿斜裙，裙面刻雙鈎的雲朵。腰間扎着優美的結扣裙帶，一條細長裙角垂在兩腿間。跣足踏高方臺。背光鏤空雕刻，身光與頭光套連在一起，背光邊沿刻花葉卷草形的火焰紋。此像是克什米爾藝術風格鮮明的藏西佛像，體量高大，十分難得。

座面刻方印，外框邊長5厘米，印文爲四個雙鈎的蘭扎體梵文字母：dha rma ta tra 排列成漢字方印式樣。dharmatatra 意爲「法性護佑」。此印文與《西藏歷代藏印》（第十七頁）所收西藏文管會所藏的一方元代梵文玉印印文相同，此印的用途尚不明。

Vajrasattva wears three-leaf crown, holding vajra pestle in the right hand and grasping vajra bell (lost) in the left hand. His upper body is uncovered and he wears an Indian leg grapevine bias skirt and sets foot on high square platform barefooted. The openwork overlapping body light and head light are carved with flower leaf rolled-up grass shaped flame grain. This statue is a Western Tibet Buddhist statue with distinguished Kashmir art style.

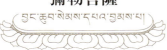

2

彌勒菩薩

བྱང་ཆུབ་སེམས་དཔའ་བྱམས་པ།

黃銅，高115厘米，12～13世紀

Bodhisattva Maitreya

Brass Height: 115cm 12th-13th century

彌勒佛身形挺拔偉岸，高扁髮髻，辮髮垂肩，髮髻前雕塔，圓塔瓶，塔刹細高。彌勒細眉長目，眼睛嵌銀，高鼻梁，厚唇嵌紅銅，明目紅唇，面帶微笑，刻畫精緻，形象英俊祥和。帶有印度人面容特點。兩腿直立，略顯僵硬。右手抬起，作説法印，左手下垂，手形似應握净瓶。指甲嵌紅銅。上身袒露，左肩披仁獸皮，下着貼體長裙，裙面淺刻花朵圖案，裝飾簡約，祇有一道長聖綫從左肩垂下盤繞右側身後。扁圓蓮座雕雲頭形蓮瓣，蓮座下承托中空的方臺座，上刻簡潔的陰綫花紋（座可能是後配），多有十一至十二世紀尼泊爾佛像特點，但身體略顯僵直，時代相對較晚。

座面刻方印，外框邊長4.5厘米，印文爲四個雙鉤的蘭扎體梵文字母：ra tna si ha 排列成漢字方印式樣。漢文意爲寶獅子。此印文與《西藏歷代藏印》（第十七頁）所收西藏文管會所藏的一方元代梵文象牙印印文相同，此印的用途尚不明。

Bodhisattva Maitreya raises the right hand in the gesture of teaching, hanging the left hand. His upper body is uncovered and the left shoulder is covered with Kylin skin. He wears a fitted long skirt printed with light flower pattern. The decoration is very simple with only a long Arya rope hanging from the left shoulder and coiling around the back of right body. The oblate lotus throne is carved with cloud cluster shaped lotus petals, and the lower part of the throne is a hollow square pedestal engraved with simple shade line pattern, which is characterized by many features of the 11-12th century Nepal Buddhist statue.

3

六臂觀音菩薩

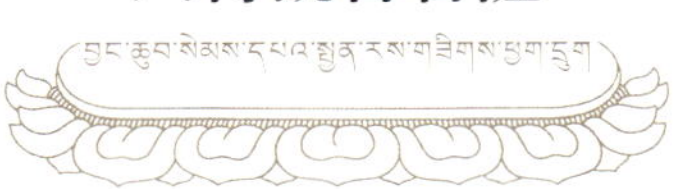

黃銅，高103厘米，14～15世紀

Six-armed Avalokiteśvara

Brass　Height: 114cm　14th-15th century

六臂觀音，長方面豐滿，頭戴三葉冠，冠葉刻珠寶下托彎月，近似克什米爾佛冠，耳上部兩股長辮垂挂肩後，辮髮雕成扁片的飄帶形，上面裝飾連續的小菱形塊。大眼睛嵌銀，刻出半圓的眼瞳，目光下視，神情莊嚴。胸前飾長短項鏈。項鏈、耳環鑲嵌銀紅銅。在頸部用紅銅鑲嵌一道裝飾圈，似衣服領邊，上刻花紋。六隻手的拇指小指戴戒指，裝飾華麗。下身着印度式的纏腿斜裙，一條細長裙角垂在兩腿間，裙上陰綫淺刻方孔銅錢、雲卷紋顯露了漢文化的影響。佛像保留了大量波羅造像因素，身軀圓潤，肌理平滑，裝飾細節繁複華麗。蓮座爲後配的。

The Six-armed Avalokiteśvara wears a three-leaf crown carved with jewelry and crescent, similar to Kashmir Buddha crown. The two long braids above the ears are hanging behind the shoulders and the braids are carved into oblate ribbon shape. The little finger of all the six hands wears a ring with gorgeous decoration. His lower part of the body is dressed in an Indian grapevine bias skirt, and a slender fringe of skirt is hanging between the two legs.

蓮花手觀音菩薩

黃銅，高119厘米，14～15世紀

Avalokiteśvara Padmapāṇi

Brass Height: 119cm 14th-15th century

蓮花手觀音身材壯健，身軀略側扭，雙腿直立仰蓮座上。大眼睛嵌銀，唇嵌紅銅，面相莊嚴。下身着貼體短裙，腰帶嵌紅銅刻花。背光由四根立柱托一橫梁，立柱間雕兩立獅踏大象背上。橫梁左右站立人身鳥足的仙人。金翅鳥展翅站立頂端，嘴中所叼與兩手握的不是長蛇，而是帶花葉長莖蔓，花葉垂掛背光頂部，設計精美，獨具匠心。蓮座下爲高層方臺，座中空，前面雕雙獅法輪，雕刻生動，打磨細緻，工藝精湛。

Avalokiteśvara Padmapāṇi stands straight on the lotus throne, wearing a fitted short skirt with his upper body uncovered. The waistband is embedded with red copper carved patterns. The aureole consists of four upright columns holding a beam and there is a pattern of two lions standing on the back of an elephant carved between the columns. Garuḍa stands on the top spreading its wings, holding a long vine with flower leaf in its mouth and grasping the two sides of the vine in its hands and the flower leaf is hanging on the top of the aureole. The lower part of the throne is a hollow square, the front of which is carved with double lion Dharma wheels.

5

菩薩

བྱང་ཆུབ་སེམས་དཔའ།

黃銅，高58厘米，14～15世紀

Bodhisattva

Brass　Height: 58cm　14th-15th century

菩薩右手作説法印，左手作禪定印，三葉寶冠，束髮冠帶翻卷，大眼睛嵌銀，唇嵌紅銅，唇帶微笑，面相祥和。裝飾項鏈、臂釧、手鐲，鑲嵌銀、紅銅。背光空靈優美，左右兩側立獅懸空，下面是兩隻俯卧的飛禽。方臺正面中層雕雙獅，兩獅中間垂臺幔，没有雕刻法輪。方臺側面中層雕大象。菩薩身份待定。

Bodhisattva makes the mudrā of teaching with the right hand and the mudrā of meditation with the left hand. He wears three-leaf crown, miter and roll and is decorated with necklace, armlet, bracelet embedded with silver and red copper. There are two standing lions hanging on the two sides of the aureole, below which are two sprawling fowls, and the middle layer of the square platform is carved with double lions.

6

唐東杰布

ཐང་སྟོང་རྒྱལ་པོ།

黃銅，高66厘米，15世紀

Thang stong rgyal po

Brass Height: 66cm 15th century

唐東杰布，約與宗喀巴同時代人，香巴噶舉派高僧，一生雲游四海，熱心公益，在西藏各地修建寺院，建造了很多鐵橋，編寫多種藏劇劇本，發明醫藥治病救人。此像雙目圓睜，眼睛嵌銀，嘴唇嵌紅銅，面相微怒，長胡鬚，左手托寶瓶，右手作觸地印。身披僧袍，袍褶邊鑲嵌紅銅、銀裝飾條，上刻花紋。全跏趺坐於三層卡墊上，卡墊下承托凸字形方臺座，座前面雕雙獅、法輪，臺角刻金剛杵。現已捐贈國家博物館。

座後背刻方印，外框邊長5.2厘米，印文爲九個雙鈎的蘭扎體梵文字母排列成漢字方印式樣：ma vā ma dvi pa ga ra thah。梵文字的含義待考。此印文與《西藏歷代藏印》（第十七頁）所收西藏文管會所藏的一方元代梵文玉印印文相同，據原印所拴布條記載該印爲薩迦和帕竹之間統治南部地區的長官之印。

Thang stong rgyal po, a comtemporary of Tsong kha pa, an eminent monk of Shangs pa bka' brgyud pa sect, traveled around the world for life full of public spirit. He built temples in various regions of Tibet and constructed many iron bridges. He wrote many kinds of Tibetan Opera and invented medicine to cure and save lives. This statue has wide open eyes embedded with silver, lips embedded with red copper, and a miffed face with long beard. He holds jeweled bottle in the left hand and make the gesture of touching the earth with the right hand. It has now been donated to the National Museum.

7

黃財神

ཛམ་ལྷ་སེར་པོ།

黃銅，高86厘米，15世紀

Yellow God of Wealth Jambhala

Brass Height: 86cm 15th century

黃財神亦稱黃布祿金剛，是多聞子的變化身之一，在密宗四部中，他被置於事續部的世間部，充當有財部、藥叉部和其餘世間部的護法神。此像身材肥碩，雙目圓睁，怒氣衝衝，高髮髻，頭戴五葉冠，右手持海螺，左手持吐寶獸。半跏趺坐仰蓮圓座，蓮座下是凸字形方臺座，座前面雕雙獅、法輪，臺角刻金剛杵。冠帶、瓔珞、珠寶、法輪等部位鑲嵌紅銅、銀，工藝精細。

The Yellow God of Wealth, also called Yellow Jambhala, is a naimanika-kaya of Vaiśravaṇa. He is a guardian god of the Kriya Tantra, and serves as a guardian god of Wealth. This statue has stout stature, wide open eyes and angry expression, and wears high bob and five-leaf crown. He holds a conch in the right hand and a treasure-producing beast in the left hand.

8

四臂菩薩

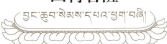

བྱང་ཆུབ་སེམས་དཔའ་ཕྱག་བཞི།

黃銅，高101厘米，15世紀

Four-armed Bodhisattva

Brass Height: 101cm 15th century

此尊菩薩四臂分上下排列，形制比較少見，身份待考。菩薩身體上部雙手捻蓮花莖作説法印，右肩花上托海螺，左肩花上托寶瓶；下部雙手作禪定印。全跏趺坐，裙面刻平行的瓔珞珠綫作裙褶裝飾。鏤空背光，門字形框架，左右立柱內側雕翻轉自然、圖案簡潔的纏枝，纏枝下部雕兩位侍從菩薩，横梁兩端爲摩羯龍，龍尾翹起聯結翻卷的卷草，正中銜接金翅鳥頭和兩隻手握的飄帶，頂端雕摩尼寶。背光的優美樣式汲取了十四世紀前後西藏壁畫唐卡中所繪背光的設計元素，如夏魯寺壁畫可見近似樣式。方座前面刻藏文六字真言。

Four arms of this Bodhisattva are arrayed up and down. The upper two hands twine the stalk of the lotus and make the mudrā of teaching; the flower on the right shoulder holds a conch whilst the flower on the left shoulder holds a jeweled bottle; the underneath hands makes the mudrā of meditation. He is seated in the diamond attitude and the skirt is carved with parallel Keyura pearl chains. The aureole is openwork. The inner side of the left and right upright columns is engraved with two simple twining stem. The two ends of the beam are engraved with Nāgas, whose tail scrolls and connects with rolled grass, middle joints the head of Garuḍa and two ribbons grasped in hands, and the top is carved with the Cintāmaṇi. The front of the square platform is carved with Tibetan Oṃ Maṇi Padme Hūṃ.

9

彌勒菩薩

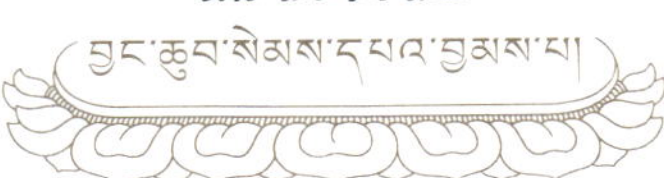

黄銅，高94厘米，15世紀

Bodhisattva Maitreya

Brass Height: 94cm 15th century

彌勒頭戴五葉寶冠，髮髻高挽，長髮辮垂肩頭，耳邊束髮冠帶呈U形上卷，長方面，寬額細眉，上眼瞼略寬，眉間白毫突起，直鼻大耳，多有漢族相貌特徵。頰頤豐滿，莊重和慈。下身着雙層長裙，垂雙足坐於束腰長方臺座上，右手捻珠寶結説法印，左手托净瓶，正在講經説法。背光同圖八，空靈秀美，別具匠心。

Maitreya wears five-leaf crown and a high bun. His long braid is hanging on the shoulder and the hair band beside the ears is U-shaped and is scrolled. He has a square face, broad forehead and slender eyebrows. The white hair between his eyebrows sticks up. He has straight nose and big ears, which is distinguished Han Chinese facial features. His cheek is full and round, solemn and amiable. His lower part of the body is dressed in double-layer long skirt. He sits on a girded long square platform hanging his feet with the right hand twining the pearl knot and making the mudrā of teaching, and the left hand holding white vase and he is seated in the gesture of teaching the Dharma.

10

蓮花生

黃銅，高95厘米，18世紀

Padmasambhava

Brass Height: 95cm 18th century

蓮花生，印度僧人，烏仗那國人。八世紀中葉應邀入藏傳播印度金剛乘密法，創建西藏第一座寺院桑耶寺，被尊爲藏密祖師，寧瑪派祖師，廣受尊奉。此像身披袈裟，長辮髮垂於肩頭袈裟外，戴寧瑪派佛冠，飾大耳璫，雙目圓睁作忿怒相，胸前挂三角形精美的珠寶配飾。右手持金剛杵，左手托嘎巴拉碗，碗中立寶瓶，左肩夾持天仗。眼睛嵌紅銅，瞳仁嵌銀，袈裟衣邊交錯鑲嵌紅銅、白銀寬邊，上刻細密的纏枝蓮纹，鑄造、鑲嵌工藝十分精湛。

座面刻藏文題記“蓮花生上師咒”。

原文轉寫：oṃ āḥ hūṃ badzra guru padma siddhi hūṃ| oṃ padma badzra hūṃ

vajragurupadmasiddhi：蓮花生上師名號，可譯爲“金剛上師蓮花成就”。

《大藏全咒》裏没有與此咒同様的咒。

Padmasambhava is an Indian monk from Udyana. He came to Tibet upon invitation to spread Indian Vajrayana tantra and established the first temple—Samye Monastery in Tibet and was considered patriarch of Tibet tantra and rNying ma pa sect and was widely respected and served. This statue wears cassock and rNying ma pa sect Buddha crown with his long braid hanging on the shoulder outside the cassock. He holds a five-pronged diamond sceptre in the right, an alms bowl in the left hand. The ceremonial staff is leaning agaist his left shoulder. On the surface of the throne there carved a Tibetan inscription: "Padmasambhava Mantra".

11

四臂菩薩

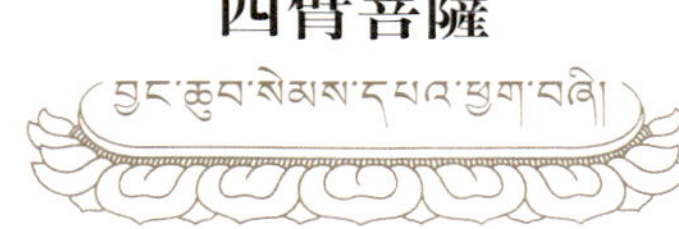

བྱང་ཆུབ་སེམས་དཔའ་ཕྱག་བཞི།

黃銅，高49厘米，明洪武十三年（1380）

Four-armed Bodhisattva

Brass Height: 49cm The 13th year of Hongwu's reign, Ming Dynasty (1380)

菩薩四臂分上下排列，此形象比較少見，身份待考。菩薩身體上部雙手捻蓮花莖作說法印，右肩花上托海螺，左肩花上托寶瓶；下部雙手作禪定印。全跏趺坐，裙面刻平行的瓔珞珠綫作裙褶裝飾。眼睛嵌紅銅，瞳仁嵌銀，珠寶瓔珞等部位大量鑲嵌紅銅白銀，特別是裙面上鑲嵌凸起的菱形、花瓣形銀片，紅銅片，是突出的裝飾工藝特點。

蓮座前沿刻漢字款識「大明洪武一十三年」單綫陰刻楷書，自右向左書。

The four arms of this Bodhisattva are arrayed up and down. The upper two hands twine the stalk of the lotus and make the mudrā of teaching; the flower on the right shoulder holds a conch whilst the flower on the left shoulder holds a jeweled bottle; the underneath hands makes the mudrā of meditation. He is seated in the diamond attitude and the skirt is carved with parallel Keyura pearl chains. His eyes are embedded with red copper, the pupils are embedded with silver, and the jewelry, Keyura, etc. are inlaid with a large amount of red copper and silver.

On the front of the lotus throne, there carved Chinese inscription "Da Ming Hong Wu Shisan nian" which is the single-line intaglio standard script written in the direction from right to left.

12

手持金剛

黃銅，高40.5厘米，17世紀

Vajrapāṇi

Brass Height: 40.5cm 17th century

此像右臂上舉，手握金剛杵（已佚），左手作期克印。頭戴三葉寶冠，未戴骷髏冠，三目圓睁，形象凶憤。胸前垂挂人頭項鬘。項鏈、手鐲、脚鐲、臂釧均爲小蛇盤繞作裝飾。虎皮短裙，腰帶從兩腿間垂下與項蔓和座面相聯。脚下踏裸體仰卧二人。銅色黝黑，鑄造精细。

蓮座背刻藏文款識：鄔孜甲金剛手咒：phyag rdor u tsa rya' i u tsa rya [śri–ucārya–Vajrapāṇi] yaksasena aṅ kusha dza dza hūṃ hūṃ phaṭa

鄔孜甲金剛手是金剛手的一個化現，有關於該本尊的儀軌論書見*sGrub thabs kun btus*［成就法集］，ga函：dpal phyag na rdo rje u tsa rya' i sgrub thabs rjes gnang las tshogs dang bcas pa' i skor rnams［聖鄔孜甲金剛手成就法隨許並羯磨］。

This statue raises the right arm, grasping a vajra pestle (lost), and makes the gesture of threatening with the left hand. He wears a three-leaved crown and his three eyes are wide open which makes a ferocious and angry expression. He wears human head vine which hangs in front of this chest. His necklace, bracelet, anklet and armlet are all decorated with coiled snakes. He wears a tiger skin skirt, and the waistband hangs down between the two legs and connects with the vine and the surface of the throne. He tramples on two naked people lying on their back. The color of the bronze is dark and the casing is refined.

13

六臂護法神

མགོན་པོ་ཕྱག་དྲུག་པ།

銅合金，高33厘米，15世紀

Six-armed Mahākāla (mGon po phyag drug pa, ṣaḍbhuja Mahākāla)

Copper alloy Height: 33cm 15th century

護法神六臂，各手所持法器已佚，身份待考。三目圓睜，怒目俯視，頭戴骷髏冠，胸前垂挂人頭項鬘，長蛇裝飾。跨騎在一神背上。此神憤怒明王面相，不戴帽冠，裸體佩戴項鏈、手鐲、脚鐲，頭略抬起，四肢着地用力爬行，身下爲橢圓型蓮花座，動感强烈。近似此神形象的護法神像有羅刹天，也騎在爬行的人背上，兩臂舉劍，持嘎巴拉碗。羅刹天與此神是否有關待考。

The six-armed Mahākāla is three eyed with a fierce expression. He wears skull garland and human head vine which hangs in front of his chest and is decorated with long snakes. With spread legs he tramples on Gaṇeśa, wears necklace, bracelet and anklet naked, raises his head slightly and crawls with his four limbs. Under his body, there is an oval lotus throne, which makes a scene full of strong movement.

13

14

米拉日巴

མི་ལ་རས་པ།

黃銅，高57厘米，18世紀

Mi la ras pa

Brass　Height: 57cm　18th century

米拉日巴是後弘期噶舉派著名僧人、詩人，以道歌傳播佛教。大師身材肥碩豐滿，右手上舉耳際，似在傾聽，右腿曲起，左腿盤坐，以游戲坐式坐在羚羊皮墊上，姿態輕鬆自如。面容平静，圖案化的卷髮貼在頭頂，形象生動有趣。銅色橘紅，光潤優美。

Mi la ras pa is a famous monk and poet of bKa' brgyud pa sect in the second Period of dissemination of Buddhism in Tibet. The master has a stout body and holds the right hand to the ear. He sits on the antelope skin cushion bending the right leg and crossing the left leg in a cozy posture with a free and relaxed stance. His face is peaceful and the patterned curl is attached to the top of the head, which makes a vivid and interesting image.

15

釋迦牟尼佛

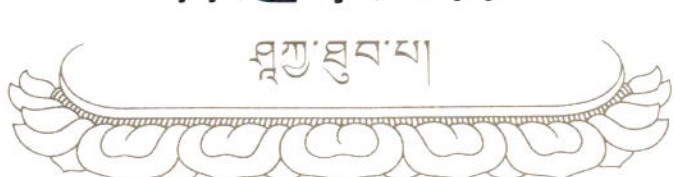

黄銅鎏金，高83厘米，17世紀

Buddha Śākyamuni

Gilt brass　Height: 83cm　17th century

釋迦佛着袒右肩袈裟，袈裟一角搭敷右肩。雙眼俯視，神情莊嚴。佛頭的每個螺髮卷高高凸起，造型獨特，袈裟衣褶起伏流暢，增强了佛像的生動氣息，巧妙地吸收了十五世紀以來內地永樂佛像衣紋表現手法。

Buddha Śākyamuni wears cassock which uncovers the right arm and the tip of the cassock is put on the right shoulder. He looks down with solemn expression. The Buddha head is covered with unique spiral hair. The pleat of the cassock is in smooth curve, which strengthens the lifelikeness. It masterly absorbs the expression technique of the Yongle period statues drapery from mainland since the 15th century.

16

阿彌陀佛

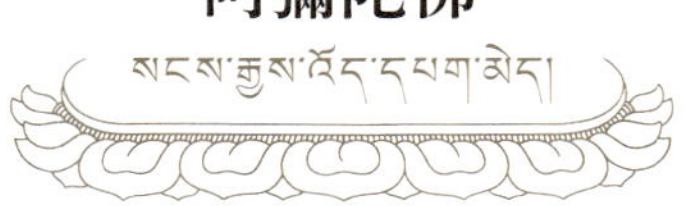

黃銅鎏金，高61厘米、寬44.2厘米、厚10厘米，14～15世紀

Buddha Amitābha

Gilt brass　Height: 61cm　Width: 44.2cm　Thickness: 10cm　14th-15th century

阿彌陀佛高浮雕像，採用鑄造方法製成，未使用常見的錘鍱方法。銅壁較厚，分量較重。佛雙手施禪定印，全跏趺坐蓮臺上，蓮座下是長方須彌座。馬蹄形背光頂雕刻金翅鳥、蛇身龍子、卷草尾摩羯龍、异獸、鳥身羽人、獅子、大象各種拿具，形象生動活潑。在背光周圍分五層，雕刻諸佛菩薩，最上層是五位五方佛、十一面觀音、手持金剛、黃財神；二層三層六位菩薩坐像；四層是佛身邊左右侍立兩站像菩薩；須彌座下第五層是棋格狀排列的七位菩薩。在不大的長方形面積內布置衆多佛菩薩像，場面宏大，形象繁複，構圖嚴密，其形象構圖採用了十二至十四世紀西藏繪畫唐卡畫法，吸收印度波羅藝術因素，夏魯寺十四世紀壁畫中可見相似背光樣式。用高浮雕方式把繪畫唐卡轉化成立體形象，設計巧妙，工藝精湛，在金銅佛像中比較少見。

Buddha Amitābha statue is a relief sculpture. Both of his hands are in the mudrā of meditation. He is seated on the lotus throne in the diamond attitude, and below the lotus throne is rectangular Sumeru throne. The top of the horseshoe shaped aureole is carved with Garuḍa, dragon with snake body, Mojie dragon with scrolled grass tail, strange animal, feather man with bird body, lion, elephant and various animals, which are vivid and vigorous. Five layers of Buddhas and Bodhisattvas are carved along the edge of the aureole; the top layer is five Dhyani Buddhas, 11 faces Avalokiteśvara, Vajradhara, the Yellow God of Wealth; the second and the third layers are six seated statues of Buddha; the fourth layer is two standing Bodhisattvas attending on the two sides of Buddha; the fifth layer below the Sumeru throne is seven Bodhisattvas arranged in checkered array.

17

釋迦牟尼佛

ཤཱཀྱ་ཐུབ་པ།

黃銅鎏金，高88厘米，17世紀

Buddha Śākyamuni

Gilt brass Height: 88cm 17th century

釋迦牟尼佛着袒右肩袈裟，雙眼俯視，神情莊嚴肅穆，右手施觸地印，左手作禪定印，寬胸闊背，身材壯碩有力。袈裟表面鑲嵌銀絲組成的法輪、雲朵圖案，頭部手脚裸露部位，蓮瓣中心局部鎏金，工藝精細、優美。蓮座前沿鑄出半露的金剛杵。此像是觸地印釋迦牟尼佛坐像，表現釋迦牟尼在菩提迦耶降服衆魔成佛，手施觸地印讓地母爲他成佛作證的情景。

Buddha Śākyamuni is seated in the diamond attitude. The left hand rests in the lap while the right hand is extended in the gesture of touching the earth. The upper monastic garment is rendered without folds in a transparent manner and covers the left shoulder only. He has a wide chest and back and a stout and powerful body. The surface of the cassock is embedded with Dharma-wheels formed in silver thread and cloud patterns. His head, hand and feet are exposed. The center of the lotus petal is partly gold plating. The half exposed vajra pestle on the front edge of the lotus throne proves the status of the Buddha statue.

18

緑度母

བླ་མ་ལྗང་གུ།

黄銅鎏金，高112厘米，16世紀

Green Tārā (Śyāma-Tārā)

Gilt brass Height: 112cm 16th century

緑度母頭戴鑲嵌松石、珊瑚五葉寶冠。肩後裝飾舟形火焰頭光，雕刻細膩，精美華麗，面相端莊英俊。右手握蓮蕾長莖，莖隨身形婉轉延伸與蓮座相連，在花枝卷曲渦旋中，巧妙地配制四位佛母小像。左右肩花中端坐佛與菩薩。緑母手握蓮花莖，右手施與願印。上身袒露，斜披絡腋，下着貼體長裙，前胸腰部裝華麗的瓔珞珠寶。女性特點鮮明，形象優美。西藏羅布林卡收藏同樣一尊緑度母像。本尊現已捐贈國家博物館。

The Green Tārā wears five-leaf crown embedded with turquoises and corals. The decoration behind his shoulder is boat shape flame head light. She holds the long stalk of lotus, which winds with the body shape and extends and connects with the lotus throne. In the curled vortex of flower branches are the four small statues of Buddha. Buddha and Bodhisattva are sitting in the left and right flowers on the shoulders. The Green Tārā holds the stalk of lotus and the right hand is in the gesture of charity. The statue has been donated to the National Museum of China.

19

六臂觀音菩薩

黄銅鎏金，高63厘米，16世紀

Six-armed Avalokiteśvara

Gilt brass Height: 63cm 16th century

觀音菩薩左舒坐於高梗的蓮臺上，高扁發髻前爲阿彌陀佛，左肩頭披瑞獸皮，是觀音菩薩的典型標識。觀音面容寧靜慈祥，長髮辮垂肩，沿面部髮髻輪廓圈一周細密的雲卷，裝飾性很强，增添了女性的美感。觀音六臂，右邊三手持拂塵、羂索、金剛杵（主手）；左邊三手持珊瑚、刻花寶瓶、手捻蓮花長莖（主手），蓮花心上刻海螺。圓形蓮花底座，蓮瓣成細長的條形，圓柱形花梗兩側裝飾翻卷飄動的纏枝蓮，底部雕雙獅，纏枝蓮頂部兩朵小蓮花上跪坐二弟子向觀音合十致禮。此像現已捐贈國家博物館。

Bodhisattva Avalokiteśvara is seated comfortably on the lotus throne with long stalk. In front of the high and flat bun is Buddha Amitābha. The left shoulder is covered with mascot skin, which is a typical mark of Avalokiteśvara. The three right hands of Avalokitésvara hold horsetail whisk, chain and vajra pestle (main hand). The left three hands hold coral, carved jeweled bottle and twine the long stalk of lotus (main hand). The center of the lotus is carved with a conch. The bottom of the round lotus throne is carved with double lion and on the two lotuses on the top squats two disciples who salute to Avalokiteśvara with arms put together. The statue has been donated to the National Museum.

20

觀音菩薩

བྱང་ཆུབ་སེམས་དཔའ་སྤྱན་རས་གཟིགས།

黄銅鎏金，高60厘米，15～16世紀

Bodhisattva Avalokiteśvara

Gilt brass Height: 60cm 15th-16th century

觀音身材修長，肌肉壯健，面相方圓豐滿，頭戴華麗的五葉寶冠，正中冠葉雕金翅鳥頭。面相、帽冠、胸前雕飾的珠寶瓔珞基本採用永樂佛像的作法，但已有很大變化。背光頂雕刻金翅鳥握蛇，上彎的横梁兩端雕卷草尾摩羯龍、肥碩的馬形異獸站立在大象背上，保留着十三至十四世紀流行的背光造型部分作法。身側兩支粗壯的蓮花，單獨鑄造，蓮莖隨身形婉轉延伸與觀音兩臂和蓮座相連。單層仰蓮座，下承托鏤空須彌座，是一尊漢藏佛像技法巧妙藝術結合的優秀作品。漢風爲主，很可能是漢族工匠的作品。

Avalokiteśvara wears gorgeous five-leaved crown the center leaf of which is the head of Garuḍa. The top of the aureole is carved with the pattern of Garuḍa holding snake, the two ends of the upswept beam with Makara with scrolled grass and stout horse shaped strange animal standing on the back of an elephant. The two stout lotuses on the side of the body are cast separately, and the stalk winds with the body shape and extends and connects with the two arms of Avalokiteśvara and the lotus throne.

21

觀音菩薩

བྱང་ཆུབ་སེམས་དཔའ་སྤྱན་རས་གཟིགས།

黃銅，高70厘米，15～16世紀

Bodhisattva Avalokiteśvara

Brass Height: 70cm 15th-16th century

觀音高髮髻不戴寶冠，髮髻前雕簡化的阿彌陀佛。身形魁梧，胸前飾項鏈珠寶瓔珞，下着長裙，左肩斜挎長珠鏈，簡單地模仿印度、尼泊爾佛像上常見的聖綫。左手握拂塵，右手握漢式花瓶，瓶内插長莖蓮花。

圓蓮花座下承托雙層的八角方臺，下面是梯形的空心高臺，臺内跪坐兩位弟子。步步升高的臺座把觀音襯托得十分高大。這顯然是漢式的觀音像，但在八角方臺面上并無漢字題記，只刻寫藏文觀音咒：

namaḥ ārya avalokiteśvarāya | bodhisatvāya | mahāsatvāya | mahākārunikāya | kārune kārune | mahākāruna | pratisthedi kārunuya svāhā |

Simplified image of Buddha Amitābha is carved in front of the bun of this Avalokiteśvara statue. The chest is decorated with necklace, jewelry and Keyura. He wears a long skirt and a long pearl necklace on the left shoulder. He holds horsetail whisk in the left hand and Han Chinese style vase in the right hand, and a lotus with long stalk is put in the base. Below the round lotus throne is double-layer octagonal platform below which is trapezoidal hollow high platform in which squat his two disciples.

22

文殊菩薩

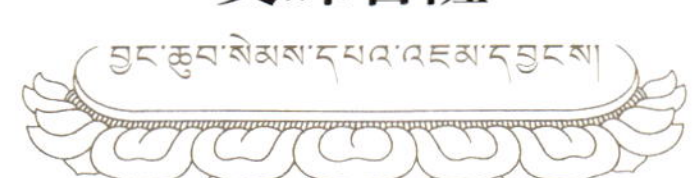

黃銅，高52.7厘米，約13世紀

Bodhisattva Mañjuśrī

Brass Height: 52.7cm 13th century

佛座、佛身、背光分三部分組合而成。文殊菩薩游戲坐姿，右手撫膝、左手輕按臺面，手心握蓮莖，粗壯的蓮花頭上置經篋。端坐在橢圓蓮花座上，蓮座下置多層疊澀的方臺座。文殊菩薩大眼睛，厚嘴唇，印度人特徵明顯。胸前斜披寬帛，戴項鏈、手鐲、臂釧，裝飾簡約。舟形大背光，頂部立圓傘蓋，頭光部位雕圓蓮花。背光上刻四座小塔，塔刹細高爲覆鉢式藏式佛塔，是元代開始流行的藏式佛塔式樣。從文殊形象、佛座、背光的式樣及細部特徵看是典型的十一至十三世紀東北印度波羅風格佛像。臺座後面刻八思巴文方印，內容爲“統領釋教大元國師”。此像具有很高的歷史研究價值。

Mañjuśrī is seated in the attitude of ease, with the right hand touching his knee and the left hand flicking at the surface of the platform and holding the lotus stalk. Sutra portfolio is put on the top of the stout lotus. Mañjuśrī has distinct Indian features including big eyes and thick lips. The aureole is boat shaped. The top is set up with round canopy, and the head light part is carved with round lotus. The aureole is carved with four towers, the top decorations of which are thin and tall and the towers are Tibetan stupas with covered alms-bowl style, a kind of style that began to be popular since the Yuan Dynasty. This Mañjuśrī is a typical 11-13th century Northeast Indian Polo style. The back of the throne is carved with a seal of 'Phags pa script stamp, it reads: "The state preceptor of the Grand Yuan Dynasty in charge of Buddhist Affairs".

23

金剛薩埵

ཪྡོ་རྗེ་སེམས་དཔའ།

黃銅鎏金，高82厘米，17世紀

Vajrasattva

Gilt brass Height: 82cm 17th century

金剛薩埵高鼻長目，神態肅穆莊嚴。高髮髻，髻頂飾金剛杵。五葉冠，冠葉寬大，鑲嵌寶石。袒胸，斜披寬帛，飾項鏈，臂釧，雕刻十分精緻。肩披寬帛翻卷繞於身側，寬帛翻起的一面鏨刻細密精美的花葉紋、聯珠綫，裝飾效果很强，顯示了高超的鏨刻技藝。蓮座雕雙層蓮瓣，蓮瓣凹心，原來每片蓮瓣都嵌寶石「現寶石已佚」，可見此像的精美華麗。

༢༣

Vajrasattva has a high bun, the top of which is decorated with vajra pestle. The five-leaved crown he wears has wide leaf and is embedded with gems. He is covered with wide silk with his chest uncovered. The necklace and armlet he wears are delicately carved. The wide silk covering the shoulder rolls and encircles the side of the body. The surface of the rolled up wide silk is carved with compact and delicate flower leaf pattern and pearl lines. The strong decoration effect shows the superior carving technique.

24

除蓋障菩薩

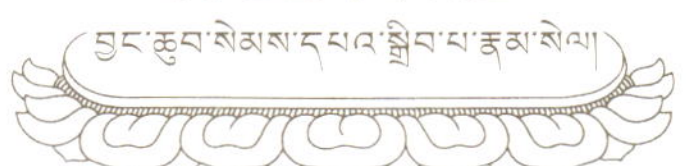

黃銅鎏金，高43厘米，15世紀

Sarvanivaraṇa Viṣkambhin

Gilt brass Height: 43cm 15th century

除蓋障菩薩身材壯碩，四肢圓實飽滿。頭戴五葉冠，髮髻頂雕金剛杵。面形方圓，彎眉長目，眉間飾毫相。鼻梁挺直，雙唇輕閉，蘊含笑意，目光柔和慈悅。全跏趺坐，雙手抬起作說法印，手大而指掌圓厚。上身袒露，佩戴項鏈、臂釧、手鐲，嵌松石、珊瑚；下身長裙，不刻衣紋褶皺，在膝頭綫刻大團花圖案，形制獨特，工藝精湛。身兩側粗壯長莖蓮花，花心雕日月。

Sarvanivaraṇa Viṣkambhin has a square face, bending eyebrows and long eyes. Urna-laksana is decorated between the eyebrows. He has a straight nose bridge and slightly closed lips. He is smiling softly with gentle and gracious sight. He is seated in the diamond attitude and holds his hands in the gesture of teaching dharma. His hands are big and have stout fingers and palms. He wears necklace, armlet and bracelet embedded with turquoise and coral with his upper body uncovered. The lower part of his body is dressed in long skirt with no carved wrinkles. Patterns of large cluster of flowers are carved on the knees. The center of the stout lotus with long stalk is carved with sun and moon.

25

般若佛母

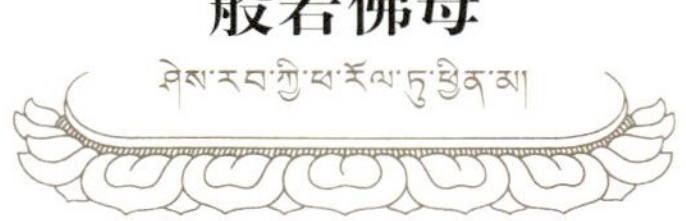

黃銅鎏金，高38厘米，15世紀

Buddha Prajñāpāramitā

Gilt brass Height: 38cm 15th century

般若佛母圓面柳眉，細目，秀口，眉間細長白毫，面容温婉秀美。五葉寶冠精緻華麗，耳飾大圓耳璫，束髮繒帶彎轉飄舉。兩肩頭覆蓋刻花披肩，胸前滿飾珠寶瓔珞，鑲嵌緑松石。雙手施説法印牽蓮花蔓，左側蓮花上置梵篋，爲般若佛母標識。長裙無衣褶，裙面刻多道纏枝蓮花纹裝飾條，雕聯珠綫。此像身材修長，比例適度，肌膚豐滿，裝飾繁縟華麗，是15世紀西藏佛像中富有尼泊爾佛像韵味的精彩佳作。中國文物交流中心收藏同樣一尊佛像。

The shoulders of Buddha Prajñāpāramitā are covered with carved cape and the chest is fully decorated with jewelry and Keyura and embedded with green turquoise. The two hands are in the gesture of teaching and holds lotus vine, and sūtra is put on the top of the left lotus, this is the mark of Buddha Prajñāpāramitā. The long skirt has no wrinkles and the surface of the skirt is carved with many decorations of lotus scrolls and pearl lines.

26

白度母

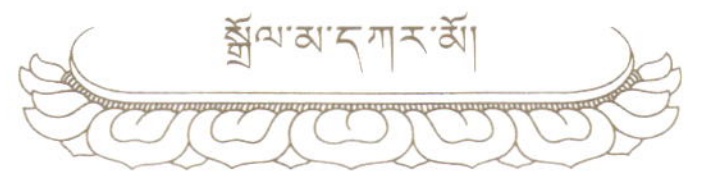

黃銅鎏金，高36厘米，17世紀

White Tārā (Sita-Tārā)

Gilt brass　Height: 36cm　17th century

白度母是藏傳佛教諸神中三長壽佛之一，胸前斜披寬帛，佩飾珠寶項鏈，下裙刻花紋，身側雕刻的蓮花婀娜多姿。方形框架式背光，圓頭光，蓮枝花邊。兩隻粗壯獅羊站立框架左右，前腿彎曲扶立柱。橫梁頂部兩隻神鳥，鳥頭上揚，鳥尾連接卷草與金翅鳥雙臂相聯，形制獨特。

White Tārā is one of the three deities of longivity in Tibetan Buddhism. Her chest is covered with wide silk aslant, adorned with necklace. The underneath skirt is carved with pattern and the carved lotus on the side of the body is graceful. The aureole is in the shape of square frame, and the head light is round and lotus branch lacework. Two stout lions stand on the two sides of the frame bending the front legs holding on to the upright column. The two holy birds on the top of the beam raise their head and their tails are connected with scrolled grass and the wings of the Garuḍa.

27

绿度母

黃銅鎏金，高42.5厘米，17世紀

Green Tārā (Śyāma-Tārā)

Gilt brass　Height: 42.5cm　17th century

༢༧

绿度母爲二十一救度佛母之首，傳爲觀世音菩薩所幻化，在西藏倍受崇信。此像右舒坐，脚踏小蓮花，臉型圓滿，修眉廣目，儀容端莊秀麗，豐乳細腰，姿態典雅，左手拇指與無名指相捻結拔濟衆生印，右手結與願印置膝上。長裙衣紋自然流暢，覆蓋蓮座。女性身材比例準確，肌體綫條勻稱柔美。

Green Tārā, one of the 21 Tārās of salvation, is said to be the incarnation of Arya Avalokiteśvara and receives much respect and worship in Tibet. This round faced statue is seated in the attitude of ease and steps on a small lotus with an elegant posture. Her left thumb and ring finger displays the gesture of saving all sentient beings, and the right hand holds the gesture of charity and is put on the knee. The wrinkles of the long skirt are natural and smooth covering the lotus throne. Her female stature is well-proportioned, and her body lines are well shaped and mellow.

28

大威德金剛

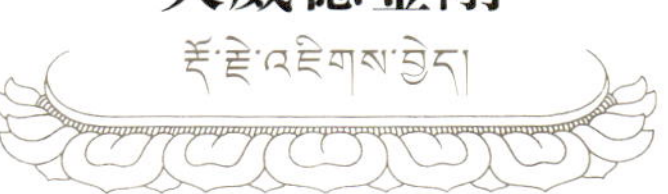

黃銅鎏金，高55厘米，17世紀

Vajrabhairava

Gilt brass Height: 55cm 17th century

大威德金剛是藏傳佛教密宗無上瑜伽部父系的本尊之一。作爲文殊菩薩的忿怒化現身，由熱譯師等人在十一世紀時從印度和尼泊爾傳播到西藏，並得到弘揚。格魯派和薩迦派都修行此尊。此尊爲大威德金剛雙尊像。主尊九面三十四臂十六足，九面表示大乘九部契經，三十四臂與身、語、意共表三十七道品，十六足代表十六空勝。十六足爲展左立姿，腳踏八獸、八禽、八大天等。鑄造工藝精緻，可惜法器全失了。

Vajrabhairava is a wrathful emanation of Mañjuśrī. He is shown with nine heads, the principal one being the head of a buffalo and the one on top in the center being that of Mañjuśrī. He has thirty-four arms and sixteen legs. He is trampling on a large number of various animals and beasts, placed on a single lotus pedestal.

29

喜金剛

ཀྱེ་རྡོ་རྗེ།

黄銅，高57厘米，17世紀

Kapāladhara Hevajra

Brass Height: 57cm 17th century

喜金剛爲藏密無上瑜伽部主尊，又稱呼金剛，薩迦派尤重此尊。喜金剛有各種變相，此爲藍色心藏喜金剛。此像八面十六臂兩腿，主像戴骷髏冠，身頸挂五十骷髏人首項鏈，兩主臂擁抱明妃無我佛母，其餘各臂呈扇形展開。佛母一面二臂，二手各持鉞刀、嘎巴拉碗。喜金剛十六隻手中都持嘎巴拉碗，左側嘎巴拉碗内盛白色水神、緑色風神、紅色火神、黄色地神等地、水、火、風、日、月、死、財等八位世間神衹，右側嘎巴拉碗内盛白鼻驢、紅牛等象、鹿、驢、牛、駝、人、獅、猫等八獸。喜金剛足下踏仰面魔羅，表示對貪、瞋、痴三毒的克服。此像多手多臂，造型生動，富有律動感。

This image depicts the sixteen-armed form of the Yi dam Hevajra with eight faces and four legs, known as Kapāladhara Hevajra, joined as a couple with Nairātmyā. In his eight right hands Hevajra holds skull-cups (kapāla) containing small effigies of an elephant, a horse, an ass, an ox, a camel, a griffin, and a cat, acting as guardians of the eight directions. The skull-cups in his left hands contain small effigies of deities, namely Pṛthivī (earth), Varuṇa (water), Vāyu (air), tejas (fire), Candra (moon), Āditya or Arka (sun), Yama or Antaka (death), and Dhanada (wealth). The two principal hands of Hevajra, turned inwards and crossed in front of the chest, embrace his consort Nairātmyā. She holds in her principal hands a ritual chopper with a vajra handle and a skull-cup, and has her right leg wrapped around the hips of Hevajra.

30

吉祥天母

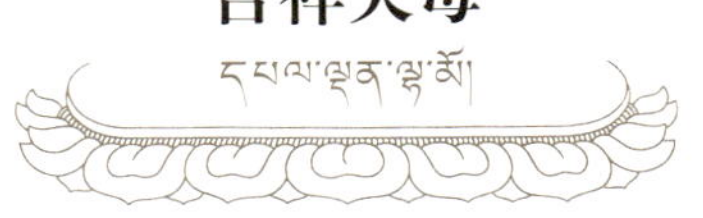

黃銅鎏金，高56厘米，17世紀

Śrī-Devī (dPal ldan lha mo)

Gilt brass Height: 56cm 17th century

吉祥天母頭戴五骷髏冠，紅色火焰形怒髮上衝，束髮冠帶兩邊雕小獅子、蛇。三目圓睜，口銜活人，凶神惡煞。右手應擧骷髏頭短杖（已佚），左手托嘎巴拉碗，跨騎騾背上，前胸垂挂人頭項鏈，騾子臀部有兩隻眼睛，一張人皮綁扎在騾背上。騾子雙耳竪起，鬃毛齊整，身形矯健。騾脚踏翻卷的波浪，表示吉祥天母在血海中奔走。底座周圍雕出綿延起伏的山巒，山頭飄着朵朵白雲，山石峻峭，借鑒了國畫筆法，頗有斧劈皴的意味。背光高浮雕連續不斷的雲卷，配合翻卷的火焰，雕刻生動，精細入微。匠師顯然是吸收了漢地繪畫藝術因素，刻畫出吉祥天母的生動形象。

Śrī-Devī wears five-skull crown. Her red flame shaped hair bristles. The two sides of the bandeau are carved with small lions and snakes. She holds a living human in his mouth with his three eyes wide open, which makes him look fierce. The right hand should be holding a short skull rod (lost), and the left hand holds a skull-cup. She bestrides on the back of a mule and hangs human head necklace before her chest. The buttocks of the mule have two eyes and a human skin is bound on its back. The aureole is carved with continuous succession of clouds and scrolled flame, which is carved vividly and subtly.

31

寶帳怙主

གུར་གྱི་མགོན་པོ།

黃銅，高52厘米，17世紀

Pañjaranātha Mahākāla (Gur gyi mgon po)

Brass Height: 52cm 17th century

寶帳怙主，大黑天神系中的一位重要神祇，具有帳房保護神、戰神的屬性。特別受到薩迦派的尊崇，格魯派也尊崇此神。清宮廷佛堂中也供奉此神，名稱漢譯爲「宮室永保護法」。此神四方面，頭戴骷髏冠，額開慧眼，三目圓鼓，怒目張口，面相凶忿。胸前垂挂珠寶瓔珞，人頭項鬘，長蛇裝飾。手持鉞刀與嘎巴拉碗，雙腿彎曲蹲踞姿態，兩肘彎托短杖。眼嵌銀，鑄造工藝精細。

蓮座後面陰刻八思巴文方印，印文待考。

Pañjaranātha Mahākāla, three-eyed with a fierce expression, is trampling with spread legs on a corpse placed on a single lotus pedestal with beaded borders. With the right hand he holds a ritual chooper with a vajra handle and with the left hand a skwll-cup. Mahākāla wears a five-leaved crown decorated with skulls, is adorned with jewellery and snake ornaments and wears a garland of skulls.

The Mahākāla cult was espercially popular during the Mongol Yuan period. Mahākāla was considered as the deity of war and the protector of the country.

32

白勇保護法

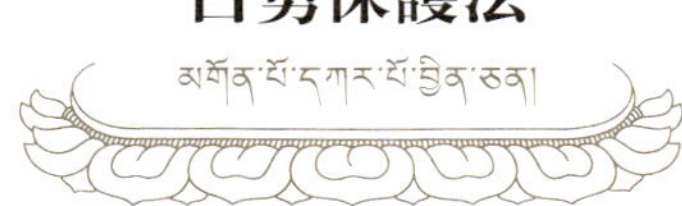

黃銅，高107厘米，17世紀

White Mahākāla

Brass Height: 107cm 17th century

༣༢

白勇保護法亦名白如意寶怙主，是六臂護法之異相，兼有護法與財神的雙重神格。此像一面六臂，赤髮上指，束五葉冠，怒目闊口，面相威猛而略帶憨態，右主臂手托摩尼珠，另兩手分持鉞刀、鼗鼓；左主臂手托顱器，內盛寶瓶，其他手持三股叉與金剛鈎。肩披長帛帶，下身着裙。胸前裝飾珍寶瓔珞，袒腹直立，腿部短粗而有力，足下踏兩位象頭神，整體造型生動有力。由纏枝卷草組合成火焰背光，上雕五位佛母。寶冠、眼睛、裙面鑲嵌紅銅，工藝十分精湛。

座面左角刻一方八思巴文印文，爲五世達賴喇嘛私章印文（見《西藏歷代藏印》第六十六頁）。説明此佛像與五世達賴喇嘛有關係。

White Mahākāla, is one form of the six-armed Dharma Protector Mahākāla, combines the dual characteristics of Dharma Protector and god of wealth. This statue has one face and six arms with brave, fierce and slightly silly appearance. The right main arm holds jewelry beads and the other two hands hold curved knife and rattle-drum; the left main arm holds a Kapāla which contains a jeweled bottle, and the other hands hold Trisula and vajra hook. He steps on two Gaṇeśas. The flame aureole is formed by floral and herbal scrolls on which five buddha mothers are carved.

33

騎鵬鳥護法

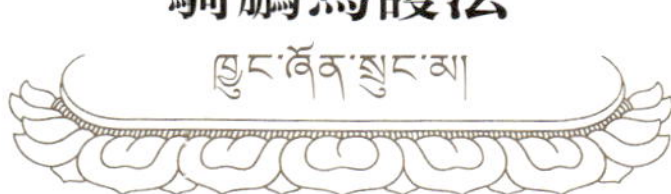

ཁྱུང་ཆེན་སྲུང་མ།

黄銅，高50厘米，17世紀

Protective Deity on a Garuḍa

Brass Height: 50cm 17th century

༣༣

護法神四方面絡腮胡，三目圓睜，張口怒吼，四臂各持法器，主手持鉞刀、嘎巴拉碗。其餘二臂右手持火焰劍，左手握人心。胸前擁抱明妃，明妃手中持嘎巴拉碗、三叉。跏趺端坐在金翅鳥背上。金翅鳥雙翅舒展，鷹嘴羊頭，毛髮竪立，口咬蛇身，胸部肌肉圓鼓，兩隻粗壯的人手臂握蛇頭尾兩端。鳥身下鎮壓着一裸形人，曲腿抬臂掙扎狀。此神形象罕見，與騎金翅鳥的遍入天近似，但面相、所持法器不同。準確名稱待考。蓮座前面刻方印印文，八思巴字，內容尚未識別。

This Protective Deity has three eyes and four arms holding a curved knife and a skull-cup bowl in his main hands. The other two arms hold flame sword and human heart respectively. He embraces his consort who is holding a skull-cup and Trisula and is seated on the back of Garuḍa in hero posture. The Garuḍa with eagle beak and goat head stretches its wings and bites the body of a snake with all its hair sticking up straight. The Garuḍa suppresses a naked human who bends his legs and raises arms in struggle.

34

六臂大黑天

མགོན་པོ་ཕྱག་དྲུག

銅合金，高59厘米，16世紀

Six-armed Mahākāla

Copper alloy Height: 59cm 16th century

༣༤

此像爲大黑天神系中的一尊，四頭六臂二腿。火焰形怒髮膨脹竪起，頭部碩大，方形明王怒相，闊口獠牙，怒目圓睜，形象凶猛。六臂持法器，左臂分别持羂索、三叉、嘎巴拉碗（已佚）；右手持鼗鼓、骷髏念珠、鉞刀。身後是展開的雙翅膀。胸前抱明妃，明妃左手托嘎巴拉碗，右手鉞刀（已佚）。佛像右弓步展立，右腿彎曲，左腿伸展，粗壯有力。四頭排列上下兩層，向左大角度傾斜，動感强烈。此像鑄造精細，打磨光滑圓潤，銅質爲淺咖啡色，色澤均匀漂亮，是一種少見的優質的銅合金材料，可能爲黄利瑪佛像。

This Mahākāla statue has four heads, six arms and two legs. His flame shaped hair swells and bristles. His eyes are wide open and his image is quite fierce. His six arms hold ritual apparatus; the left hands hold chain, Trisula and Kapāla bowls (lost) respectively; the right hands hold rattle-drum, skull, prayer beads and curved knife. Behind his body are two stretched wings. He embraces his consort who holds a Kapāla bowl in her left hand and a curved knife (lost) in her right hand. The Buddha statue bends the right leg and stands in lunge and stretches the left leg.

35

六臂大黑天

མགོན་པོ་ཕྱག་དྲུག

銅合金，高51厘米，16世紀

Six-armed Mahākāla

Copper alloy Height: 51cm 16th century

34

六臂大黑天，又稱六臂永保護法，爲大自在天的化身，是藏密中最高護法神。民間又傳爲戰神，禮祀此神可增威德，又爲施福之神，在西藏極受尊崇。這尊佛像火焰髮，戴五骷髏冠，面目猙獰。上身赤裸，飾瓔珞，戴人骨念珠。中間兩手執嘎巴拉碗和鉞刀；右面兩手執𧏚鼓、人骨念珠；左面兩手執索、三叉。雙足微弓，足下踏象頭神。此像鑄造精緻，打磨光滑圓潤，銅質爲淺咖啡色，色澤均勻，是一種稀見的優質的銅合金材料，可能爲黃利瑪佛像。

Six-armed Mahākāla, also called six-armed mGon po, an emanation of Maheśvara, is the highest guardian god of the Tibetan tantric Buddhism. This statue has flame-shaped hair, wears five-skull crown and ferocious appearance. He wears Keyura and human bone prayer beads with his upper body uncovered. The middle two hands hold a Kapāla bowl and curved knife; the right two hands hold rattle-drum, human bone prayer beads; the left two hands hold chain and Trisula. He stands on two Gaṇeśas with his legs slightly bent.

36

金剛亥母

རྡོ་རྗེ་ཕག་མོ།

黃銅鎏金，高81厘米，15世紀

Vajravārāhi

Gilt brass Height: 81cm 15th century

金剛亥母舞立姿，左脚獨立踏裸體人。戴骷髏冠，裸體，胸佩十字交叉珠鏈，腰部垂飾網狀瓔珞，身挂人頭項鬘。怒目圓睁，相貌猙獰。曲起的右腿下立蓮花莖支撑，使佛像重心平衡穩固。一條寬大的飄帶從髮髻後蜿蜒曲折垂下，飄帶下部爲纏枝蓮形，鑲嵌松石、珊瑚。飄逸優美，工藝精湛，别具匠心。西藏博物館收藏有一尊相同式樣的金剛亥母。

The three-eyed goddess, identified as Vajravārāhi, dances with her left foot on a corpse lying on a double lotus pedestal with beaded border. The Ḍākinī is naked except for the pañcamudrā ornaments carred of human bone and a garland of seveved heads. In the raised right hand she brandishes a ritual chopper with a vajra handle; in the left she holds a skull-cup. The Tibet Museum collects a Vajravārāhi with the same style.

37

金剛亥母

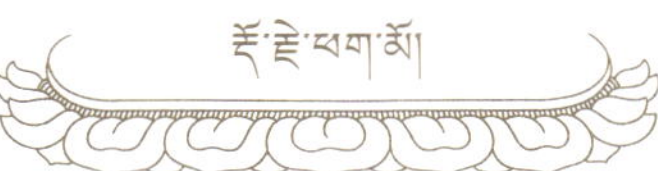

黄銅，高39.5厘米，18世紀

Vajravārāhi

Brass Height: 39.5cm 18th century

金剛亥母以主首側另有一猪首爲其形象特徵，此像把猪首立在髮髻前，形制特别。在藏傳佛教中她常以上樂金剛明妃的身份出現。主面三目圓睁，猪面右向，挺鼻張口。豐乳束腰，體態嫵媚，肌膚表現富於質感。頭戴骷髏冠，項挂骷髏蔓，右手持鉞刀上舉，左手托嘎巴拉碗於胸前，雙腿曲叠獨立，呈顯優美的舞蹈立姿，左足下踏裸體人。蓮座後面刻圓形印押，經查證爲清代西藏拉薩第穆活佛拉讓（府邸）丹吉林庫房印章（见《西藏歷代藏印》第八十三頁），説明此像與第穆活佛有關。

Vajravārāhi is named after the excresceuce in the shape of a sow's head on the side of the main head. She is often taken as the consort of Saṃvara. She is three-eyed. The pig face faces right, straightens her nose and opens her mouth. She wears skull crown and hangs skull vine on the neck holding and raising a curved knife in her right hand and holding a skull-cup in front of her chest. She stands on one leg with another leg bending and overlapping on another, which makes an elegant dancing posture. She steps on a naked human body with her left leg.

38

財神大黑天

ནོར་ལྷ་མགོན་ནག

黃銅，高36.5厘米，18世紀

Mahākāla of Wealth

Brass　Height: 36.5cm　18th century

༣༨

大黑天神系中財神，頭戴骷髏冠，火焰形怒髮膨脹豎起，方形明王怒相，闊口獠牙，怒目圓睜，形象凶猛。身着大袍，穿靴，背後披人皮。兩手執嘎巴拉碗和鉞刀。右腿弓步展立，明妃騎在伸開的左腿上，身披人皮，手持嘎巴拉碗和鉞刀。右足踏卧牛，牛身下壓一裸形人；左足踏卧馬，馬身下壓裸形人。座面刻藏文財神咒：Oṃ Jambhala jalendraya svāhā.

The Mahākāla of wealth wears skull crown with his flame-shaped hair swollen and bristled. His eyes are wide open and his image is quite ferocious. Dressed in a big robe, he wears boots and his back is covered with human skin. His two hands hold a skull-cup and curved knife. He stands in lunge with the right leg and stretches the left leg on which his consort rides. The consort wears human skin and holds a skull-cup and a curved knife. The right leg steps on a lying cattle which suppresses a naked human body; the left leg steps on a lying horse suppresses a naked human body. The Mantra of the Mahākāla is carved on the surface of the throne.

39

喇呼拉護法

སྒྲ་གཅན་འཛིན།

黄銅鎏金，高78.5厘米，18世紀

Rāhula

Gilt brass Height: 78.5cm 18th century

喇呼拉護法又稱毗紐天、羅睺星。上身人形，下身龍身，九頭四臂，頭分三層排列，頂層髮髻上雕鳥頭。腹部另有一頭，皆闊口獠牙，怒目圓睁，身披人皮，腰纏虎皮，袒胸露腹，猙獰可怖。前面兩手拉弓射箭，後面兩手持摩羯龍頭勝幢與蛇。環形中空的火焰背光。三角形須彌底座，座上邊雕起伏的山巒，每角雕一人頭。束腰處雕雙獅、交杵。此神爲寧瑪派主供的大護法神，在唐卡中偶然可以見到，在銅佛像中十分罕見。

Rāhula, also called Vishnu and Rahu, is the great guardian god mainly worshipped by the rNying ma pa sect. The upper body is humanoid and the lower half is in dragon shape. He has nine heads and four arms. His heads are arranged in three arrays. The bun on the top head is carved with bird head. There is another head on the belly which has wide mouth and bucktooth. He is dressed in human skin and girdled with tiger skin with his chest and belly uncovered. His image is very ferocious. The two front hands pull the bow and shoot arrow; the two rear hands hold the head of dragon and snake. The aureole is flame-shaped. Curved chain of mountains is carved on the side sculpture of the triangular Sumeru pedestal. Each angle is carved with one human head. The girdle is carved with double lion and crossed pestles.

40

空行母

མཁའ་འགྲོ་མ།

黃銅鎏金，高41厘米，17世紀

Ḍākinī

Gilt brass　Height: 41cm　17th century

空行母在密宗裏是代表智慧與力量的空中飛行女神，立姿弓箭步，左手高舉嘎巴拉碗，右手向下持鉞刀弓步立姿，頭高昂，是充滿力量憤怒迎敵的戰鬥姿態。軀體造型準確，肌膚豐滿，動態感强烈，充分表現了空行母降妖伏魔的威猛氣勢。頭戴五葉骷髏冠，雙耳戴大耳環，全身赤裸，上身飾瓔珞，乳部豐滿，女性特徵鮮明。天杖倚右臂彎內（已佚），雙足微弓，足下各踏一人。此像製作風格粗獷豪放，表情生動。

Ḍākinī is a flying goddess who stands for wisdom and power in Tantrism. She stands in lunge raising a skull-cup high with her left hand and holding curved knife in her left hand in the stance of lunge. She holds her head up in an attacking stance full of anger and power to confront any enemy. Her well proportioned and well developed body is full of dynamics, which fully shows her brave and fierce momentum with which she subdues demons and monsters. She is fully naked and the garland she wears and her boobs clearly show her femaleness.

41

黃財神

རྫམ་བྷ་ལ་སེར་པོ།

黃銅鎏金，高46厘米，15世紀

Píta-Jambhala

Gilt brass Height: 46cm 15th century

黃財神，多聞子的變化身之一，在密宗四部中，他被置於事續部的世間部，充當有財部、藥叉部和其餘世間部的護法神。肥頭大耳，兩目，眼圓睜，火焰眉，高髮髻，頭戴五葉冠，佩大耳璫。右手持芒果，左手持吐寶如意獸。袒上身，大腹，袒胸飾珠寶項鏈、臂釧、右舒坐，脚踏蓮花，單層蓮花座下承托立柱連接圓蓮座。蓮座覆鈴造型表面采用減底陽刻手法雕刻精美的卷草纹、蓮花瓣。四周圍繞纏枝蓮花組成的八個渦旋，如八瓣蓮花，正前方装饰飘动的帛带，造型異常優美。

Jambhala is one of the eight assistants of Navātmaka-Mahāpita-Vaiśravaṇa. He is seated in the attitude of ease on a lotus pedestal. There is a supporting round lotus pedestal under the single-layer lotus throne. He is fat and bulky and has three wide open eyes and flame-shaped eyebrows. He wears high bob, five-leaved crown and big ear-ornaments. He holds mango in the right hand and treasure-producing beast in the left hand. With his upper body uncovered and a big belly, he is decorated with jewelry, necklace and armlet.

42

菩薩

བྱང་ཆུབ་སེམས་དཔའ།

黃銅鎏金，高65厘米，18世紀

Bodhisattva

Gilt brass Height: 65cm 18th century

這是幾位神靈疊羅漢式的組合形象，以俯臥的麒麟爲底座，人身鳥頭的金翅鳥手握長蛇蹲踞在麒麟背上。四臂菩薩蹲踞在麒麟肩膀上，菩薩手持海螺、蓮花、短杖等法器。八臂菩薩蹲踞在四臂菩薩肩膀上，手中持念珠、三叉、經篋、索繩、蓮花、寶瓶，胸前右手施無畏印。這種多尊組合的形象在金銅佛像中十分罕見，人物組合形式近似北京故宮收藏唐卡中的哈里哈里羅世自在觀世音（北京故宮博物院藏文物珍品全集《藏傳佛教唐卡》圖130）。唐卡所繪畫的形象有明顯的觀音的標志，此像未見觀音標志，身份待考。

It is a combined image of several deities in pyramid. The base is a Kylin lying on its stomach. The Garuḍa with human body and bird head holds long snake and squats on the back of the Kylin. The four-armed Bodhisattva squats on the shoulder of the Kylin holding ritual apparatus such as conch, lotus, short rods, etc. The eight-armed Bodhisattva squats on the shoulder of the four-armed Bodhisattva holding prayer beads, Trisula, sutra box, rope, lotus and jeweled bottle and making the mudrā for bestowing fearlessness with the right hand in front of his chest.

43

蓮花生

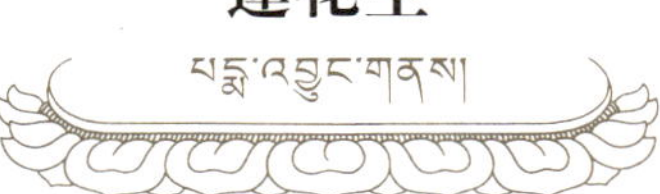

黃銅，高31厘米，17世紀

Padmasambhava

Brass Height: 31cm 17th century

蓮花生爲印度密宗大師，公元八世紀進入西藏弘揚佛法，被尊爲藏傳佛教寧瑪派之開山祖師。蓮花生頭戴尖頂帽，長圓面，眉頭緊蹙，雙目圓睜，目光炯炯，神情威嚴。右手當胸持金剛杵，左手結禪定印，上托嘎巴拉碗（已佚）。脚穿靴半跏趺坐蓮花座。蓮座前左右站立手托佛鉢供養菩薩。圓形鏤空背光，雕刻六拿具，爲清代內地流行圖案。下爲須彌方座，雕刻法輪珠寶。底面刻藏文六字真言。

座面後部刻有八思巴印一方，根據《西藏歷代藏印》（第七十頁）查對，此印爲第司桑結嘉措「壽」字印，該印是他的私章，藏布達拉宫。

Padmasambhava is a tantric master from India. He went to Tibet to spread tantric Buddhism in the 8th century and was regarded as the founder of the rNying ma pa sect. Padmasambhava wears peaked cap, holds vajra pestle in front of his chest with the right hand and holds a skull-cup (lost) with the left hand while displaying the gesture of meditation. He is seated on the lotus throne in the attitude of ease.Two Bodhisattvas stand in the left and right side making offerings with alms bowls. The round openwork aureole is carved with six animals, which was a popular pattern in the Qing Dynasty. The underneath Sumeru throne is carved with Dharma-wheels and jewels.

44

宗喀巴

ཙོང་ཁ་པ།

黄銅鎏金，高30.5厘米，18世紀

Tsong kha pa

Gilt brass　Height: 30.5cm　18th century

宗喀巴上師作爲藏傳佛教格魯派的開山祖，被視爲文殊菩薩的化身而享有至尊的地位，他的形象標志也與文殊菩薩相同。此尊身穿喇嘛僧袍，全跏趺禪坐蓮臺之上，雙腿遮於袍下，衣紋處理細緻自然，在大袍衣緣等部位鏨刻精美的蓮花纏枝圖案。長圓面温厚慈祥。雙手當胸結説法印，手中各引花蔓至身兩側。左右肩頭蓮花上各托經、劍，代表文殊之大智。整體造型給人以平和安詳之感。

As the founder of the dGe lugs pa sect, Tsong kha pa is regarded as an emanation of Mañjuśrī and thus enjoys the most revered and respected status. His image is identical with that of Mañjuśrī. The statue wears Lama frock and is seated on the lotus throne in the diamond attitude with both his legs covered under the frock. The wrinkles of the frock are delicate and natural. Exquisite patterns of lotus scrolls are carved on the edge of the frock. His long and round face looks gentle and kind. Both of his hands display the gesture of teaching the dharma, and the flower vines in the hands stretch to the two sides of the body. The lotuses on the left and right shoulders hold sutra and sword, which stands for the great wisdom of Mañjuśrī.

45

高僧像

མཁས་གྲུབ་ཆེན་པོ།

黄銅，高54厘米，14～15世紀

Eminent Monk

Brass Height: 54cm 14th-15th century

高僧豐面大耳，雙目細長，嘴唇輕啓，唇邊挂着微笑，手作説法印，正在給衆人講經説法。體形魁梧，身着交領大袍，内衣未着喇嘛穿的坎肩背心，大袍遮住全跏趺坐的雙腿，在大袍衣緣淺刻精美的纏枝蓮紋。造型簡潔，比例準確，綫條流暢，工藝手法精到嫻熟，以寫實肖像技法生動刻畫了一位佛法精深的高僧形象。没有題記參考，無法判斷其身份，從着裝看可能是一位漢僧。

造像後背刻印文一方，漢字雙鈎「夾實堅藏」，此印爲明宫廷永樂年間所賜。現存兩方同樣文字印，一象牙印，一青玉印，收藏在拉薩羅布林卡。象牙印刻款識，右上：「永樂十三年五月日」；左上：「賜思裸般領葛剌」（見《西藏歷代藏印》第四十四頁）。「思裸般領葛剌」是何人待考。

The eminent monk has plump face, big ears and slender smiling eyes. His hands are in the gesture of teaching. He has a burly figure and wears robe with crossed collars which covers the legs in the diamond attitude. The edge of the robe is carved with exquisite lotus scroll patterns. The back of the statue is carved with a seal, which is written in Chinese character and double hooked "Jia shi jian zang"[bKra shis rgyal mtshan]. This seal was bestowed by the Ming court in the Yongle Years. There exist two seals of same word, one is ivory seal and another is grey jade, both collected in Norbulingka, Lhasa.

46

咱雅班智達

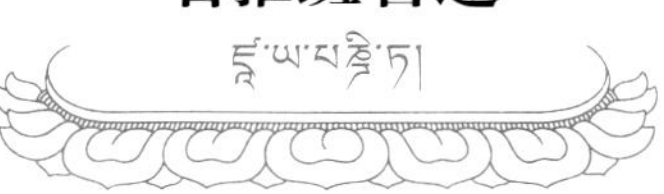

黃銅，高37厘米，17世紀

Zaya paṇḍita

Brass Height: 37cm 17th century

咱雅班智達（一五九九至一六六二年）出身於衛拉特和碩特部蒙古貴族，原名納木海嘉木措，是明末清初衛拉特蒙古和碩特部著名高僧。青年時期在西藏格魯派寺院長期學佛，一生致力於藏傳佛教在西部蒙古的傳播，在衛拉特蒙古軍事力量支持格魯派取得在西藏的统治地位的鬥争中，發揮過重要作用。他創制了托忒蒙古文，用托忒文翻譯藏文佛教典籍，在溝通蒙藏文化，保留衛拉特民族歷史文獻方面做了重大貢獻。此像以全跏趺式坐於三層座墊上，右手施説法印，左手施禪定印。面容清瘦，皺紋滿布，慈顔含笑，雙耳大張，一副飽經滄桑但意志堅定的睿智老僧形象。肥大的袈裟裹住全身，下擺落於座墊上，綫條流暢生動。從其栩栩如生的面部表情，及内在氣質的强烈渲染力可以看到十五世紀以來典型的西藏肖像寫實風格。此像與北京故宫博物院收藏的咱雅班智達像形象完全一致，是新發現的又一尊咱雅班智達像，具有重要歷史價值。此像現已捐贈國家博物館。

Zaya paṇḍita or Namkhaijantsan (1599-1662) was the most prominent Buddhist scholar of Oirat Mongol origin in the transitional period between the Ming and Qing Dynasty. He was studying and practicing Buddhism in Tibet under the guidance of the 4th Panchen lama during his youth. Later Zaya paṇḍita spread Tibetan Buddhism to the Oirats, the Khalkha and even the Kalmyks in far away Russia.This statue sits on the three-layer cushion in the diamond attitude. His right hand makes the gesture of teaching and his left hand displays the gesture of meditation. This statue has exactly the same image with the Zaya paṇḍita preserved in the Palace Museum. It is a newly founded Zaya paṇḍita statue with important historical value. It has been donated to the National Museum.

47

格魯派高僧像

དགེ་ལུགས་པའི་མཁས་གྲུབ་ཆེན་པོའི་སྐུ་བརྙན།

黃銅，高40.5厘米，17世紀

Eminent Monk of the dGe lugs pa

Brass Height: 40.5cm 17th century

高僧頭戴班霞帽，內着坎肩式僧裝，外披僧袍，其裝束表明他是藏傳佛教格魯派的高僧。面龐豐圓，眼睛嵌白銀，眼仁再嵌深色銅，兩目圓睜，炯炯有神，面相生動寫實。全跏趺坐於梯形方墊之上，右手胸前結説法印，左手結禪定印，掌心覆蓋長袍一角。僧袍、方座表面採用陽刻與陰刻結合銀絲鑲嵌等多種藝術手法，巧妙地雕出朵花、卷草、雲卷。綫條流暢，疏密得當，精緻華美。其精彩的肖像藝術在明清祖師像中十分罕見。臺座後背刻四行工整的藏文，內容是獻給宗喀巴大師的頌詞。

The clothing of the eminent monk indicates his identity of dGe lugs pa origin. His face is round and plump. His eyes are embedded with silver and the pupils are inlaid with dark bronze. He is seated in the diamond attitude on the trapezoidal square cushion with the right hand in front of the chest displaying the gesture of teaching and the left hand in the gesture of meditation. The surface of the frock and the square pedestal employs many means of artistic expression such as the combination of relief sculpture and intaglio and silver line embedding etc. to carve flowers, scrolled grass and clouds.

明宫廷藝術風格佛像

明代宫廷製作佛像，多爲明代中央政府賞賜西藏來朝貢的各派宗教領袖的珍貴禮品，見證了永樂、宣德時期宫廷與藏區的緊密聯繫。永宣佛像造型優美，工藝精湛，題材豐富，品相完好，可以啓發我們認識永樂、宣德佛像的藝術成就，以及它在明清佛教雕塑藝術史中的深遠影響。永宣佛像造型來源不僅是西藏，直接影響則來自於元代以來内地漢藏佛教藝術的發展，其式樣在藏區長期流傳，影響久遠。永宣佛像取得的藝術成就是元代以來藏傳佛教在内地傳播、發展藏漢藝術交流的碩果。

48

旃檀佛

黃銅鎏金，高30.5厘米，明永樂年間（1403～1424）

Sandalwood statue of Buddha Śākyamuni

Gilt brass　Height: 30.5cm　Yongle reign, Ming Dynasty (1403-1424)

釋迦牟尼佛身着圓領通肩式大袍，雙腿直立在圓蓮座上，面容莊重，慈祥可親。右手曲臂向上結施無畏印，左手下垂結與願印。突出兩隻有力的大手，傳達對佛陀精神的贊頌和崇敬。寬大衣袍緊貼佛的雙肩和身體，胸前下垂形成U字形的密集衣紋呈水波紋狀，衣袍至腋部隨佛手勢的提垂又形成有動感的衣褶。依稀可見公元四、五世紀印度笈多王朝佛像藝術的遺韵。

旃檀佛是最早的佛陀造像樣式之一，相傳佛成道以後思報母恩，遂升忉利天爲母說法，僑薩羅國優填王（utrayang，鄔陀衍那）思念佛。乃請目犍連主持用旃檀木雕刻了佛像，佛從忉利天復降人間，王率臣民前往迎佛，旃檀佛像升空謁佛，佛爲之摩頂授記說：我滅度千年後，汝往震旦，廣利人天。後來這尊旃檀佛像果然流傳中國，在中國演繹了一個時間久遠、內容神奇的佛像流傳故事。佛像由旃檀木雕刻得名，成爲一種規範樣式。後來人們仿照此樣式造佛，無論是木雕、銅鑄或泥塑，凡此形象的釋迦牟尼佛像統稱爲旃檀佛，成爲佛陀形象中歷史最悠久，流傳最廣泛的一種，尤爲中國歷代皇帝歷朝宮廷所重視。

蓮座正面由左至右陰刻“大明永樂年施”楷書款。封底完好，底蓋陰刻金剛交杵圖形，明永樂宮廷作品。

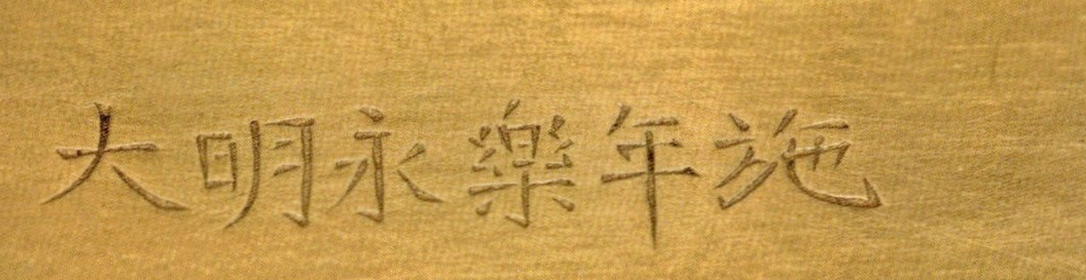

Sandalwood statue of Buddha Śākyamuni is one of the earliest Buddha statues, and got his name "Sandalwood Buddha" from the sandalwood carving. This Sandalwood Buddha wears big robe with round collars and stands straight on the round lotus throne with solemn and amiable facial appearance. He raises his right hand and makes the gesture of bestowing fearlessness with his arms bent, and his left hand displays the gesture of supreme generosity.

The front of the lotus throne is carved in intaglio with the six-character Yongle reign mark "Da Ming Yongle nian shi" (granted during the Yongle reign of the Grand Ming) in standard script in the direction from left to right. The back cover is intact and the bottom cap is carved in intaglio with patterns of crossed vajra pestles.

藥師佛

སངས་རྒྱས་སྨན་ལ།

黄銅鎏金，高25厘米，明永樂年間（1403～1424）

Medicine Buddha (Bhaiṣajyaguru)

Gilt brass　Height: 25cm　Yongle reign, Ming Dynasty (1403-1424)

此藥師佛像是永樂皇帝賜予西藏佛教領袖的珍貴禮品，在存世的永樂佛像中較爲稀少。藥師佛形象與釋迦牟尼佛一樣，螺髮高髻，面容端嚴慈祥，彎眉長目，嘴角眉目間充溢着笑意，洞徹一切的和熙目光，關注着衆生的病痛疾苦。身着袒右袈裟，衣紋流暢，曲伏自如。全跏趺坐，左手禪定印托鉢，右手與願印，二指輕捏棗核形藏青果，以精準流暢的綫條完美地表現了藥師佛誓願救度病苦衆生的佛性。

蓮座正面由左至右陰刻「大明永樂年施」楷書字款，字體端正，刻寫清晰。封底完好，底蓋陰刻金剛交杵圖形，上有塗朱砂痕迹，永樂宮廷作品。

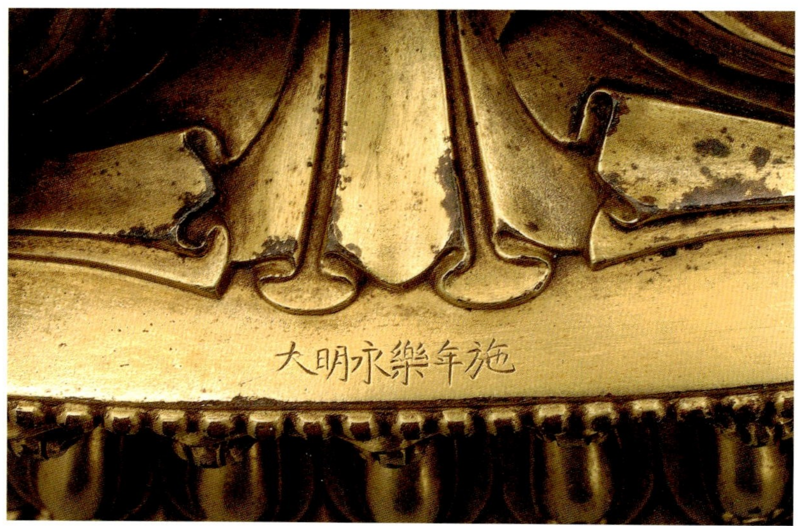

The Medicine Buddha statue was a precious gift bestowed to the leader of Tibetan Buddhism by Emperor Yongle, and was relatively rare in the existing Buddhist statues of the Yongle reign. The image of the Medicine Buddha is similar to that of Buddha Śākyamuni. He has screw-like hair in high bun and solemn and kind facial appearance. He is seated in the diamond attitude with the left hand holding bowl displaying the gesture of meditation and the right hand pinching the date pit-shaped myrobalan in the gesture of charity.

The front of the lotus throne is inscribed the six-character Yongle reign marks in standard script in the direction from left to right. The back cover is intact and the bottom cap is carved in intaglio with patterns of crossed vajra pestles. It is coated with cinnabar.

50

無量壽佛

སངས་རྒྱས་ཚེ་དཔག་མེད།

黃銅鎏金，高24.2厘米，明永樂年間（1403～1424）

Buddha Amitāyus

Gilt brass Height: 24.2cm Yongle reign, Ming Dynasty (1403-1424)

◎無量壽佛，頭戴五葉寶冠，葫蘆形高髮髻鎏金，不刻髮絲，上飾摩尼寶珠，雕飾精美。垂目俯視，高鼻薄唇，略含笑意，面相清秀，神態和悅。長髮披肩，裝飾大耳璫。袒上身，長帛帶繞身，下着長裙自然流暢。端坐在仰覆蓮座上，蓮瓣瘦長挺拔，蓮瓣尖端上卷雕卷雲紋，上下邊緣飾聯珠紋。

◎蓮座正面由左至右陰刻「大明永樂年施」楷書字款，字體端正，刻寫清晰。封底完好，底蓋陰刻金剛交杵圖形。永樂宮廷作品。

Buddha Amitāyus wears a five-leaved crown. His calabash-shaped high pun is gold-decorated without being carved with hairline and is adorned with jewelry bead. He has his upper body uncovered and circled with long silk. The underneath long skirt is natural and smooth. He is seated in the diamond attitude on a double lotus pedestal, the front of which clings to each other. The petal of the lotus is slender and straight, the top of which is carved with cirrus cloud patterns and the upside and underside are decorated with bead-like patterns.

The front of the lotus throne is inscribed with the six-character Yongle reign mark in standard script in the direction from left to right. The bottom cap is carved in intaglio with patterns of crossed vajra pestles.

51

四臂觀音菩薩

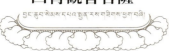

黃銅鎏金，高18厘米，明永樂年間（1403～1424）

Four-armed Avalokiteśvara (Ṣaḍakṣarī-Lokeśvara)

Gilt brass　Height: 18cm　Yongle reign, Ming Dynasty (1403-1424)

四臂觀音又稱六字觀音，是由六字真言所化現的觀音，在藏傳佛教諸多觀音形象中極爲重要，廣受尊崇。菩薩全跏趺坐，面相莊嚴，胸前兩手合什，後右手捻佛念珠串（僅剩一顆念珠），左手持蓮花。胸前裝飾精美的雙股瓔珞項鏈，項鏈式樣是永樂、宣德佛像特有的。左肩未雕常見的觀音標識仁獸皮。

蓮座正面由左至右陰刻「大明永樂年施」楷書字款，字體端正，刻寫清晰。

The four-armed form of Avalokiteśvara known as Ṣaḍakṣarī is seated in the diamond attitude on a double lotus pedestal with an upper beaded border. With the principal pair of hands he displays the gesture of respectful salutation. The upper left hand holds a lotus flower. In the upper right hand Ṣaḍakṣarī originally holds a rosary. The front of the chest is well-ornamented with two-ply Keyura necklace, the style of which was peculiar to the Buddhist statues of the Yongle and Xuande Periods.

The front of the lotus throne is inscribed with the six-character Yongle reign mark in standard script in the direction from left to right.

52

彌勒菩薩

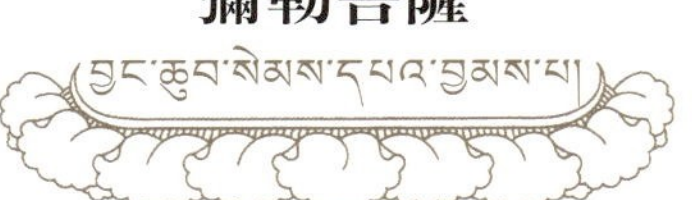

黄銅鎏金，高38.2厘米，明永樂年間（1403～1424）

Bodhisattva Maitreya

Gilt brass Height: 38.2cm Yongle reign, Ming Dynasty (1403-1424)

彌勒菩薩爲八大菩薩之上首，因他是釋迦牟尼佛的繼承者，亦被稱爲未來佛，他的形象也因而有菩薩裝與佛裝的不同表現。此像菩薩裝，雙腿直立仰覆蓮座，身體略側扭。臉形方圓，高卷髮髻，頭戴寶冠，束髮冠帶翻卷，大圓耳璫。袒露上身，胸前裝飾項鏈瓔珞，下着雙層長裙，裙褶曲復自然，有輕柔的波動感，裙面垂飾華麗瓔珞。長帛繞身飄垂身側，身後兩條短飄帶鈎挂在腰帶兩邊。雙手各牽蓮花長莖，左手施説法印，右手施與願印。身側的蓮花束枝條婀娜多姿，造型別致，爲永樂佛像特有。蓮花頂部雕净瓶、法輪。形體圓潤豐滿，與瞿曇寺觀音像風格一致。鑄造鎏金工藝精湛，是一尊罕見的永樂宫廷佛像珍品。

蓮座正面由左至右陰刻「大明永樂年施」楷書字款。字體端正，刻寫清晰。原封底完好，底蓋陰刻金剛交杵圖形，交杵部位鎏金。

Bodhisattva Maitreya stands in a slightly beat attitude on a lotus pedestal. With the right hand he displays the gesture of charity and holds the stalk of a nāgakeśara branch. The left hand displays the gesture of teaching. He is ornamented with a five-leaved crown.

The front of the lotus throne is carved in intaglio with the six-character Yongle reign mark in standard script in the direction from left to right. The back cover is intact and the bottom cap is carved in intaglio with patterns of crossed vajra pestles. The crossed part is gold-decorated. This is a work of the Yongle court of the Ming Dynasty.

53

觀音菩薩

黃銅鎏金，高24.5厘米，明永樂年間（1403～1424）

Bodhisattva Avalokiteśvara

Gilt bras　Height: 24.5cm　Yongle reign, Ming Dynasty (1403-1424)

此尊觀世音菩薩一面二臂，作正觀音形。尊像方面闊額，嘴角上挑，修眉朗目，寂靜慈祥。頭戴五葉寶冠，繒帶束髮，雙垂耳璫。菩薩袒上身，帛帶自雙肩繞臂婉轉飄垂。左手豎三指，屈無名指與拇指相捻當胸，右手掌心向外置右膝上結與願印。上體頭右身左，略呈三折肢勢。舒右腿，足踏蓮花，左腿盤曲，呈游戲坐姿。通常稱此造型者爲“自在觀音”，也名“世間尊觀音”。

蓮座正面由左至右陰刻“大明永樂年施”楷書字款。字體端正，刻寫清晰。原封底完好，底蓋陰刻金剛交杵圖形。永樂宮廷作品。

This Avalokiteśvara has one face and two arms. He wears a five-leaved crown with his upper body uncovered. The silk ribbon rotates around the arm from the shoulders. The three fingers of the left hand sticks up and the ring finger and the thumb are bent and twined together in front of the chest. The right palm faces outward and is put on the right knee in the gesture of charity. He steps on the lotus with his right leg stretched. He bends and crosses his legs in the stance of larkishness.

The front of the lotus throne is carved in intaglio with the six-character Yongle reign mark in standard script in the direction from left to right. The bottom cap is carved in intaglio with patterns of crossed vajra pestles. This is a work of the Yongle court of the Ming Dynasty.

43

54

思惟觀音菩薩

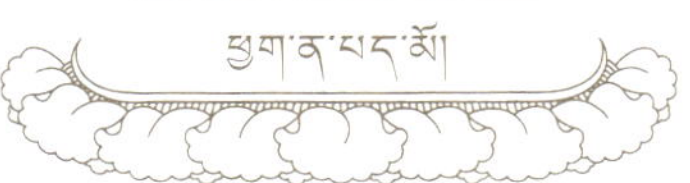

銅鎏金，高29.5厘米，明永樂年間（1403～1424）

Bodhisattva Avalokiteśvara in Meditation

Gilt brass　Height: 29.5cm　Yongle reign, Ming Dynasty (1403-1424)

觀音菩薩，長眉細目，鼻梁挺括，頭略低，兩眼俯視，左手彎曲托腮靜默思維。胸前飾珠寶瓔珞，雙聯珠綫樣式。長裙衣褶起伏自然，裙邊透迤垂於座面。高蓮座，蓮瓣細長。寬肩細腰，右腿盤坐，左腿曲起，姿態閑適。

蓮座正面由左至右陰刻“大明永樂年施”楷書字款。字體端正，刻寫清晰。原封底完好，底蓋整體鎏金，陰刻金剛交杵圖形，永樂宮廷作品。

Bodhisattva Avalokiteśvara with slender eyebrow and eyes holds his chin with bent left hand in meditation. The front of his chest is decorated with jewelry Keyura which is in the style of dual bead line. The high lotus throne has slender petals. He has wide shoulders and slender waist. He is seated in the attitude of ease with his right leg hunkered and his left leg bent.

The front of the lotus throne is inscribed the six-character Yongle reign mark in standard script in the direction from left to right. The gold-decorated bottom cap is carved in intaglio with patterns of crossed vajra pestles. This is a work of the Yongle court of the Ming Dynasty.

55

思惟觀音菩薩

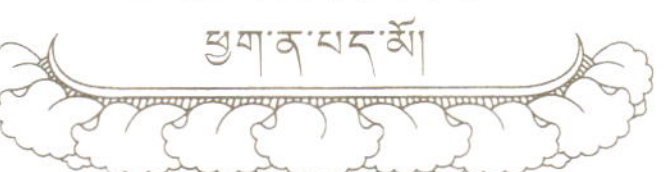

黄銅鎏金，高49厘米，明永樂年間（1403～1424）

Bodhisattva Avalokiteśvara in Meditation

Gilt brass Height: 49cm Yongle reign, Ming Dynasty (1403-1424)

觀音菩薩，眉目疏朗，兩眼俯視，静默思維。右腿盤坐，左腿曲起，游戲坐姿。左臂肘支于膝上，手掌彎曲托腮，右手放右腿上。胸前飾珠寶瓔珞，雙聯珠綫樣式。長裙衣褶起伏自然，裙邊逶迤垂於座面。高蓮座，蓮瓣細長，姿態閑適。

蓮座正面由左至右陰刻“大明永樂年施”大字楷書字款，下有藏文一行，意爲“大明永樂之年賜”。

Bodhisattva Avalokiteśvara in meditation is seated in the attitude of ease with his right leg hunkered and his left leg bent. The left elbow is put on the knee; the bent palm holds the chin; the right hand is put on the right leg. The front of his chest is decorated with jewelry Keyura which is in the style of dual bead line. The wrinkle curve of the long skirt is natural, and the winding edge of the skirt is hung on the surface of the throne.

The front of the lotus throne is inscribed with the six-character Yongle reign mark in standard script in the direction from left to right. There is a line of Tibetan which means “Bestowed in the Yongle Years of the Ming Dynasty”.

44

56

大持金剛

黃銅鎏金，高38.2厘米，明永樂年間（1403～1424）

Vajradhara

Gilt brass　Height: 38.2cm　Yongle reign, Ming Dynasty (1403-1424)

◎大持金剛傳爲大乘密宗佛法的直接傳授者，在密宗諸派中享有崇高的神性地位。此像頭戴五葉冠，細眉朗目，容貌慈藹。上身袒露飾瓔珞環釧，全跏趺坐，腰部收束，下着長裙。雙手交叉於胸前，手中持金剛鈴、金剛杵。

◎此像鑄造精細，鎏金純厚，裝飾華麗，工藝精良；造像氣度端莊，比例和諧。蓮座没有刻年款，其精湛的工藝說明此像爲永樂宮廷作品。

The image of Vajradhara is seated in the diamond attitude on double lotus pedestal with beaded border. The right hands holding five-pronged diamond sceptres and the left hands holding prayer-bells are turned inwards and crossed over the chest. He is clad in cloth tied by belts with attached beaded strands around the hip. He wears bejewelled ornaments, namely five-leaved crown fastened with ribbon with swirling ends in front of the knot of hair with jewelled tips, pairs of circular earrings, necklaces with beaded strands of pearls attached, bracelets on the upper arms and wrists, ornaments on the legs, and anklets.

57

觀音菩薩

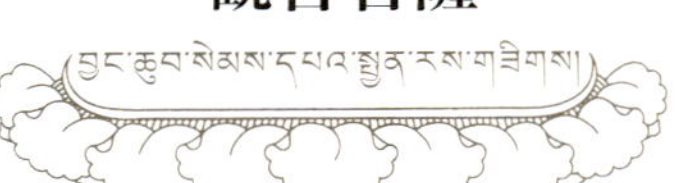

銅鎏金，高105.5厘米，明永樂年間（1403～1424）

Bodhisattva Avalokiteśvara

Gilt brass　Height: 105.5cm　Yongle reign, Ming Dynasty (1403-1424)

◎觀音雙腿直立仰覆蓮座，身體略側扭。臉形方正，鼻梁挺括，鼻綫鋭利。高卷髮髻，頭戴八葉華麗寶冠，束髮冠帶翻卷，大圓耳璫。袒露上身，胸前裝飾繁密的項鏈瓔珞，下者雙層長裙，裙褶曲復自然，裙面裝飾華麗的繁密瓔珞。長帛繞身垂落臺面，身後兩條短飄帶鈎挂在腰帶兩邊。身側的兩朵蓮花呈寶塔形，碩大無朋。比較青海瞿曇寺永樂觀音站像，此像基本保持了永樂佛像的做法，只是帽冠式樣稍有變化。面相身材綫條略方硬，没有瞿曇寺觀音圓潤豐滿，然而工藝相當精湛，是一尊難得的永樂風格佛像佳作。

◎座下沿陰刻藏文題記一圈，內容爲贊頌觀音功德。漢譯：如同幼苗受陽光，得享悲心大恩情，菩薩聖者具大力，頂禮聖者觀世音！

Bodhisattra Avalokiteśvara stands straight on double lotus pedestal with beaded border. He wears eight-leaved gorgeous jeweled crown with his upper body uncovered. The front of his chest is decorated with intricate Keyura necklace. A round of Tibetan inscription is carved in intaglio along the bottom of the throne, and the content is to eulogize the merits and virtues of Avalokiteśvara.

58

文殊菩薩

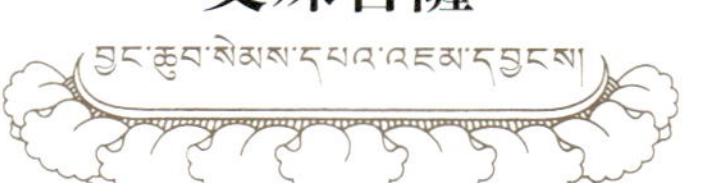

黃銅鎏金，高25厘米，明永樂年間（1403～1424）

Bodhisattra Mañjuśrī

Gilt brass Height: 25cm Yongle reign, Ming Dynasty (1403-1424)

文殊菩薩面相豐滿端正，神態静穆。頭戴五葉寶冠，高髮髻，袒上身，瓔珞、臂釧雕飾精美。腰束長裙，衣褶折疊流暢，右舒坐，右腿自然下垂踏小蓮花，左腿盤曲架在右膝上。身體呈三折扭姿態，閑適自如。右手牽蓮花莖撫座面，左手握經篋。端坐於仰覆蓮座上，蓮瓣尖上卷成三顆圓珠狀，上下邊緣飾聯珠紋。

蓮座正面由左至右陰刻“大明永樂年施”楷書字款。封底完好，底蓋陰刻金剛交杵圖形。明永樂宫廷作品。

Mañjuśrī wears a five-leaved crown and girdled long skirt with his upper body uncovered. The wrinkle of the clothes is smooth. He is seated in the attitude of ease with his right leg falling naturally and stepping on small lotus and his left leg coiled on the right knee. The body is in the free and smooth stance of three twists. The right hand holds the lotus stalk and touches the surface of the throne and the left hand holds a sutra box.

The front of the lotus throne is inscribed with the six-character Yongle reign mark in standard script in the direction from left to right. The bottom cap is carved in intaglio with patterns of crossed vajra pestles. This is a work of the Yongle reign.

59

吉祥天母

དཔལ་ལྡན་ལྷ་མོ།

黃銅鎏金，高25.5厘米，明永樂年間（1403～1424）

Śrī-Devī (dPal ldan lha mo)

Gilt brass　Height: 25.5cm　Yongle reign, Ming Dynasty (1403-1424)

吉祥天母又稱吉祥天女，藏密護法女神之首。因騎騾子，俗稱“騾子天王”，象徵她可以在天上、地上、地下三界遍走飛行。火焰形髮髻，佩五骷髏冠，怒目圓睜，凶神惡煞，張開的大口伸出細細的長舌，舌爲一具捆住雙手的人體形象。胸前右手托盛血的嘎巴拉碗，左手握金剛索繩。後兩臂，右臂高舉寶劍，左臂舉戟，兩種兵器相交於頭頂。跨騎騾背上，兩脚腕戴脚環鎖鏈，一張人皮綁扎在騾背上。摩羯面佛母手牽繮繩站在騾子頭下。騾子脚下刻出翻卷的波浪，波浪中刻漂浮的人頭，表示她在血海中奔走。周圍刻劃一圈起伏的山巒，雕刻精細入微。

蓮座前立面刻“大明永樂年施”楷書小字，由左至右書寫。封底完好，底蓋刻交杵圖案。這是一尊珍稀的明永樂宫廷佛像，現已捐贈國家博物館。

This image presents a four-armed form of Śrī-Devī, a chief guardian-goddess of the Tibetan Buddhist pantheon. The three-eyed fearsome Śrī-Devī is riding a mule on a sea of blood, all set on a single lotus base. The upper right arm is holding a sword, the upper left hand a ritual staff. The lower right hand holds a skull-cup, the lower left hand a noose. She wears a garment tied around the hips and is decorated with a diadem of skulls, a garland of heads, and bone ornaments. The top of the lotus pedestal is inscribed with the six-character Yongle mark. This image has been donated to the national museum.

大明永樂年施

60

寶帳怙主

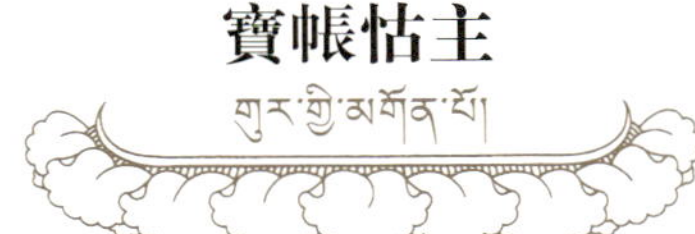

གུར་གྱི་མགོན་པོ།

黄銅，高52厘米，約明永樂年間（1403～1424）

Pañjaranātha Mahākāla

Brass Height: 52cm Yongle reign, Ming Dynasty (1403-1424)

寶帳怙主，圓面，絡腮胡鬚，頭戴骷髏冠，額開慧眼，三目圓鼓，怒目張口，面相凶憤。胸前垂挂珠寶瓔珞，人頭項鬘，長蛇裝飾。手持鉞刀與嘎巴拉碗，兩肘彎托短杖，杖與常見的圓棍形不同，呈扁片形，兩端翹起，雕刻蓮花珠寶。雙腿彎曲蹲踞姿態，雙脚踏在一俯卧的裸形人頭和臀上。造型生動，肌膚豐滿，綫條圓潤，鑄造工藝精細。

座面陰刻「大明永樂年施」雙鈎楷書款識，自右向左行。座後刻藏文一行，其意爲：本护法神的咒语。原文轉寫：Oṃ āḥ hrī siṅha nara hū phaṭa

Pañjaranātha Mahākāla, three-eyed with a fierce expression, is trampling with spread legs on a corpse placed on a single lotus pedestal with beaded border. With the right hand he holds a ritual chopper with a vajra handel and with the left hand a skull-cup. He carries a wooden implement across the crooks of his elbows.

The front of the lotus throne is inscribed with the six-character Yongle reign mark in double hooked standard script in the direction from left to right.

61

馬頭金剛

རྟ་མགྲིན།

黃銅鎏金，高27.2厘米，明永樂年間（1403～1424）

Hayagrīva

Gilt brass　Height: 27.2cm　Yongle reign, Ming Dynasty (1403-1424)

◎馬頭金剛亦稱馬頭明王，是觀音菩薩的忿怒化身。形象有八臂、六臂、二臂多種。此像二臂二腿，右手高舉寶杖，杖爲寶劍外形無刃，劍身陽刻卷草花，劍端雕骷髏；左手托嘎巴拉碗。火焰形怒髮，頭頂髮髻中雕馬頭，前胸人首項鬘垂地，長蛇盤身，表鎮壓龍王之意。身形粗壯有力，弓步立姿氣勢凶猛。飄飛的長帛繞身翻卷，增加了强烈動感。

◎蓮座面刻「大明永樂年施」楷書小字，由左至右書寫。底蓋刻交杵，交杵部位鎏金。明永樂宮廷作品。

Hayagrīva is an important deity for all traditions of Tibetan Buddhism and is one of the eight great meditation deities. Hayagrīva is three-eyed and steps to the right with the right leg bent and the left straight on a single lotus pedestal. In the raised right hand he brandishes a staff surmounted by a skull, the left hand in front of the chest holds a skull-cup.

Hayagrīva wears a tiger skin tied below belly. He wears a crown composed of skulls with a horse' s head in front of the prominent knot of hair, a pair of circular earrings, a necklace with attached pendants, bracelets, anklets, the sacred thread in the form of a snake, and a garland composed of heads. The image is encircled by a ribbon-like scarf with swirling ends.

The top of the pedestal is inscribed with the six-charater Yongle mark "Da Ming Yongle nian shi". The bottom of the pedestal is sealed with a gilt brass plate decorated with a viśvavajra.

62

四臂大黑天

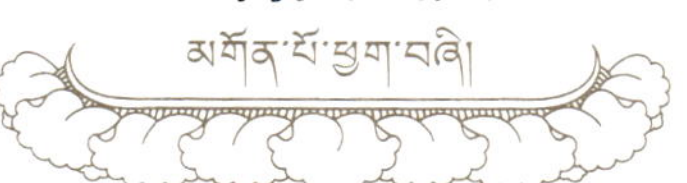

黃銅鎏金，高24厘米，明永樂年間（1403～1424）

Four-armed Mahākāla (Caturbhuja Mahākāla)

Gilt brass Height:24cm Yongle reign, Ming Dynasty (1403-1424)

四臂大黑天，是大黑天神系中重要的一神。紅色火焰形髮髻，盤繞長蛇，髮髻前立化佛。頭戴骷髏冠，裝飾華麗的珠寶，流蘇垂額前，方圓形明王怒相，三目圓睜，胡鬚眉毛精雕細刻成藝術化的雲卷形。一頭四臂，主臂持鉞刀嘎巴拉碗。身後右臂舉寶劍，左臂舉喀章噶。游戲坐姿，坐在兩位菩薩背上，兩菩薩半身抬起，一位注目黑天，一位凝視前方，形象生動，工藝精湛，是珍貴的永樂宮廷作品。

蓮座面刻"大明永樂年施"楷書小字，由左至右書寫。底蓋刻交杵圖案。

The four-armed form of Mahākāla is seated on two unidentified Brahmanical deities on a single lotus pedestal with beaded border. In the upper right hand Mahākāla holds a sword as a symbol of "pure knowledge" and the "destruction of ignorance", in upper left hand a trident as a symbolic weapon against evil energy. With the two principal hands Mahākāla holds a chopper with a vajra handle and a skull-cup.

The top of the pedestal is inscribed with the six-character Yongle mark: "Da Ming Yongle nian shi". The bottom of the pedestal is sealed with a plain plate decorated with a viśvavajra.

63

紅閻魔敵

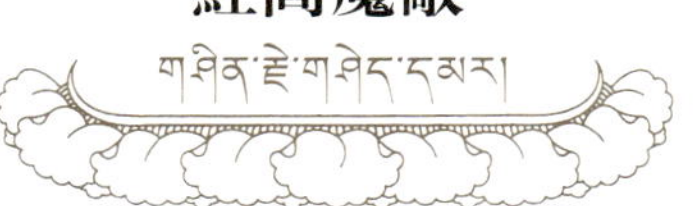

黄銅鎏金，高26厘米，明永樂年間（1403～1424）

Rakta-Yamāri

Gilt brass　Height: 26cm　Yongle reign, Ming Dynasty (1403-1424)

◎紅閻魔敵，右手高舉喀章噶，左手托嘎巴拉碗，懷抱佛母，佛母手持嘎巴拉碗、骷髏杖。展左立姿踏在一魔神頭部和臀部上，魔神緊緊俯身在牛背上。牛在重壓之下四腿蜷伏，頭略抬起，張口喘息，形態生動逼真。一條寬大的飄帶繞身往復翻卷，裝飾繁密的珠寶瓔珞。覆蓮座，蓮瓣細長，瓣尖爲三顆圓珠，是一尊工藝精湛、造型生動的永樂宫廷佛像。

◎蓮座面刻「大明永樂年施」楷書小字，由左至右書寫。封底完好，底蓋刻交杵圖案。

63

The top of the pedestal is inscribed with six-character Yongle mark: "Da Ming Yongle nian shi". The bottom of the pedestal is sealed with a brass plate decorated with a viśvavajra.

Rakta-Yamāri is a red form of Yamāntaka, who is one of the tantric manifestations of Mañjuśrī. The three-eyed deity steps to the right with the right leg bent and the left straight embracing his consort Svābha-Prajña. Rakta-Yamāri tramples on the prostrate body of Yama, symbolizing the victory over the Brahmanical god of death, who lies on top of a buffalo supported by a single lotus pedestal with beaded border. In the raised right hand Rakta-Yamāri brandishes a club decorated with a head, a skull, and a vajra finial, in the left hand he holds a skull-cup. The defeated Yama holds a noose in the left hand and a club in the right. Svābha-Prajña holds a skull-cup in the right hand and a ritual chopper with a vajra handle in the left. Rakta-Yamāri and his consort are decorated with the pañcamudrā ornaments carved of human bone and wear garland of severed heads around the necks.

64

時輪金剛

དུས་འཁོར།

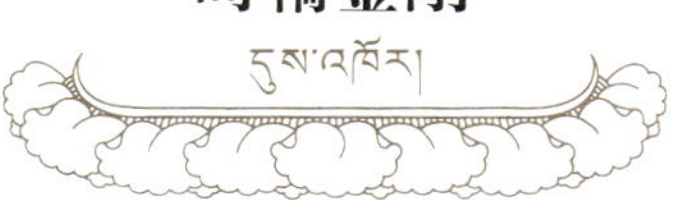

銅合金，高94厘米，約明永樂年間（1403～1424）

Kālacakra

Copper alloy　Height: 94cm　Yongle reign, Ming Dynasty (1403-1424)

༦༤

◎時輪金剛雙尊像，主尊四面二十四臂，每面各三目，頭戴寶冠，嗔怒相。赤裸全身，肩披帛帶，腰束虎皮裙，佩飾耳璫、項鏈、臂釧、手鐲、脚鐲。藏傳佛像有嚴格的圖像標准，以故宮梵華樓時輪金剛銅像與唐卡畫像爲標准：左元手持金剛鈴，右元手持金剛杵，雙臂相交，擁抱明妃；副手分兩層，內層左副手持獸面盾牌，右副手持火焰寶劍；外層左副手自上而下分別持喀章喀、嘎巴拉碗、弓、羂索、摩尼寶、蓮花、海螺、寶珠、金剛鎖、梵天頭，右副手自上而下分別持三尖叉、鉞刀、三枝箭、金剛鉤、嘎巴拉鼓、金剛錘、法輪、槍、針、金剛斧；兩腿展右立單層覆蓮底座上；明妃四面三目八臂，赤裸全身，佩飾耳璫、項鏈、臂釧、手鐲、脚鐲，腰纏瓔珞；左手自上而下分別持嘎巴拉碗、羂索、蓮花、摩尼寶，右手自上而下分別持鉞刀、金剛鉤、嘎巴拉鼓、念珠；展左立。對比故宮時輪金剛像形象，此像除法器位置錯亂，一些法器缺失外，形象持物都吻合，如此像尚存的十六件法器與故宮時輪金剛完全一致。主尊與明妃足下共踏一人，皆仰卧。蓮座中間二人跪坐。此像身體比例合度，肌膚豐滿圓潤，鑄造工藝精湛。是一尊珍貴的大尺寸永樂風格時輪金剛銅像。

◎蓮座面刻「大明永樂年施」雙鈎楷書款識，由右向左書，字體端正有力。

Kālacakra is the principal deity of the Śrīkālacakra Tantra. The four-headed and twenty-four-armed Kālacakra steps to the left with the left leg bent and the right one straight. He tramples on the Brahmanical gods Kāma and Maheśvara, both of them have a female attendant squatting next to their prostrate bodies on the double lotus pedestal. The two principal hands of Kālacakra hold a five-pronged diamond sceptre and a prayer-bell, and are turned inwards and crossed in front of the chest embracing his four-headed and eight-armed consort Viśvamātā.

65

大成就者毗盧巴

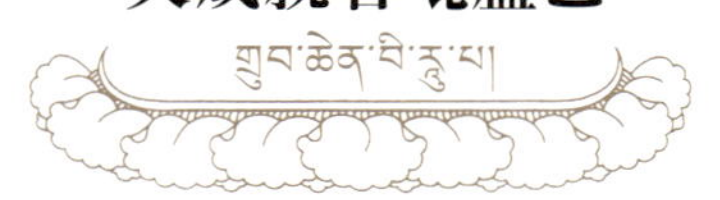

黄銅鎏金，高28厘米，明永樂年間（1403～1424）

Mahāsiddha Virūpa

Gilt brass Height: 28cm Yongle reign, Ming Dynasty (1403-1424)

大成就者毗盧巴是藏傳佛教著名的八十四大成就者之一，他有定住太陽不動的超凡功能，在衆多印度大成就者中以其神奇的事迹爲西藏各教派所尊，尤爲薩迦派所推崇，其形象元代就傳入内地，入明以後又得到永樂宫廷的尊崇。此像表現的即是他定日的形象。輪王坐姿，以虎皮爲墊端坐蓮花座上。大腹便便，四肢肥壯，頭髮卷曲，戴花冠，兩目圓睜。左臂抬起，食指伸出指日，右手在胸前托嘎巴拉碗。袒露的上身垂挂珠寶瓔珞，爲永樂佛像特有的瓔珞樣式。左肩斜披一條花朵組成的綬帶，下身着印度短裙，花鬘腰帶，裙面均匀分布條帶，條帶内鑄出細密精美的纏枝蓮花紋。永樂宫廷佛像作品。

在蓮座底沿刻“大明永樂年施”楷書小字，由左至右書寫。封底完好，底蓋刻交杵圖案。

Mahāsiddha Virūpa, one of the eighty-four siddhas, is seated in the attitude of royal ease on the skin of a tiger placed on a single lotus pedestal with beaded border. He holds a skull-cup in the right hand and arrests with the left hand the sun in its course.

The top of the pedestal is inscribed with the six-character Yongle mark. The bottom of the pedestal is sealed with a brass plate decorated with a viśvavajra.

64

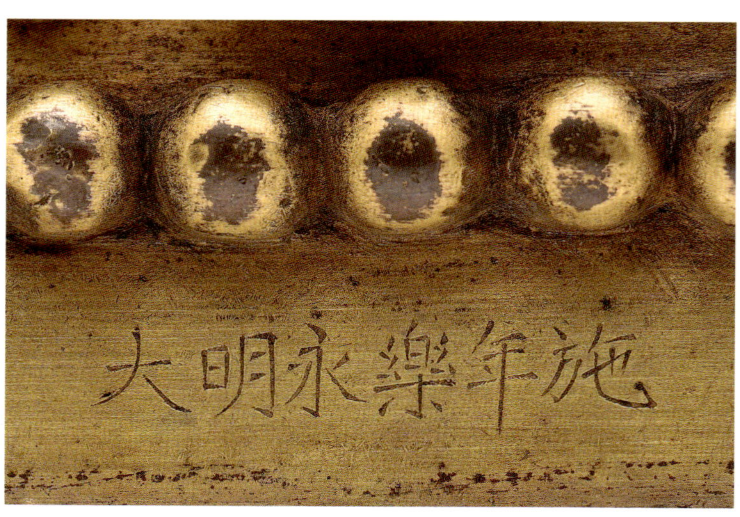

大明永樂年施

66

普賢菩薩

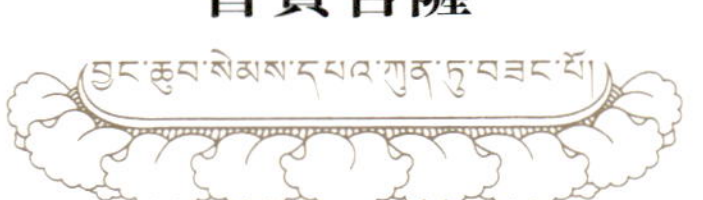

黃銅，高29厘米，明永樂年間（1403～1424）

Samantabhadra

Brass Height: 29cm Yongle reign, Ming Dynasty (1403-1424)

66

普賢菩薩，頭戴五葉寶冠，髮髻高卷，長髮辮垂肩。面相方正，眉間有水滴形白毫，長眉細目，俯視衆生，神態祥和。雙手作説法印，游戲坐姿坐在大象背上。長裙下垂，裙褶曲復自然，覆蓋象背。披肩長帛，人字形左右展開，對稱上卷。象頭裝飾瓔珞珠寶，大耳翻卷，長鼻勾起，温順可愛。造型巧妙生動，是一尊精美的永樂宮廷風格作品。

Samantabhadra wears a five-leaved crown and high bun. His long braids are hung on the shoulders. He has a square face. There is water drop-shaped white hair between the eyebrows. He has slender eyebrows and eyes. Both hands display the gesture of teaching. He is seated on the back of an elephant in the stance of larkishness. The wrinkle of the long skirt is curved and natural covering the back of the elephant. The head of the elephant is adorned with Keyura jewelry. The ears of the elephant are scrolled and its long nose rises. It is a work of the Yongle style.

67

文珠菩薩

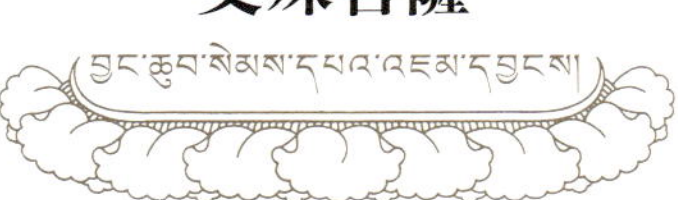

黃銅鎏金，高23.2厘米，明永樂年間（1403～1424）

Bodhisattva Mañjuśrī

Gilt brass　Height: 23.2cm　Yongle reign, Ming Dynasty (1403-1424)

◎文殊菩薩身姿挺拔，面相豐滿端正，神態靜穆。頭戴五葉寶冠，高髮髻，袒上身，瓔珞、臂釧雕飾精美。雙手持蓮花長莖，結說法印，左右肩蓮花上分別托劍和梵篋。腰束長裙，衣褶折疊流暢，全跏趺坐於仰覆蓮座上，蓮座蓮瓣寬肥，瓣尖上卷雕象鼻狀卷雲紋。上下邊緣飾聯珠紋。

◎座面陰刻「大明永樂年施」楷書款。封底完好，底蓋刻交杵圖案。永樂宮廷佛像作品。

Mañjuśrī is seated in the diamond attitude on a double lotus pedestal with beaded border. The two hands, each holding the stalk of a flower attached to the shoulder, form the gesture of the wheel of the doctrine. The two principal attributes of Mañjuśrī, a sword and a manuscript of the *Prajñāpāramitā Sūtra*, are attached to the flowers. He wears a five-leaved crown in front of the knot of hair, with jewelled tips, pairs of circular earrings, necklaces with beaded strands of pearls attached, bracelets on the upper arms and wrists, ornaments on the legs, and anklets.

The back of the pedestal is inscribed with the six-character Yongle mark. The bottom of the pedestal is sealed with the brass plate decorated with a viśvavajra.

68

金剛手菩薩

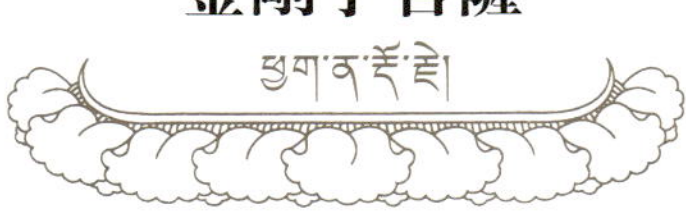

黃銅鎏金，高23厘米，明永樂年間（1403～1424）

Vajrapāṇi

Gilt brass Height: 23cm Yongle reign, Ming Dynasty (1403-1424)

金剛手菩薩面相豐滿，雙目俯視，嘴角含笑，神態安詳。頭戴五葉冠，冠帶呈U字型緊貼耳部向上卷曲，垂輪式耳環，帔帛由肩前下垂纏繞雙臂垂於身後，寶冠佩飾規整，雕飾精美。全跏趺坐，雙手牽蓮花莖，施説法印，身側兩枝蓮花花蕊中立金剛鈴、金剛杵。形象端莊，工藝精美。座面陰刻“大明永樂年施”楷書款。封底完好，底蓋刻交杵圖案。永樂宮廷佛像作品。

Vajrapāṇi has round and plump bearing with his drooping eyes and a faint smile on his lips. His U-shaped crown clings to his ears, which wears torus-like earrings, and rolls up with elegant accessories and delicate decorations. He is seated in the diamond attitude with his hands holding lotus stalks and displaying the gesture of teaching. By his side are two lotuses, the buds of which hold a Vajra Bell and a Vajra-pestle. The back of the pedestal is inscribed with the six-character Yongle mark. The bottom of the pedestal is sealed with a brass plate decorated with a viśvavajra.

69

持世菩薩

ནོར་རྒྱུན་མ།

黃銅鎏金，高28.8厘米，明宣德年間（1426～1435）

Vasudhārā

Gilt brass Height: 28.8cm Xuande reign, Ming Dynasty (1426-1435)

◎持世菩薩原爲印度教的財富女神，後爲佛教吸收成爲黃財神之妻，稱爲財續佛母，能予人以豐收與財富。持世菩薩一頭六臂，頭戴華麗寶冠，方圓面，五官緊湊，清秀俊美。左腿盤曲坐在厚坐墊上，右腿下伸，右舒坐式。六手各持寶瓶、穀穗、梵篋、珠寶。上身袒露，裝飾項圈、臂釧、手鐲。下着長裙，寬大的裙擺下垂，平鋪在坐墊前。裙腰前後裝飾華麗的瓔珞珠串，臀部瓔珞鏤空雕刻垂於蓮座面，工藝精湛，是珍貴的宣德宮廷作品。

◎蓮座面由左至右陰刻「大明宣德年施」楷書款。封底完好，底蓋刻交杵圖案。

The six-armed goddess identified as Vasudhārā is seated in the attitude of ease on a double lotus pedestal with a beaded border and rests the foot of the pendent right leg on a lotus flower. She is clad in a cloth tied around the hips by a belt with attached beaded strands, and carries a shawl over both shoulders, the ends falling over the arms to the pedestal. Vasudhārā has bejewelled ornaments, namely a five-leaved crown fastened with a ribbon with swirling ends in front of the knot of hair with a jewelled tip, a pair of circular earrings, necklaces with beaded strands of pearls attached, bracelets on the upper arms and wrists, ornaments on the legs, and anklets.

The top of the pedestal is inscribed with the six-character Xuande mark: “Da Ming Xuande nian shi”. The bottom of the pedestal is sealed with the brass plate decorated with a viśvavajra.

70

金剛薩埵

黄銅鎏金，高25.5厘米，明宣德年間（1426～1435）

Vajrasattva

Gilt brass　Height: 25.5cm　Xuande reign, Ming Dynasty (1426-1435)

金剛薩埵頭戴五葉寶冠，象徵五佛嚴頂，束髮繒帶雙飄耳後，雙耳垂飾大耳璫。方面朗目，嘴角上揚，微含笑意。着菩薩天衣裝束，上身袒露，肩披帛帶，胸前、腰際佩挂瓔珞，四肢手足各以臂釧、手鐲、脚鐲等爲裝飾。左手持金剛鈴作拳，安於腰側，表以大智慧清净法音驚覺一切有情歸於正道；右手持五股金剛杵安立心際，象徵着如來五佛五智。

蓮座正面由左至右陰刻「大明宣德年施」楷款。封底完好，底蓋陰刻金剛交杵圖形。明宣德宮廷作品。

Vajrasattva wears a five-leaved crown representing solemness. His hair is bound up with silk lace floating behind his ears. Both his earlobe is decorated with loops. His left hand clenched a Vajra Bell to the side of his waist, meaning that the Sacred Dharma Sound will make all emotions return to the right way. His right hand holds a Vajra-pestle to the chest signifying the five wisdom of the Five Buhddas.

The top of the pedestal is inscribed with the six-character Xuande mark: "Da Ming Xuande nian shi". The bottom of the pedestal is sealed with the brass plate decorated with a viśvavajra.

71

四臂文殊菩薩

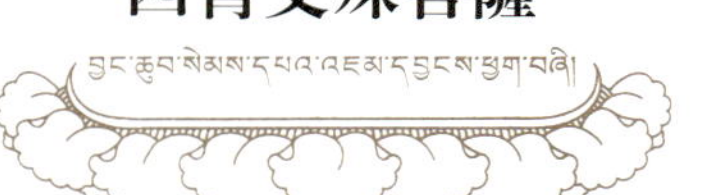

黄銅鎏金，高36.5厘米，明宣德年間（1426～1435）

Four-armed Mañjuśrī

Gilt brass Height: 36.5cm Xuande reign, Ming Dynasty (1426-1435)

文殊菩薩一頭四臂，面相方正，垂目俯視，神態静穆。頭戴五葉寶冠，袒上身，細腰束裙，褶紋轉折自如，流暢起伏，瀟灑飄逸。主臂右手上舉持劍，左手牽蓮花莖，肩旁蓮花頂雕經篋；另外兩手右手持箭，左手上舉持弓，全跏趺坐。端坐仰覆蓮座，蓮瓣細長挺拔，上下邊緣飾聯珠紋。座面陰刻“大明宣德年施”楷書款。封底完好，底蓋刻交杵圖案。明宣德宫廷作品。

Four-armed Mañjuśrī wears a five-leaved crown with his upper body uncovered and waist wrapped by slender skirt. His principal right hand holds a sword and left lotus stalks. His other right hand holds an arrow and left a bow. He is seated in the diamond attitude.

The top of the pedestal is inscribed with the six-character Xuande mark: "Da Ming Xuande nian shi". The bottom of the pedestal is sealed with the brass plate decorated with a viśvavajra.

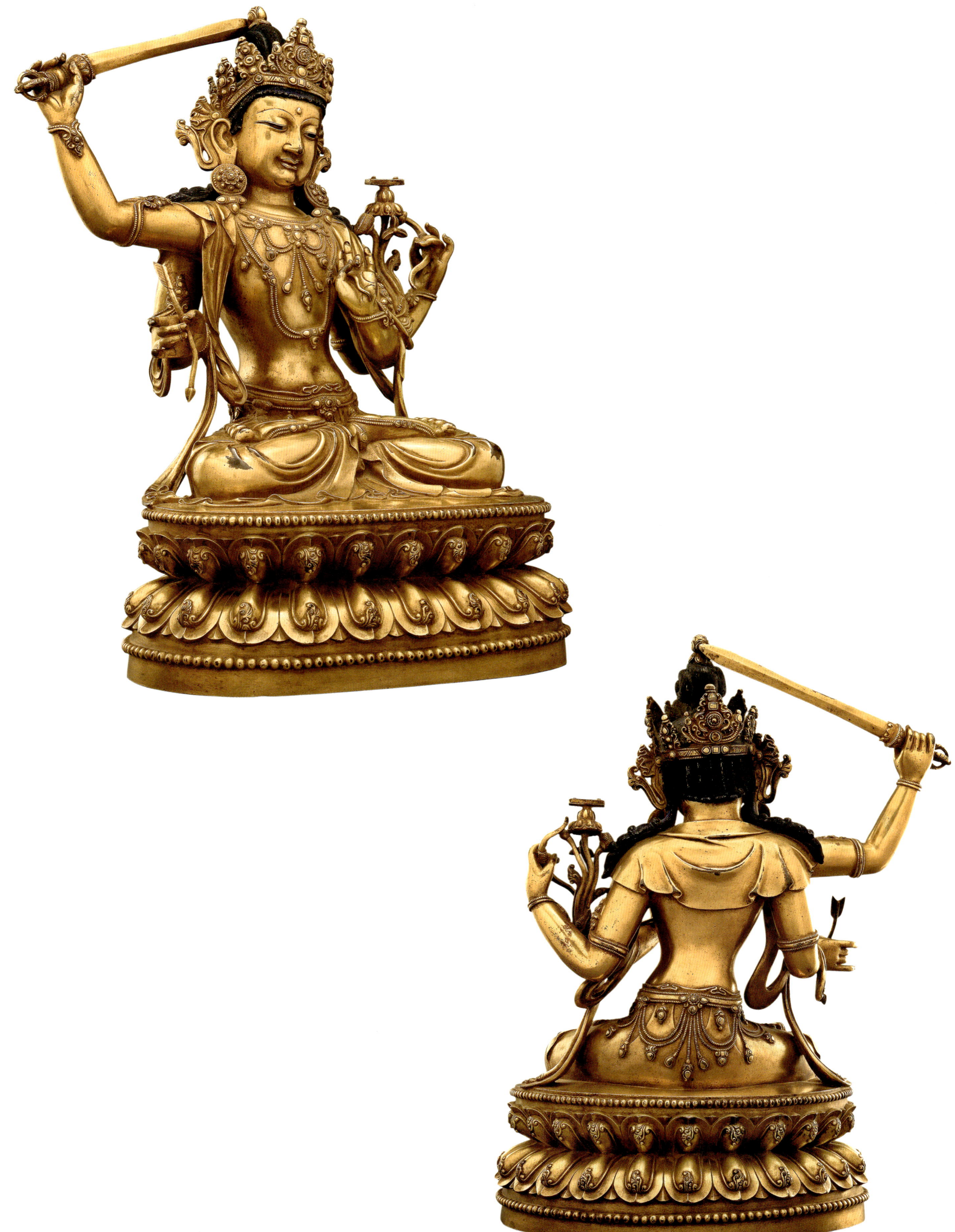

72

大黑天

黃銅鎏金，高58.2厘米，明宣德年間（1426～1435）

Pañjaranātha Mahākāla

Gilt brass　Height: 58.2cm　Xuande reign, Ming Dynasty (1426-1435)

大黑天梵文音譯爲瑪哈噶拉，起源於印度，原爲財富之神、戰神，傳入西藏成爲藏傳佛教中護法大神，具有帳房保護神、戰神的屬性。大黑天三目圓睁，鬚眉立起，怒目而視。頭戴五骷髏冠，髮髻正中坐阿彌陀佛，左手托嘎巴拉碗，右手持銀制鉞刀。胸前挂人首項鬘、珠寶瓔珞，長蛇裝飾。兩短腿作蹲踞姿勢踏仰卧神。全身披挂華麗繁密的瓔珞珠飾，長帛繞身翻卷，動感强烈，裝飾繁縟華麗，雕刻精細入微，形象怒而不凶，憨態可掬。

蓮座正面由左至右陰刻“大明宣德年施”楷書字款，字體端正，刻寫清晰。原封底完好，底蓋陰刻金剛交杵圖形，交杵部位鎏金。是一尊珍貴的大尺寸宣德宮廷佛像作品。

Pañjaranātha Māhākāla, three-eyed with a fierce expression, tramples with spread legs on a corpse prostrate on a single lotus pedestal with beaded border. In the right hand he holds a ritual chopper with a vajra handle, in the left hand a skull-cup. He carries a wooden implement accross the crooks of his elbows. Mahākāla wears a five-leaved crown decorated with skull.

The top of the pedestal is inscribed with the six-character Xuande mark: “Da Ming Xuande nian shi”. The bottom is sealed with the brass plate decorated with a viśvavajra.

༧༢

73

舞蹈菩薩

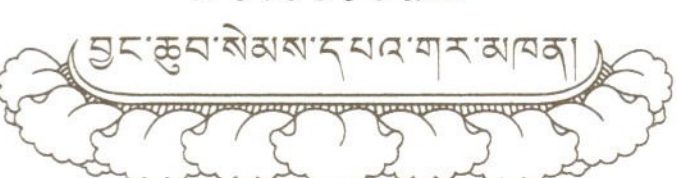

黃銅鎏金，高29.5厘米，明宣德年間（1426～1435）

Dancing Bodhisattva

Gilt brass　Height: 29.5cm　Xuande reign, Ming Dynasty (1426-1435)

舞蹈菩薩，右腿獨立，左腿曲起，金鷄獨立姿態，左臂高舉，手掌上翻平伸；右臂下伸，掌心朝下呼應，姿態輕松優美，其舞姿來源於印度舞蹈。菩薩面相方正，高卷髮髻，頭戴寶冠，束髮冠帶翻卷，大圓耳璫。袒露上身，胸前裝飾項鏈瓔珞，下着雙層長裙，裙褶曲復自然，似輕柔的絲綢波動，長帛繞身飄垂身側，呈u形上卷，增加了舞姿的靈動感。菩薩後背留有方形裝藏封蓋。

蓮座面由左至右陰刻「大明宣德年施」楷書字款，字體端正，刻寫清晰。原封底完好，底蓋陰刻金剛交杵圖形。明宣德宮廷作品。

Dancing Bodhisattva stands on his right leg with left leg bent upward. He raises his left arm high with upturned palm. His right arm extends downwards in the same manner. His dancing posture is relaxing and graceful and has its origin from Indian dance. The upper body of the Dancing Bodhisattva is decorated with pearl and jade necklace on the chest. The lower part of his body is covered by two-layered long skirt.

The top of the pedestal is inscribed with the six-character Xuande mark: "Da Ming Xuande nian shi". The bottom of the pedestal is sealed with the brass plate decorated with a viśvavajra.

74

觀音菩薩

བྱང་ཆུབ་སེམས་དཔའ་སྤྱན་རས་གཟིགས།

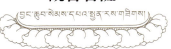

黄銅鎏金，高37.5厘米，明宣德年間（1426～1435）

Bodhisattva Avalokiteśvara

Gilt brass Height: 37.5cm Xuande reign, Ming Dynasty (1426-1435)

◎觀音菩薩右腿輕舒踏小蓮花，左腿盤坐。兩手牽蓮花長莖，左手作説法印，方額廣頤，長眉細目，雙眼微眯，神態莊嚴沉静。身側兩束蓮花枝，爲永樂、宣德固定樣式，雕盛開、凋謝、含苞的三種不同形態蓮花。雕刻綫條準確，鎏金明亮厚實。

The right leg of Avalokiteśvara treads lightly on the small lotus, his left leg crossed. His hands hold the long lotus stalk and his left hand displays the gesture of teaching. He looks rather solemn. The two bunches of lotus at both of his sides follows the conventional style in Yongle and Xuande Years, consisting of full flowering, withered and budding lotus.

清宫廷藝術風格佛像

佛像的樣式與藝術風格與故宫所藏清代宫廷製造的佛像一致，出自同一模本，同一設計造型，細部有差别，但其母型是一致的。一些佛像刻寫清晰的漢文款識與印章圖記，説明了清宫廷佛像與甘青地區民間佛像之間的相互影響和緊密聯繫。藝術現象往往會直接或間接地反映出歷史長河中民族文化交流融合的痕迹，佛像造型樣式工藝技法，更多地采用了漢地佛像藝術的表現手法，漢風爲主，在裝飾細部上吸收西藏佛教藝術的樣式。以明清宫廷爲代表的内地佛像藝術對甘青地區佛教藝術的發展影響深刻，漢藏交融是甘青地區明清佛像藝術風格的主旋律。

75

釋迦牟尼佛

黄銅，高43.5厘米，清康熙年間（1662～1722）

Buddha Śākyamuni

Brass　Height: 43.5cm　Kangxi reign, Qing Dynasty (1662-1722)

◈釋迦牟尼佛，長圓形臉，隆鼻闊目，神態寂静安詳，全跏趺式端坐於單層蓮座上。左手施禪定印，右手作觸地印，蓮座下爲須彌方座。佛着袒右袈裟，以均勻平行的陰刻綫表現衣紋，領口袍邊刻多層褶邊，爲清宫廷佛像常見作法。背光澆注成型，銅板厚重，在精緻的卷草紋襯托下，高浮雕摩尼寶、釋迦牟尼佛、文殊菩薩、四臂觀音菩薩、力士。須彌座正中垂臺簾，邊沿刻精美細密的纏枝蓮紋，正中刻金剛杵。左右兩邊雕造型生動、刻劃精細的獅子，爲漢族傳統獅子樣。須彌座底後背平面滿雕精美的八寶圖案，雕鑄工藝精細、綫條規整流暢，爲内地清宫廷風格作品。

◈背光後面刻八思巴文方印，三厘米見方，印文爲第司桑結嘉措壽字印（見《西藏歷代藏印》第七十頁），説明此佛像與第司桑結嘉措有關係。

Buddha Śākyamuni is seated in the diamond attitude on a single lotus pedestal. His left hand makes the gesture of meditation and the right the gesture of touching the earth. The Buhhda wears cassock with right chest uncovered, the evenly carved lines represents drapes and the edge of neckline is manifold. The front of the sitting throne is carved delicately with intertwined lotus and crossed pestles and its left and right sides with lively shaped lions. The whole statue follows the royal style of the Qing Dynasty.

76

無量壽佛

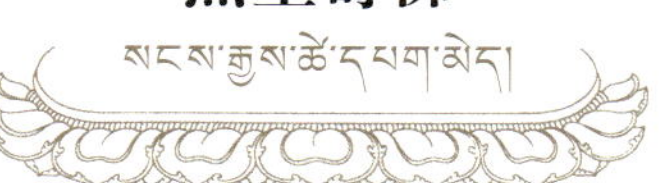

黄銅，高43.5厘米，清康熙年間（1662～1722）

Buddha Amitāyus

Brass Height: 43.5cm Kangxi reign, Qing Dynasty (1662-1722)

◈無量壽佛，頭戴五葉寶冠，方圓臉，長髮披肩，裝飾大耳璫，面相清秀，神態莊嚴，全跏趺坐，雙手結禪定印，捧寶瓶。長帛帶繞身，下着長裙，雕刻起伏的衣紋自然流暢。佛像帽冠服飾，胸前裝飾的項鏈、瓔珞仍可見明永樂、宣德佛像的作法。蓮座背光已變化，與圖75相同，須彌座底後背平面滿雕精美的八寶圖案，精細華麗的藝術設計是清宮廷佛像的突出特色。

◈背光後面刻八思巴文方印，三厘米見方，印文爲第司桑結嘉措壽字印（見《西藏歷代藏印》第六十九頁）。

༧༦

Buddha Amitāyus wears a five-leaved crown and is seated in the diamond attitude. His hands display the gesture of meditation and hold a jeweled bottle. His whole body is intertwined with long silk laces and he wears a long skirt carved with smooth lines. The back of his Sumeru throne is full of delicately carved eight treasures pattern. The splendid art style gives prominence to the feature of the imperial Buddhist statue in the Qing Dynasty.

77

觀音菩薩

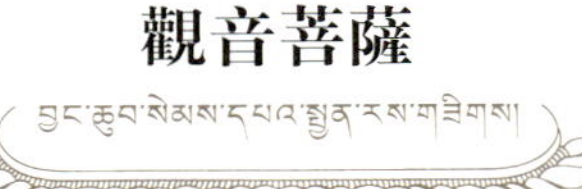

黃銅鎏金，高98厘米，清康熙年間（1662～1722）

Bodhisattva Avalokiteśvara

Gilt brass　Height: 98cm　Kangxi reign, Qing Dynasty (1662-1722)

༧༧

觀音菩薩雙腿直立雙層蓮臺上，頭上戴五葉寶冠，冠葉高聳。辮髮垂肩，身材壯碩，面相豐滿。雙肩雕兩朵蓮花，枝葉交錯，婀娜多姿。雙手作説法印，手牽蓮花長莖。下身着雙層長裙，肩披長帛，貼身飄下直垂地面，翻卷上揚，造型穩重、莊嚴。

座面刻“大清康熙年禮部造”雙鈎寫法，由右向左書，字體端莊有力。此像爲清宫廷所造。

Avalokiteśvara stands uprightly on the double lotus pedestal, wearing a five-leaved crown with erect crown petals. His braids droop to his shoulders. He has a strong body and plump bearing. His shoulders are carved with two lotuses and his hands display the gesture of teaching, holding the long stalks of lotus. The front of the pedestal is inscribed with "Made by the Board of Rites in the Years of Kangxi of the Qing Dynasty" in double-hooked writing style, all the characters look solemn and powerful.

78

財寶天王

རྣམ་ཐོས་སྲས།

黄銅鎏金，高53.5厘米，清康熙年間（1662～1722）

Vaiśravaṇa

Gilt brass Height: 53.5cm Kangxi reign, Qing Dynasty (1662-1722)

◈財寶天王頭戴寶冠，身着鎧甲、戰袍、戰靴，威風凛凛跨騎在獅子背上。左手托吐寶獸，右手握勝利寶幢（已佚）。方面小胡鬚，擰眉竪目，神情威嚴生動。寶冠鎧甲雕刻精細寫實，前胸、雙臂、腹部雕刻三種式樣不同的鎧甲片，精雕細刻，一絲不苟。漢族傳統風格的獅子俯卧地面，轉頭張口，憨態可掬。此像爲内地工匠所造，漢藏結合，以漢族造型爲主的佳作。

◈座面刻「大清康熙年禮部造」單綫陰刻款識，由右向左書寫，圈雙綫框。

Vaiśravaṇa wears a crown on his head and loricae, armor and caliga on his body. He is seated on the back of a lion in a solemn manner. His left hand holds the treasure-producing beast and right hand jeweled banner (lost). Both the crown and the armor are delicately carved, there are various kinds of neatly carved armor sheets. This statue is made by Han Chinese artisan and is one of the best works that combine Han Chinese and Tibetan art style. The top of the pedestal is inscribed with the Kangxi reign mark: "Da Qing Kangxi nian Libu zao" (Manufactured by the Ministery of Rite during the Kangxi Reign).

79

增長天王

འཕགས་སྐྱེས་པོ།

黃銅鎏金，高36.5厘米，清康熙年間（1662～1722）

Virūḍhaka

Gilt brass Height: 36.5cm Kangxi reign, Qing Dynasty (1662-1722)

增長天王顰眉怒目，面相凶猛，身着鎧甲戰袍，右腿盤曲，左腿伸出，坐於須彌座上。天王右手握劍把，平端寶劍，左手持劍刃前端，動感强烈，生動地刻畫出天王的威猛和劍拔弩張的氣勢，其造型與常見的增長天王形象迥異，顯示了高超的雕塑藝術水平，十分接近於居庸關雲臺雕刻的增長天王拔劍出鞘的形象。

Virūḍhaka frowns and looks angrily with fierce bearing. He wears loricae and armor and is seated on the Sumeru throne with twisting right leg and extending left leg. The right hand holds a sword flatly and his left hand touches the front part of the blade in a vivid manner.

80

四臂觀音菩薩

黄銅鎏金，高56厘米，約清康熙年間（1662～1722）

Four-armed Avalokiteśvara (Ṣaḍakṣarī-Lokeśvara)

Gilt brass　Height: 56cm　Kangxi reign, Qing Dynasty (1662-1722)

四臂觀音長圓臉豐滿圓潤，神情慈祥，頭戴五葉寶冠，前胸佩飾項鏈、瓔珞，衣紋起伏自然，蓮瓣圓鼓，還保持着永樂、宣德造像的一些特點。蓮座形式已多有變化，蓮座下承托凸字形華麗的須彌座，座立面高浮雕雙獅、摩尼寶，配以精美的花紋、聯珠綫裝飾。舟形大背光内側頂部雕金翅鳥口銜長蛇，兩手抓住蛇身；左右是兩條騰起的行龍。背光外圈高浮雕雲卷圖案。雖工藝不太細緻，基本造型具有清初宮廷佛像的特徵。

座後正中刻印一方，印文爲漢滿藏三體，漢文篆書，「西天大善自在佛所领天下释教普通瓦赤喇怛喇达赖喇嘛之印」。此印文内容格式與順治九年清朝廷頒賜給五世達賴喇嘛的大印一致（見《歷代西藏藏印》第六十頁）。印文兩邊刻漢文題記「大清康熙年」，「布達拉宮供」。

Four-armed Avalokiteśvara wears a five-leaved crown on his head and pearl and jade necklace on his chest. He is seated in the diamond attitude on the lotus pedestal, the bottom of which combines with splendid Sumeru throne. The surface of the pedestal dotted with relief sculpture of double lion and maṇi treasury.

On the back of the pedestal a trilingual seal of the Fifth Dalai Lama is inscribed. There is an inscription which indicates that the statue was made during the Kangxi reign of the grand Qing dynasty and offered by the Potala Palace.

81

藥師佛

黄銅，高48厘米，清康熙年間（1662～1722）

Medicine Buddha (Bhaiṣajyaguru)

Brass Height: 48cm Kangxi reign, Qing Dynasty (1662-1722)

藥師佛，全稱“藥師琉璃光如來”，亦稱“大醫王佛”，是東方净琉璃世界的教主。此佛眉間刻白毫，眉骨凸起，神情莊嚴肅穆。全跏趺坐，身姿挺拔，右手持藥草，左手托鉢。着袒右袈裟，薄衣貼體不刻衣褶，在衣緣下擺處刻花邊。蓮座下承托凸字形華麗的須彌座，座立面高浮雕雙獅、摩尼寶。舟形大背光雕纏枝蓮團花。佛像背光與底座爲分鑄，在底座内藏樺樹皮寫漢字藥方。座後背刻五行藏文。

原文轉寫：

'Jam dpal dbyangs kyi gzungs/

漢譯：曼殊室利陀羅尼

原文轉寫：

Oṃ arapacana dhih/

漢譯：唵 阿囉跛者娜 地

咒名：曼殊室利菩薩心陀羅尼（參《大藏全咒》卷六，頁511）

原文轉寫：

thugs rje chen po'i gzungs

漢譯：大悲心陀羅尼

Oṃ maṇipadme hūṃ//

咒名：六字大明陀羅尼

原文轉寫：

gsang bdag phyag rdor gyi gzungs/

漢譯：金剛手菩薩陀羅尼

原文轉寫：

Oṃ badzra pāṇi hūṃ phaṭ/

梵文轉寫：

Om vajrapāṇi hūṃ phaṭ/

漢譯咒文：

唵拔雜喇巴呢吽噝

咒名：振鈴印真言

The Medicine Buddha is seated in the diamond attitude on double lotus pedestal with beaded border. In the right hand extended in the gesture of charity it holds myrobalan fruit, with the left hand resting in the lap it holds alms bowl. Under the lotus pedestal is the gorgeous convex Sumeru throne, the surface of which is carved with relief sculpture of double lions and maṇi treasury. The aureole of the Buddha statue is made separately from the pedestal. Prescription written in Chinese on the birch-bark is stored in the pedestal.

82

四臂觀音菩薩

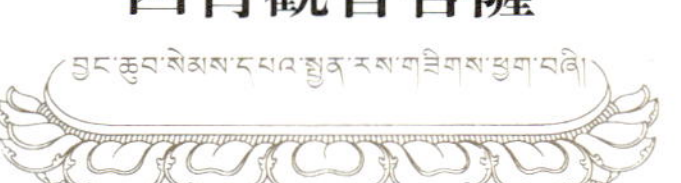

黄銅，高53.5厘米，清康熙年間（1662～1722）

Four-armed Avalokiteśvara (Ṣaḍakṣarī-Lokeśvara)

Brass Height: 53.5cm Kangxi reign, Qing Dynasty (1662-1722)

觀音菩薩面相豐腴，永樂、宣德佛像常見的典型的漢族臉形，四方臉，下頦渾圓，神態安詳和悦。鏤空的寶冠，正中冠葉爲獸面的金翅鳥，上部摩尼寶，樣式與圖七十八財寶天王一致。大圓耳璫覆蓋肩頭，鏤空刻花，秀美華麗十分突出。胸前飾仁獸皮、瓔珞、項鏈，簡潔精緻。全跏趺坐，前雙手合掌于胸前，後左手持一朵蓮花，右手持念珠。衣褶起伏流暢自如，仍可見永樂佛像意蘊。此像鑄造精湛，具有康熙宫廷佛像特點。

座面刻「大清康熙年施」雙鈎正楷字，由右至左行。

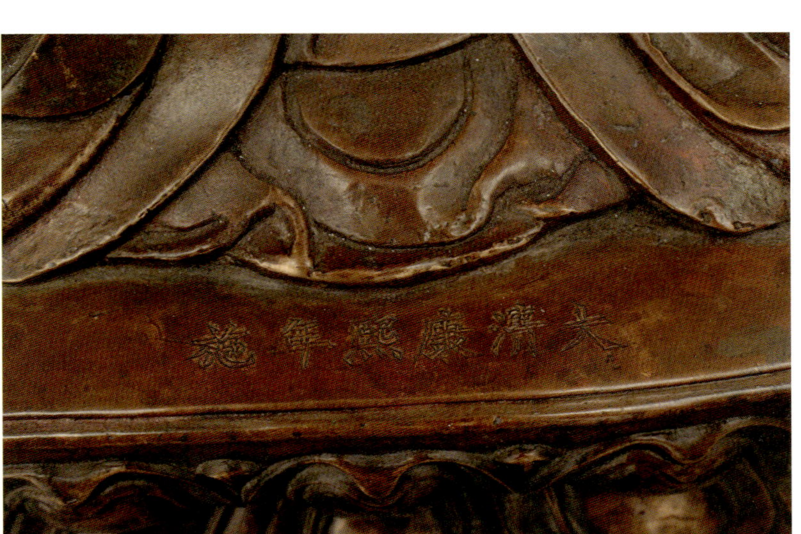

The four-armed form of Avalokiteśvara known as Ṣaḍakṣavī (Yi ge drug ma) is seated in the diamond attitude on double lotus pedestal with beaded border and displays with the principal pair of hands the gesture of respectful salution. He holds in the upper right hand a rosary and in the upper left hand a lotus flower. The image is clad in cloth lied around the hip by a belt, and has ribbon-like scarve placed over the shoulder falling over the arm to the pedestal.

On the top of the pedestal is inscribed with the six-character Kangxi mark: "Da Qing Kangxi nian shi".

83

彌勒菩薩

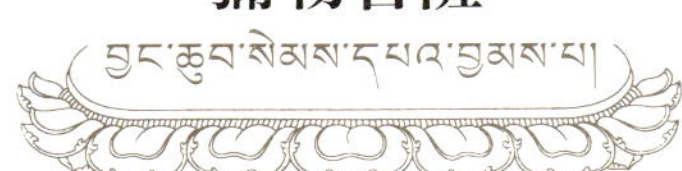

黄銅，高51厘米，清康熙年間（1662～1722）

Bodhisattva Maitreya

Brass Height: 51cm Kangxi reign, Qing Dynasty (1662-1722)

彌勒菩薩半跏趺坐，面容豐腴祥和。寶冠、珠寶、瓔珞雕刻細緻優美。臂釧、手鐲裝飾一圈小葉片邊，增加了華麗之感。最值得稱道的是，裙面鏨刻的纏枝蓮花圖案，是典型的漢族傳統風格。花朵枝葉均勻分布裙面，綫條自然流暢，溝刻陰綫粗細一致，毫無滯澀之感，如筆畫一般，顯示了高超的鏨刻技藝。

༨༣

Bodhisattva Maitreya is seated in an unconventional attitude with plump and peaceful facial appearance. The crown, jewelry and necklace are delicately carved. The armlet and bracelet are carved with a roll of small leaves. The surface of the skirt is engraved with pattern of lotus scrolls, which is traditional pattern of Han Chinese Buddhist Art.

84

彌勒菩薩

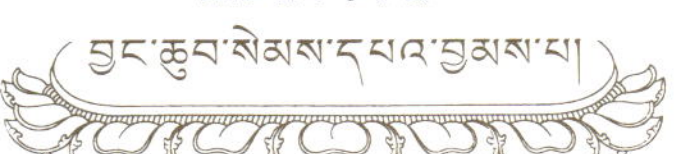

黃銅，高54.8厘米，清康熙年間（1662～1722）

Bodhisattva Maitreya

Brass　Height: 54.8cm　Kangxi reign, Qing Dynasty (1662-1722)

彌勒菩薩雙腿直立覆蓮臺上，頭戴五葉冠，髮髻頂立佛塔，身材壯碩，面相豐滿，右手作説法印，左手握蓮花莖。下身着雙層長裙，身側蓮枝纏繞盤升，隨身長帛翻卷垂地，造型優雅，工藝精緻。蓮座面刻「大清康熙年施」雙鈎楷書字，由右向左書寫，字體端正有力。

Bodhisattva Maitreya stands erectly on the two-layered lotus pedestal. He wears a five-leaved crown and on his bob is a stūpa. He has plump bearing with his right hand making the gesture of teaching and left hand clenching the stalk of a lotus. He wears two-layered long skirts with the lotus stalks intertwining at his side. The top of the pedestal is inscribed with the six-character Kangxi mark: "Da Qing Kangxi nian shi".

85

彌勒菩薩

銅鎏金，高46厘米，清康熙年間（1662～1722）

Bodhisattva Maitreya

Gilt brass Height: 46cm Kangxi reign, Qing Dynasty (1662-1722)

在藏傳佛教中，彌勒信仰廣泛深入，藏語謂“强巴”。有單獨供奉的强巴佛殿，如西藏日喀則扎什倫布寺高達26米的强巴佛銅像；也有作爲八大菩薩之上首，侍立在釋迦牟尼佛前。此彌勒菩薩細目微垂，神態莊嚴，頭戴五葉寶冠，耳邊繒帶彎曲上卷，耳飾圓形大珠寶耳璫。雙手施説法印，掌心持蓮花蔓，身側雕長莖蓮花，枝葉婀娜多姿。左肩蓮花芯中立净水瓶，是彌勒的顯著標識。一條長帛搭覆雙肩，繞臂展開。胸前腰部裝飾項鏈瓔珞，長裙褶曲復垂疊座前。配飾華麗，綫條規整。

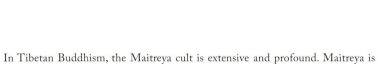

In Tibetan Buddhism, the Maitreya cult is extensive and profound. Maitreya is called “byams-pa” in Tibetan. This Maitreya slightly hangs down his slender eyes and eyebrows. He wears a five-leaved crown and big round ear-ornaments. Both his hands are in the gesture of teaching. The palm holds the vine of the lotus. The lotus with long stalk carved by the side of his body has beautiful branches and petals. The white vase standing on the center of the lotus on the left shoulder is a distinguished mark of Maitreya.

86

宗喀巴

ཙོང་ཁ་པ།

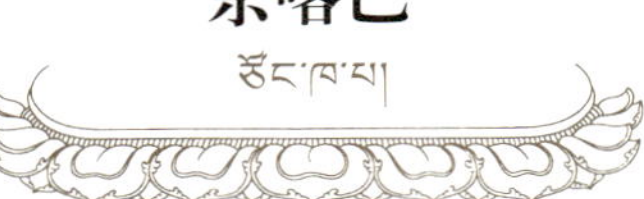

黄銅，高40.8厘米，清康熙年間（1662～1722）

Tsong kha pa

Brass Height: 40.8cm Kangxi reign, Qing Dynasty (1662-1722)

◈宗喀巴大師頭戴班霞帽，面容豐滿，笑意盈然。眼嵌銀，嘴唇嵌紅銅。設計緊湊的五官，加上銀銅兩種不同金屬色澤對比，顯得年輕而有活力。雙手牽蓮花莖作説法印。身側兩枝蓮花上立寶劍與經篋，表明其爲文殊菩薩化身。全跏趺坐，袈裟衣褶起伏自然，衣緣鑲嵌刻花銀邊。袈裟面用銀絲鑲嵌卷雲，鏨刻花朵。下擺、坐墊鏨刻細密精美的花邊。凸字形須彌座，下加圓臺角，形制獨特。須彌座後平面陰綫刻整幅精美的花卉圖案。此像鑄造、鑲嵌、鏨刻工藝俱佳，表現了清宮廷造像精工華美的藝術追求。

◈座面「大清康熙年施」雙鈎楷書字，由右向左書寫。

Tsong kha pa, founder of the dGe lugs pa sect, is seated in the diamond attitude on a single lotus pedestal. He displays the gesture of the wheel of the doctrine. Each hands holds the stalk of a lotus flower attached to a shoulder, the one on the right supports a sword, the one on the left a manuscript. He wears monastic garments and the pointed cap of the dGe lugs pa sect.

Tsong kha pa wears heart-shaped hat of versatile person with plump facial appearance. His eyes are embedded with silver and his lips are inlaid with red copper. The two hands hold the stalk of the lotus in the gesture of teaching. The sword and sutra box standing on the two lotuses by the side of the body indicate that he is the incarnation of Mañjuśrī. The inscription "Made in the Years of Kangxi of the Qing Dynasty" in double hooked standard script is written in the direction from right to left in the front of the pedestal.

87

思惟觀音菩薩

黄銅，高44.5厘米，清康熙年間（1662～1722）

Bodhisattva Avalokiteśvara in Meditation

Brass Height: 44.5cm Kangxi reign, Qing Dynasty (1662-1722)

◈思惟觀音菩薩，亦稱「莲花手菩萨」。長眉細目，鼻梁挺括，頭略低，兩眼俯視，左手彎曲托腮静默思維。胸前飾珠寶瓔珞，雙聯珠綫樣式。長裙衣褶起伏自然，裙邊透迤垂於座面。高蓮座，蓮瓣細長。寬肩細腰，右腿盤坐，左腿曲起，姿態閑適。造型顯然是吸收了永樂佛像的技法，但已變化，風格更加簡潔硬朗。

◈座面刻雙鈎楷書「大清康熙年施」，字體端莊有力，由右向左書寫。

The so-called Bodhisattva in meditation is identified as Avalokiteśvara Dadmapāṇi. He is seated in the attitude of royal ease on a double lotus pedestal with beaded border. The right hand is placed on the right leg with the palm facing up. The Bodhisattva rests his head against the left hand raised in a variation of the pensive gesture with the elbow supported by the left knee.

The top of the pedestal is inscribed with the six-character Kangxi mark: "Da Qing Kangxi nian shi".

88

四臂觀音菩薩

黄銅，高61厘米，清康熙年間（1662～1722）

Four-armed Avalokiteśvara (Ṣaḍakṣarī-Lokeśvara)

Brass Height: 61cm Kangxi reign, Qing Dynasty (1662-1722)

四臂觀音又稱六字觀音，是由六字真言所化現的觀音，在藏傳佛教諸多觀音形象中廣受尊崇。此像由觀音身像、雙層圓蓮座、背光三部分分鑄合而成。觀音頭戴花鬘寶冠，以阿彌陀佛爲頂嚴。着耳環、項鏈、胸飾等珠寶八飾。神情静穆安詳，雙目微眯，以菩薩慧眼凝視衆生，表現觀音悲憫衆生的情懷。上身袒露，左肩頭披羊皮，下身着裙，薄衣貼體，不刻衣紋。肩披短短的帛帶，没有繞臂翻卷，直垂肘前。雙層圓蓮座，中間由圓柱支撑連接，柱兩側爲三顆寶珠串，外圈卷雲裝飾，蓮瓣雕刻華麗的卷雲邊。葫蘆形鏤空背光，圖案化的卷雲邊組成火焰紋，裝飾簡約而不失精緻。

此像與北京故宫博物院藏乾隆時期清宫廷所造金四臂觀音，形象近似，雙層圓底座形制完全一樣（見《故宫博物院藏文物珍品全集——宫廷珍寶》圖一八五），説明二者間的密切關係。此像早於乾隆，具有康熙宫廷佛像的特點。此像作爲一種優美的佛像樣式流傳久遠。

The four-armed form of Avalokiteśvara known as Ṣaḍakṣarī is seated in the diamond attitude and displays with the principal pair of hands the gesture of respectful salution. He wears bejewelled ornaments, namely a five-leaved crown in front of the knot of hair with jewelled tips, pairs of circular earrings, necklaces with beaded strands of pearls attached, bracelets on the upper arms and all four wrists, ornaments on the legs, and anklets. Note the effigies of Amitābha attached to his hair.

89

四臂觀音菩薩

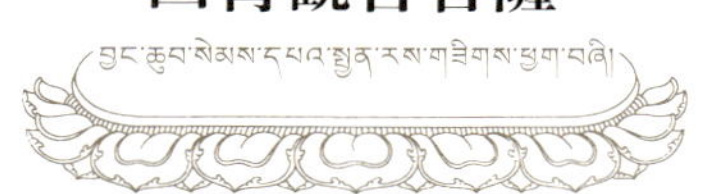

黃銅，高72厘米，清康熙年間（1662～1722）

Four-armed Avalokiteśvara (Ṣaḍakṣarī-Lokeśvara)

Brass Height: 72cm Kangxi reign, Qing Dynasty (1662-1722)

四臂觀音，葫蘆形髮髻，髻頂飾蓮座珠寶，五葉冠精緻華麗，繒帶U形上卷。胸前三圈精美的瓔珞珠寶項鏈，左肩頭披羊皮。在乳頭處雕刻大菱形珠寶飾件，左邊飾件上部刻羊頭，羊口叨珠寶。蓮座大蓮瓣圓鼓，雕刻華麗的卷雲邊，均爲康熙佛像的典型作法。佛像的樣式、尺度與北京故宮所藏康熙二十五年清宮廷製造的四臂觀音基本一致，出自同一模本，說明了兩者間的密切關係。此像現已捐贈國家博物館。

四臂觀音的蓮座前面刻藏文題記：

spyan ras gzigs phyag bzhi pa'i gzungs/

漢譯：四臂觀音之總持

蓮座後部光素没有蓮瓣，刻寫藏文題記：

一、Oṃ maṇipadme hūṃ// Oṃ maṇipadme hūṃ//

漢譯咒文：唵嘛呢巴達（二合）墨吽唵（二合）唵嘛呢巴（二合）墨吽唵（二合）

二、Oṃ maṇipadme hūṃ zhes pa'i gzungs kyi phan yon/

Oṃ gyis lha skye'i 'chi'i sdug bsngal sel/ ma yis lha ma yin 'thab rtsa'i sdug bsngal sel/ ni yis mi skye rgan 'chi'i sdug bsnal sel/ pad kyis dud 'gro bkol spyad kyi sdug bsnal sel/ me yis yi dwags bkres skom gi sdug bsngal sel/ hūṃ gis dmyal ba tsha grang gi sdug sngal sel/ sangs rgyas kun kyi snying po'i dbang/ de ring khyod la bskur bar bgi/ sangs rgyas thams can bsdus nas ni/ rig sngags rgyal po'i dbang cig bskur/ oṃ ri sbyin pa'i pha rol phyin/ ser sna med pa'i bcom ldan 'das/ sangs rgyas kun 'dus chos kyi sku/ dbang bskur byin gyis brlab tu gsol//

Oṃ phe laṃ hūṃ/ nag po ti pa tsa nāga raksha oṃ phe le laṃ hūṃ//

漢譯：

嘛呢巴達（二合）墨吽唵（二合）（六字大明咒）之功德

「唵」遮止了天趣生死之苦；

「嘛」遮止了阿修羅趣鬥争之苦；

「呢」遮止了人趣老死之苦；

「巴達（二合）」遮止了畜牲趣奴役之苦；

「墨」遮止了餓鬼趣饑渴之苦；

「吽唵（二合）」遮止了地獄趣寒熱之苦。

成諸佛之真言，聚一切正法之精要，爲衆生利益而升。授一六字真言灌頂，一切諸佛之心灌，今於你作。集一切諸佛，授明咒之最勝灌頂，極授灌之究竟。啓請集一切諸佛之法身，無有吝嗇之出有壞攝授灌頂！

The four-armed form of Avaolokiteśvara has calabash-shaped bun, the top of which is decorated with lotus throne jewels. The five-leaved crown is exquisite and gorgeous. The front of the chest is decorated with exquisite necklace. The left shoulder is covered with sheep skin. The round petal of the lotus pedestal and the gorgeously carved clouds are both typical expression of Buddhist statues made in the Kangxi period. It has been donated to the National Museum.

སྤྱན་རས་གཟིགས་ཕྱག་བཞི་པའི་གཟུངས།

90

觀音菩薩

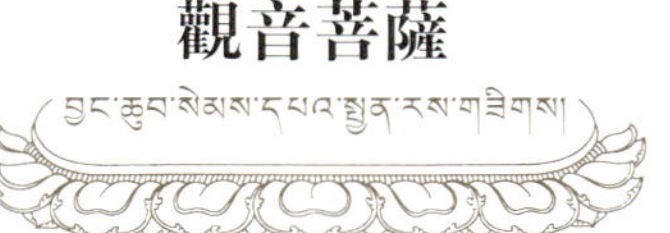

銅鎏金，高34.2厘米，清康熙年間（1662～1722）

Bodhisattva Avalokiteśvara

Gilt brass Height: 34.2cm Kangxi reign, Qing Dynasty (1662-1722)

觀音菩薩呈漢族淑女形象，雲鬟高挽，没有戴五葉寶冠，髮髻前雕小阿彌陀佛，面容豐滿清秀，目光俯視，神情寧静慈祥。未戴耳璫，裝飾簡約。胸前戴一條雕花項鏈，中間五朵蓮花，樣式精美，與藏式佛像佩飾瓔珞珠寶有别。寬松的刻花雲肩覆蓋兩肩和上臂。下着高腰長裙，衣褶曲復自然垂疊座前。全跏趺坐，右手抬起作説法印，左手施禪定印。手指柔軟秀美，雕塑技藝不凡，這是一尊藝術水平很高的漢族風格觀音像，只有蓮座採用了清初藏傳佛像做法。

座面刻款識漢字：「大清康熙年制」，由右向左書寫。

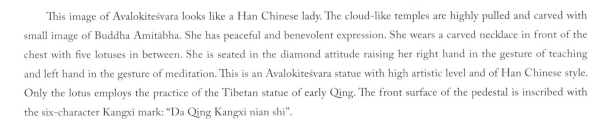

This image of Avalokiteśvara looks like a Han Chinese lady. The cloud-like temples are highly pulled and carved with small image of Buddha Amitābha. She has peaceful and benevolent expression. She wears a carved necklace in front of the chest with five lotuses in between. She is seated in the diamond attitude raising her right hand in the gesture of teaching and left hand in the gesture of meditation. This is an Avalokiteśvara statue with high artistic level and of Han Chinese style. Only the lotus employs the practice of the Tibetan statue of early Qing. The front surface of the pedestal is inscribed with the six-character Kangxi mark: "Da Qing Kangxi nian shi".

91

大黑天

གུར་གྱི་མགོན་པོ།

黃銅，高39厘米，清康熙年間（1662～1722）

Pañjaranātha Mahākāla

Brass Height: 39cm Kangxi reign, Qing Dynasty (1662-1722)

◈大黑天右手握鉞刀（已佚），左手托嘎巴拉碗（已佚），短腿作蹲踞姿態踏一仰卧神。三目圓睜，怒目俯視，眉毛胡鬚刻成精緻細密的雲卷，頭戴骷髏冠，冠葉上部雕刻圓形法輪珠寶。額前垂一圈流蘇式的珠串瓔珞。胸前裝飾永樂佛像特有的繁密瓔珞，腹前垂人頭項鬘，長蛇腰帶。一條長帛繞身翻卷，帛帶上滿綴着珠寶瓔珞。單層覆蓮座，蓮瓣細長，每個蓮瓣雕刻細密的卷雲邊，蓮瓣之間的端部一絲不茍地雕出細密的瓔珞流蘇，此種蓮座樣式是永樂宮廷所造大黑天銅像特有的。北京故宮博物院收藏一尊鐵鋄金永樂大黑天，高二十一厘米，采用鐵鑄造，鐵上鎏金。比較北京故宮大黑天，可見此尊裝飾繁縟華麗做工精緻，其細部造型，工藝特點與北京故宮大黑天像基本一致。可見永樂大黑天樣式到清代還在流傳。

◈座後刻「大清康熙年製」雙鉤楷書，由右向左書寫。現已捐贈國家博物館。

Mahākāla holds a ritual chopper (lost) in the right hand and holds a skull-cup (lost) in the left hand. He tramples on a lying god. His three eyes are wide open. He wears a five-leaved crown decorated with skulls. The leaf of the crown is carved with round Dharma wheel jewelry. Human body vine is hung in front of the belly. He is girdled with long snake-shaped waistband. The back of the pedestal is inscribed with the six-character Kangxi mark:“ Da Qing Kangxi nian shi” in double-hooked standard script in the direction from right to left. It has been donated to the National Museum.

92

大持金剛

རྡོ་རྗེ་འཆང་ཆེན།

黄銅，高61厘米，17世紀

Vajradhara

Brass Height: 61cm 17th century

大持金剛傳爲大乘密宗佛法的直接傳授者，在密宗諸派中享有崇高的神性地位。此像頭戴五葉冠，細眉朗目，容貌慈藹。上身袒露飾瓔珞環釧，全跏趺坐，腰部收束，下着長裙，裙邊刻花，裙面刻雲卷嵌銀絲。雙手交叉胸前施金剛吽迦羅印，手各牽花鬘，持金剛鈴（已佚）和金剛杵（已佚）。身側兩枝蓮花，枝條細密樣式别致，實爲牡丹花形。披肩帛帶由内外翻轉，作法獨特。

座面刻藏文咒：金剛力菩薩明

藏文轉寫：Oṃ tāre tuttāre ture svāhā |

om phe lam hūm | nag po ti pa tsa nāga raksa om phe le lam hūm |

Vajradhara wears a five-leaved crown and is clad in cloth tied by belts with attached beaded strands around the hips. He is seated in the diamond attitude on double lotus pedestal with beaded border. The right hand holding five-pronged diamond sceptre (lost) and the left hand holding prayer-bells (lost) are turned inwards and crossed over the chest.

93

釋迦牟尼佛

黃銅鎏金，高59厘米，清乾隆年間（1736～1795）

Buddha Śākyamuni

Gilt brass　Height: 59cm　Qianlong reign, Qing Dynasty (1736-1795)

◈釋迦牟尼佛面帶微笑，祥和可親。左手托鉢（鉢佚失）結禪定印，右手結降魔印，全跏趺坐。身着華麗袈裟，袈裟田相格内高浮雕千佛，衣褶細密流暢，刀法爽利。佛前立兩位托鉢侍從菩薩，菩薩雙腿直立小蓮花座上，佩飾齊整，肩披繞身長帛，在外側長帛卷起呈u字形，左右對稱。寬大的雙層須彌方座，底層雕八寶圖形和五位菩薩。姿態各异，均裝飾馬蹄形背光。二層正中立金剛杵，左右兩邊雕大黑天、吉祥天母、雙獅。正方形大背光上部爲五拱圓形，背光鏤空，滿雕枝繁葉茂的蓮花纏枝，在花枝中雕九尊佛像端坐蓮花座上，左右兩側雕兩條騰起的行龍，爲皇家專用的飛龍形象。高大華麗的須彌座，精美的大背光，巧妙地烘托出釋迦牟尼佛偉岸崇高的形象。豪華精美的大場面設計，顯示出鮮明的清宫廷特色。其宏大的廟堂氣魄，是民間普通佛像難以具備的。

Buddha Śākyamuni holds an alms bowl in his left hand and makes the gesture of meditation. His left hand makes the gesture of subduing Mārā. He is seated in the diamond attitude. He wears gorgeous cassock carved with thousand Buddhas. Two bowl-holding attendent Bodhisattvas stand in front of the Buddha in bilateral symmetry. Wide double sumeru square platform is carved with eight treasures pattern and five Bodhisattvas and its second layer stands vajra pestle in the midest, Mahākāla, Śrī-Devī and double lion carved in both sides. The aureole is full of carved lotus twines and among flower branches Buddha statue and Bodhisattva are carved with flying walking dragons on both sides. The royal flying dragon image and luxurious and elegant design in big occasion are distinctive features of the imperial workshop of the Qing dynasty.

94

釋迦牟尼佛

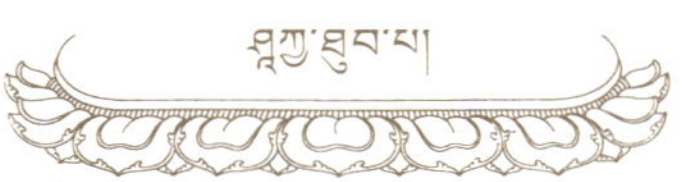

黃銅，高53.5厘米，清乾隆年間（1736～1795）

Buddha Śākyamuni

Brass Height: 53.5cm Qianlong reign, Qing Dynasty (1736-1795)

佛面長圓，高肉髻，髻頂立寶珠，彎眉長目，生動有神。着袒右袈裟，全跏趺坐於刻花圓墊上，左手施禪定印，右手作觸地印。高脖頸，上身略長，身姿挺拔。背光與圖93相似。

座後刻藏文咒：釋迦能仁陀羅尼

原文轉寫：

rGyal ba śākya thub pa'i gzungs/

Namaḥ sarvatathāgata hridaya/ anugate/ Oṃ kuruṃ gini svāhā//

Oṃ namaḥ śākyamunaye tathāgata svāhā/

tathāgaya svāhā tad yathā/

Oṃ mune mune mahāmunaye svāhā//

Buddha Śākyamuni has a long and round face with high moulds of flesh, on top of which stands pearls. His eyebrows are bending, eyes long in vivid and vigorous expression. Wearing cassock which uncovers the right arm, he is seated in the diamond attitude on carving patterned planchet and makes the gesture of meditation with left hand and the gesture of touching the earth with the right hand. He has long neck and relatively long upper body in upright posture.

95

釋迦牟尼佛

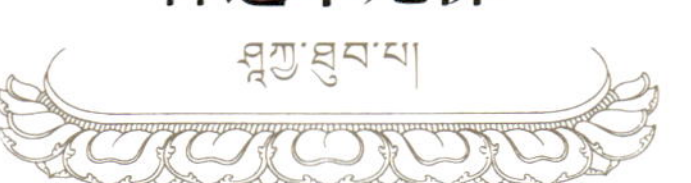

黄銅，高99厘米，清乾隆年間（1736～1795）

Buddha Śākyamuni

Brass　Height: 99cm　Qianlong reign, Qing Dynasty (1736-1795)

◈ 釋迦牟尼佛，面相方圓豐滿，螺髮肉髻，高鼻闊目，大耳垂肩，五官端正開朗，雙目微啓，神情静穆慈祥。臂膀渾圓，肌膚飽滿，符合佛像的相好標准。全跏趺坐，左手施禪定印，右手作與願印。身着華麗袈裟，每個田相格内浮雕千佛，形象各異，花紋優美，鏨刻精湛，右臂下多層衣褶細密流暢，刀法勁爽。仰覆蓮座下沿用減底法雕刻纏枝蓮。是一尊難得的清代精彩佛像。

◈ 座後部藏文題記爲釋迦牟尼佛咒，同前圖94。

Buddha Śākyamuni has a full round face with unique spiral hair of moulds of flesh. His big ears are long hanging on the shoulders with a solemn and quiet face in kindness. He is seated in the diamond attitude, makes the gesture of meditation with left hand and the right hand displays the gesture of charity. He wears gorgeous cassock, on which every cornfield-like lattice is carved with relief thousand Buddhas in all sorts and beautiful patterns. On the double lotus pedestal, the front of which clings to each other, relatively high relief was used for carving lotus twine.

96

彌勒菩薩

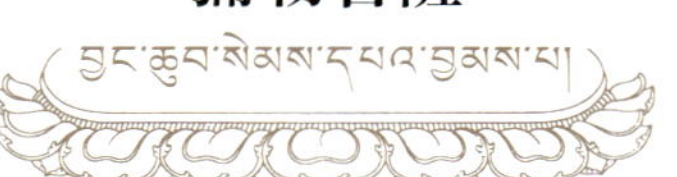

黄銅，高49.5厘米，清乾隆年間（1736～1795）

Bodhisattva Maitreya

Brass　Height: 49.5cm　Qianlong reign, Qing Dynasty (1736-1795)

◈彌勒菩薩雙腿直立雙層蓮臺上，頭戴五葉寶冠，髮髻頂立佛塔，身材壯碩，面相豐滿，右手作説法印，左手握蓮花莖，下身着雙層長裙，身側蓮枝纏繞盤升，隨身長帛翻卷垂地，造型優雅，工藝精緻。此像與圖84是同一模型。

◈蓮座面刻「大清乾隆年禮部造」雙鈎楷書字，由右向左書寫，字體端正有力。

Bodhisattva Maitreya stands on two legs above the double lotus pedestal with a five-leaved crown on his head. On top of high bob is stūpas. He makes the mudrā of teaching with right hand and holds stalk of the lotus in left hand, wearing double-layer long skirt in lower part of the body with winding rising stalks of lotus around. Rolling long silk is falling on the ground in elegant shape with refined craftwork. The surface of the lotus pedestal is carved with the inscription in double hook regular script in the direction from right to left, which indicates that this image is made by the ministery of Rite in the Qianlong reign of the Grand Qing Dynasty.

97

紅閻魔敵

黃銅，高55厘米，清乾隆年間（1736～1795）

Rakta-Yamāri

Brass　Height: 55cm　Qianlong reign, Qing Dynasty (1736-1795)

◈紅閻魔敵，右手高舉喀章噶，左手托嘎巴拉碗，懷抱佛母，佛母手持嘎巴拉碗、鉞刀。展左立姿踏在一魔神背上，魔神在重壓之下，緊緊俯身在牛背上。一條寬大的飄帶繞身往復翻卷，裝飾繁密的珠寶瓔珞。覆蓮座，蓮瓣細長，瓣尖爲三顆圓珠。整個佛像樣式及細部裝飾都仿自永樂佛像。

◈蓮座面刻「大清乾隆年施」雙鉤楷書字，由右向左書寫，字體端正有力。

Raktā-Yamāri is a red form of Yamāntaka who is one of the tantric manifestations of Mañjuśrī. The three-eyed deity steps to the right with the right leg bent and the left straight embracing his consort. He tramples on the prostrate body of Yama. In the raised right hand he brandishes a club decorated with a head, a skull, and a vajra finial, in the left hand he holds a skull-cup. The top of the pedestal is inscribed with the six-character Qianlong mark:" Da Qing Qianlong nian shi".

98

馬頭金剛

黄銅，高50厘米，清乾隆年間（1736～1795）

Hayagrīva

Brass Height: 50cm Qianlong reign, Qing Dynasty (1736-1795)

◈馬頭金剛亦稱馬頭明王，是觀音菩薩的忿怒化身。形象有八臂、六臂、二臂多種。此像二臂二腿，右手高舉火焰劍，左手持火焰。弓步立姿足踏二魔神。頭頂髮髻中雕馬頭，三目圓睁，張口怒吼，形象凶猛。前胸人首項鬘垂地，長蛇盤身，表鎮壓龍王之意。弓步立姿足踏裸體二魔神，一位頭部掙扎抬起，手臂托頂金剛脚跟；一位面朝下趴在地上，頭無力地垂在蓮座面外，動感强烈，栩栩如生，雖然跳不出造像量度經的制約，仍顯示了工匠出色的雕塑技巧和豐富的藝術表現力。

◈座面前沿刻「大清乾隆年施」漢字款識，由右向左行書，字體端正有力。

Hayagrīva is a wrathful form of Avalokiteśvara. The statue holds flame sword high in his right hand and flames in left hand. Horse head is carved on his high bob and his three eyes are wide open for yelling, which makes a ferocious and angry expression. The human head vine of his front chest is hanging nearly on the ground with long snake around body, which means to suppress the dragon king. In forward stance he tramples on two naked demogorgons. The top of the pedestal is inscribed the six-character Qianlong mark :"Da Qing Qianlong nian shi", written in the direction from right to left.

99

文殊菩薩

བྱང་ཆུབ་སེམས་དཔའ་འཇམ་དབྱངས།

黃銅，高41厘米，清乾隆十六年（1751）

Bodhisattva Mañjuśrī

Brass Height: 41cm The 16th year of Qianlong's reign, Qing Dynasty (1751)

◈ 文殊菩薩面相豐滿端正，頭戴五葉寶冠，高髮髻，袒上身，瓔珞、臂釧雕飾精美。腰束長裙，衣褶折疊流暢，右舒坐，右腿自然下垂踏小蓮花，左腿盤曲架於右膝上。身體呈三折扭姿態，閑適自如。右手牽蓮花莖撫座面，左手握經篋。端坐仰覆蓮座，瓣尖上卷成三顆圓珠狀，上下邊緣飾聯珠紋。佛像樣式及細部裝飾都仿自永樂佛像。

◈ 蓮座後面刻藏文題記，藏文轉寫漢譯，其中有「乾隆十六年」記年，說明永樂佛像樣式流傳時代之久遠。

原文轉寫：

da'i ching chen lung rgyal lo bcu drug lo'i zla bcu gnyis ba'i tshes gsum rgyal ba'i dka' yi ge ltar dan la bzos//

漢譯：大清乾隆十六年十二月三日如佛經定准造。

Mañjuśrī has a round regular face, wearing a five-leaved crown and a high bun in uncovered upper body. Necklace and armlet are decorated finely. The statue is seated in the attitude of ease and his right leg hangs naturally stepping on a small lotus and his coiling left leg rests on the right knees. His right hand holds the stalk of lotus and touches the surface of the pedestal while sutra portfolio in the left hand. Behind the lotus pedestal there is a Tibetan inscription which gives the date of the manufacture of the statue as the third day of the twelfth month of the sixteenth year of the Qianlong reign.

佛像精華　國之瑰寶

སངས་རྒྱས་སྐུ་བརྙན་ཕུལ་བྱུང་ནི་རྒྱལ་ཁབ་ཀྱི་གཅེས་ནོར་ཡིན།

呂章申

我與李巍先生認識時間並不長，但一見其人就生發出相見恨晚之感嘆。在這之前，國家發改委當時的領導同志和文化部一位部領導說，李巍收藏有大批珍貴佛像，看看國家博物館是否能夠收藏一部分。當我第一次觀瞻李先生的佛像藏品時，不禁感到吃驚。他收藏佛像的數量之多、質量之高，是我平生看到的個人收藏之最。我想，若國家博物館能收藏其中若干尊，無疑是一樁盛世美舉。

佛家動念，以善爲本。從初次交談中我了解到，李巍先生雖不信佛，却有一顆弘揚佛教文化的赤子之心，希望有個展館，將收藏的佛像供世人觀瞻。順遂因緣，共生吉祥。我即向李先生介紹說，國家博物館正在改擴建，國務院將其定爲國家重大文化工程項目，二〇一〇年五月工程竣工投入使用，建築面積達十九萬二千平方米，是世界建築面積最大的博物館。新的國博將是歷史與藝術並重的綜合性國家博物館，是國家的最高藝術殿堂。新國博開館後的陳展，不僅有五千年「古代中國」陳列，還有古代主要藝術門類的專題陳列，和近現代歷史與藝術的重大陳展。其中的「佛教造像藝術」陳列，將是國家博物館展品中一個新的亮點。

在不斷地接觸交往中，得知李巍先生收藏佛像始於上世紀六十年代。在近四十年的寒來暑往中，無論是作爲測繪大地的跋涉者，還是搏擊商海的企業家，他始終以收藏佛像和研究佛教造像藝術爲最執着、崇高的追求。有時爲收藏一尊佛像，無數次往返雪域戈壁，風餐露宿，艱苦尋覓。由此可見其堅忍不拔的精神寄託和以呵護民族文化藝術瑰寶爲己任的極高境界。

佛教造像，不僅僅是鑄造或雕塑一尊偶像，而是通過造像更藝術地傳達和表現佛陀真善美的偉大思想，是修行者學佛頓悟的一種殊勝法門，是引導佛徒心靈走向慈悲與喜樂、觀想與禪修、本尊與自我融合爲一的修習過程與驗證途徑。這其中的一切藝術行爲都是神聖虔誠的宗教行爲，一切宗教行爲也都是認識和把握佛陀精神的必要過程。就像佛陀的莊嚴美好不祇是外在的三十二相的美好，佛教造像亦是佛陀思想、慈悲、智慧和寶相的美好體現。

藏傳佛教，自松贊干布迎娶漢地文成公主和尼泊爾赤尊公主爲吐蕃帶去佛像、經典及工巧匠師後，就開始了引進和模仿印度、尼泊爾、漢地、克什米爾等地的造像藝術。自元代開始，漢地藝術深刻影響了藏傳佛教的造像藝術。特別是明清時期，由於多封衆建的民族政策，中央政府對於朝貢的藏傳佛教領袖進行賜贈，其中就有大量的佛像。這種貢賜關係中出現的佛像，一方面是藏區地方造像精品，一方面是漢地宮廷造像，而這種漢地造像則是集西藏樣式與漢地風格於一身的作品，如永樂款、宣德款的宮廷造像等。由於這種造像製作規格最高，屬於皇家宮廷造像，專用於頒賜西藏宗教領袖，因此在製作上集中了漢藏最優秀的工匠，藝術上融合了當時漢藏兩地典型的風格。製作不計工本，造型精美，鎏金細緻，工藝性和藝術性極强，是這一時期宮廷佛造像的顯著特點。此類造像一般都鐫有「大明永樂年施」、「大明宣德年施」的楷書陰識，成爲見證明初中央政府民族政策的最好歷史文物。

雖然藏傳佛教造像藝術有着嚴格的宗教儀軌要求，但是千餘年來，藏漢兩族的優秀工匠以其充滿智慧的想象力和藝術創造力，以宗教的虔誠和追求藝術完美的情操，製作了一尊尊充滿魅力、感染心靈、啓迪智慧的佛造像藝術精品，這既是珍貴的宗教遺産，也是我們民族、國家之藝術瑰寶。

老子曰：「上善若水，水善利萬物而不争。」如今，李巍先生將自己心愛的二十二尊（包括十分珍貴的明代永樂「吉祥天母」）佛造像藝術精品捐贈給了中國國家博物館。當國博的文物專家從李先生手中接過這些佛造像時，李先生落泪了……由此可見這批佛造像在他心中的地位。這一上善之舉，李巍先生實現了一個崇高宿願，國家得到了珍貴文物。國博開館後將把這些精美的佛造像長期陳列展示給廣大公衆。

佛教造像藝術卓著，佛陀思想博大精深。李巍先生捐贈的珍貴佛像，豐富了國博的館藏珍品，爲國博拓展研究領域提供了新的實證材料，這必將讓佛造像藝術綻放出新的光彩。

李巍先生即將出版金銅佛像藝術精品圖集，我應邀寫此短文，乃從命之作，如有不妥，懇請專家學者指正。

Buddhist Statues: A Treasury of the Country

Lv Zhangshen

I got to know Mr. Li Wei through the recommendation of the chairman of the National Commission of Development and Reform and the minister of the Ministry of Culture quite recently. I was told that Mr. Li Wei had a large collection of precious Buddhist statues and had plan to donate part of his collection to the National Museum. When I saw Mr. Li's Buddhist statue collection for the first time, I could not help feeling amazed. In terms of both the quantity and quality Mr. Li's collection is certainly the greatest of all private collections I have ever seen in my life. I am fully convinced that it will be a great thing if the National Museum is able to collect a certain number of statues from Mr. Li's collection.

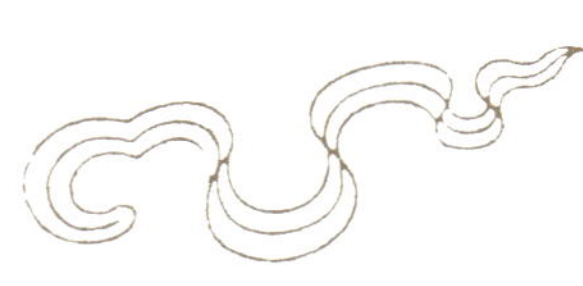

One of the major Buddhist teachings is the one of compassion. From our first conversation, my impression is that though Mr. Li is not a Buddhist, he is a very compassionate person. He has great passion for promoting Buddhist culture and wishes that there would be an exhibition dedicated to the Buddhist statues he had collected. Let nature run its course and it brings auspice. I immediately told Mr. Li that the National Museum was under reconstruction and expansion, and that the State Council regarded it as a national major cultural project. It will be completed and put into use by May 2010. With the construction area of 192,000 sq. meters, the new National Museum of China will be the museum with the biggest construction area in the world. It will be a comprehensive museum, where there is equal emphasis on both history and arts, and it will become the biggest museum on the arts and history of the country. The exhibition of the newly opened National Museum will not only include the display of the five-thousand-year history of China, but it will also devote an exclusive exhibition on selected topics in ancient Chinese arts. Among them, the exhibition of the Buddhist Art of Copper Statue will be a highlight among all exhibitions in the National Museum.

In following communications, I was informed that Mr. Li began collecting Buddhist statues as early as in the 1960s. In nearly forty years, whether as a trudger who surveys and draws the land or as an entrepreneur who has prospered in the business world, he has always regarded the collection of Buddhist statues and the study of Buddhist art as his ultimate pursuit in life. There were times when he had to battle treacherous terrains in order to collect one statue. It proves his stamina and persistence in protecting Chinese national cultural and artistic treasures.

Building a Buddhist statue is more than just casting or sculpting an idol, it is done to express and show the great ideology of the Buddhist truth through the beautiful artistry. It is a skillful mean for the gymnosophist to study Buddhist teachings and to comprehend the truth instantaneously. It is a cultivation and verification path, on which the Buddhist soul is led towards benevolence and happiness. The artistic endeavour can be considered a sacred and pious religious act which is essential to the understanding of the Buddhist spirit. The solemnity and wonderfulness of the Buddha lie not only in the exterior thirty-two faces, but the Buddha statue is also a splendid embodiment of Buddhist ideology, benevolence, wisdom and compassion.

Buddhism was introduced into Tibet when the Tibetan king Srong btsan sgam po married to the Chinese princess Wen Cheng and Nepalese princess Bhrikut, both of whom brought Buddha statues, scriptures and skillful craftsmen to Tibet. Tibetan Buddhists started erecting Buddhist statues very early by copying the style of the Buddhist statue built in India, Nepal, Kashmir, China Proper and the surrounding regions. Since the Mongol-ruled Yuan Dynasty, the Han Chinese art has made a profound influence on the art of statue building in Tibetan Buddhist tradition. Especially in the Ming and Qing Dynasty, the central government conferred numerous

Tibetan Buddhist leaders who paid tribute to the court grand titles and lavish gifts. Among the gifts there are a large number of Buddhist statues. On the one hand, these Buddhist statues are exquisite artworks of Tibet, and on the other hand, they were statues from the imperial court of the Yuan, Ming and Qing dynasties. Moreover, these statues of Han Chinese origin integrated Tibetan and Han Chinese styles. For example, the statues produced during the Yongle and Xuande reigns were made specifically for the purpose of bestowing them to both religious and lay leaders of Tibet. The quality of these statues is extremely high and the production of them involved concerted efforts of the best craftsmen from China Proper, Tibet and other places. They integrate all characteristic features of Han Chinese and Tibetan artistic styles. It is a distinguished feature of the Buddhist statues from the imperial court of this period, during which the production of the statues was greatly supported by the government. With the backing of the court, these works enjoyed delicate modeling and refined gilding, and are of extremely high manufacturability and artistry. These kinds of statues are usually engraved with intangible inscriptions of the six-character script "Da Ming Yongle nian shi (Bestowed during the Yongle Reign of the Grand Ming)" or "Da Ming Xuande nian shi (Bestowed during the Xuande Reign of the Grand Ming)."

There was a large demand for Tibetan Buddhist statues for strict religious rituals, and for over a thousand years, the excellent craftsmen of Tibetan and Han Chinese were able to successively make many exquisite works of Buddhist art with their imagination and artistic creativity, religious piety and of the desire for artistic perfection. They are important part of our religious heritage as well as the treasury of our country.

Today, Mr. Li Wei decided to generously donate twenty two Buddhist statues, among which includes the statue of Śrī Devī (Dpal ldan lha mo) of the Yongle period of the Ming Dynasty, to the National Museum of China. When our experts received these Buddhist statues from him, Mr. Li shed tears. These statues were certainly placed highly in his heart. However, Mr. Li also recognized the importance of protecting and showcasing them on the national stage. And indeed, they will be treasured both artistically, culturally, and will certainly promote high quality studies into our cultural and religious heritage. After the opening of the National Museum of China, these Buddhist statues will be displayed in long-term exhibition for the public. It is on the occasion of the publication of the collection of gilt copper Buddhist statues that I wrote this short essay. I cordially invite experts and scholars to appreciate this great collection.

Lv Zhangshen, Director of the National Museum of China

收藏金銅佛像珍品　保護民族文化遺産

གསེར་ཟངས་སྐུ་བརྙན་འགངས་ཆེན་བསྡུ་རུབ་བྱ་རྒྱུ་ནི་མི་རིགས་
རིག་གནས་ཀྱི་ཤུལ་བཞག་དངོས་རྫས་སྲུང་སྐྱོབ་བྱེད་པ་ཡིན།

李　巍

京華秋夜，皓月當空。

明天，我多年的夙願就要實現了！面對即將捐贈給中國國家博物館的二十多尊稀世金銅佛像，我心潮起伏，久久不能平靜。終於，强忍的泪水如同一粒粒佛珠，滾落在安祥恬靜、精美絶倫的佛像面前。被泪水模糊的目光中，衹見幾位氣韵生動、神采典雅的高僧，正在佛祖座前誦經弘法，爲我的祖國和同胞祈福。

向國家捐贈金銅佛像珍品，是我幾十年的期盼，這讓我感到無比欣慰，也勾起我收藏佛像的往事回憶。

我不是佛教徒，但在心靈深處從小就埋下了虔誠敬佛的種子。我的外祖母篤信佛教，家中設有佛堂供奉菩薩。早晚一爐香，晨昏三叩首，是老人每日必做的功課。母親去世後，不到周歲的我由外祖母收養。隨着年齡增長，在外祖母燒香拜佛的潛移默化中，我逐漸消除了失去母親的精神孤獨，也知道了佛家普度衆生、大慈大悲的淺顯道理。七八歲時，外祖母又專門帶我去洛陽的白馬寺等寺廟燒香拜佛。這些烙印成了我後來收藏和保護佛像的潛意識和原動力。

上世紀六十年代後期，我們的民族和國家還處在文化劫難之中，看到一些寺廟和佛像在「破四舊」中損毀，我心中有說不出來的難過，但怕禍從口出，也衹能暗自惆悵。一九七二年冬，我到青海出差，在一户老百姓家中借住。天灾人禍讓這户人家的日子十分貧困，六七歲的小男孩在零下二十多度的寒冬季節衣不遮體。我不忍心孩子受凍，便把自己携帶的毛背心和襪子送給孩子穿。後來我辭别這家人時，孩子的漢族父親和藏族母親在連聲道謝中，給我提兜裏塞了一個小包，我不知道裏面包的是什麼東西，再三不肯收下。孩子的父親見我拒收，便悄悄對我說：「請收下吧，好人！佛祖會保佑你的。」聽到「佛祖」二字，我心裏一怔，連忙收好紙包告辭。返回西寧途中，我到背人處打開小包一看，原來確是一尊鎏金小銅佛，在驚喜交集中，我把這尊小佛藏了起來。就是這尊小佛，唤起了我童年對佛像的美好記憶，也點燃了藴藏在我心底收藏佛像的熱情。

我從此開始留意散落在民間的佛像。一九七三年夏天，我去西寧出差，聽說西寧鋼廠要把一批佛像和廢銅爛鐵回爐，我立即趕到鋼廠詢問。一位藏族老工人告訴我確有其事，並帶我到廢料場去看大堆廢料。看到即將回爐的金銅佛像都已傷痕纍纍，殘缺不全，我呆呆地站着，不知道說什麼好。老工人唉聲嘆氣地說：「造孽呀，連佛像都砸成這樣！」並告訴我，這些廢料都是各地「破四舊」繳來的。在這位工人師傅的同意下，我從廢料堆中選了幾尊殘缺不全的小佛像，打算帶回後請人修補，看看能否恢復原貌。老工人是一位虔誠的佛教徒，當我把幾尊殘缺佛像捧在手裏時，老人雙手合十，喃喃自語，慈祥的眼神把我打量了好久。我把身上僅有的錢和烟留給了老工人，離開鋼廠時我特意叮嚀老人，請他幫我留心散落在老百姓家裏的佛像。然而我想修復佛像的願望落空了，我既没有找到會修復佛像的人，也没有找到敢修復佛像的人。但令我至今不解的是，從此之後，我喜歡收藏佛像的名聲却在西北一些藏族地區悄悄地傳開了。

十年動亂結束後，黨的致富政策、宗教政策逐步貫徹落實，散落在民間的佛像也慢慢地走出百姓家門，成爲文物收藏者競相追逐的熱點。隨着給我提供佛像信息的渠道增多，我發現有些受境外委託的文物販子已經把佛像列入收藏重點。爲了不使佛像珍品流失到境外，我和妻子變賣了家裏能换錢的所有財物，以至全家三口連着幾年席地而眠。但就是這樣節衣縮食，我收藏佛像的資金依然捉襟見肘。眼睁睁地看着許多精美的佛像落到文物販子手中，我急得滿嘴起泡也無可奈何。

資金的短缺使我萌發了下海經商的念頭。在丢掉「鐵飯碗」、重新找飯碗的猶豫徘徊中，我的精神倍受煎熬。在家人和親友的支持下，我終於下定決心：經商、賺錢、收佛。經過反復調查，我把開發洮硯作爲賺錢的突破口，開始同市場打交道。

洮硯是我國四大名硯之一，洮硯的原材料産地，就在洮河流經的卓尼縣。在當地政府和各族群衆的大力支持下，經過兩年多時間的不懈努力，我的洮硯廠終於恢復了洮硯的傳統生産工藝，並針對海外市場的需求，聘請高級工匠，在選料、造型、構圖和雕刻上進行創新，把審美情趣和人文内涵凝聚在洮石之上，硯池之中。一批接一批承載着中華民族文化内涵的精美洮硯，很快在香港、臺灣、日本及新加坡等地打開銷路，一段時間甚至供不應求。一大批漢藏群衆在開發、推銷洮硯産品中積纍了財富，我在夜以繼日地組織洮硯生産中，聚積了收藏佛像的經濟實力。

金銅佛像收藏市場並不是風平浪静的樂土。在常年纍月的收藏交往中，我發現有些佛像收藏者實際上就是境外文物販子在境内的代理人。他們或壓低價格蒙騙持佛人；或抬高價格同文物部門競争，在這種情况下，老百姓經常被坑蒙拐騙，文物部門則爲經費所困，不少金銅佛像就這樣被走私到境外，甚至流失到異國他鄉。有一次，我看到被一家境外拍賣公司拍賣的一尊鎏金佛像，正是我幾年前多次想收藏都因資金短缺而未能收藏的，我連續幾天吃不下飯、睡不着覺，心靈受到重創。我暗自立誓，即便傾家蕩産，也不能讓佛像珍品流失海外。我以破釜沉舟的决心，東拼西凑，用借貸的所有資金，組建了一家酒廠——三星堆古酒廠。由於管理經營好，酒品信譽高，酒的銷路很快打開，我的佛像收藏也有了同境外文物販子一較高下的經濟實力。有一次，我在新加坡接到國内電話，説一尊永樂年間的稀世鎏金佛像可能在近幾天被境外文物販子拿走。我放下電話直奔機場，買下了最後一張機票。飛機落地後，我未出首都機場，又搭最後一班飛機飛往蘭州。飛機在蘭州中川機場落地時，已是滿天繁星。我跑出機場，跳上早已聯繫好的出租車，加大油門，連夜趕到西寧，終於搶在文物販子下手之前幾個小時，以高出外商的價格把這尊佛像收藏下來。再過不久，這尊佛像的的莊嚴寶相，將在國家博物館正式面世，供人們敬奉瞻仰。

如果説收藏佛像的資金曾使我幾度處於困境，那麽收藏佛像的艱難則使我多次處於險境。一九八九年秋，我到青海牧區收藏一尊佛像，因爲道路泥濘，趕到牧場時天已摸黑，正在我四顧無人時，一隻大藏獒突然從黑暗中向我猛撲過來。儘管我是個將近一米八的大塊頭，又穿着厚厚的皮大衣，但因赤手空拳，也被這隻猛犬撲着連連倒退，危急時刻，多虧一位藏族老阿媽喝退了藏獒，我纔僥幸脱險。一九九六年春節前，青海一位熟人告訴我，有個老鄉希望我收藏他家的一尊四臂觀音。核實清楚地址後，我立刻從西寧租了一輛夏利車，想在午飯前趕到目的地，誰知汽車開了三百多公里就拋錨了。車子趴在海拔三千多米的高山便道上，大風揚雪，寒氣透骨，司機使出渾身解數，也未能排除故障。這時已是凌晨四點多鐘，氣温降到零下三十多度，隨身携帶的食物早已吃完，體内的熱量也幾乎耗盡。我和司機凍得全身上下没有知覺，凍僵的雙手甚至連修理工具也拿不住。經驗告訴我們，如果再凍幾個小時，我們不凍死也要凍殘。真是善有善報。就在我們身陷絶境，求生無望，眼看要踏上死亡邊沿的時候，一輛卡車的燈光從遠處山上射了過來。恍惚中，我感到山上的燈光如同佛光，把我的眼前照亮了，把我心頭的恐怖驅散了，我知道我們有救了。俗話説「男兒有泪不輕彈」，當卡車司機把車停在我們面前時，我和夏利車的司機再也控制不住自己的泪水了。從卡車司機口中知道，他原來是個藏族高原汽車兵，聽説我們是爲了請一尊佛像，才在這裏陷入困境，立即動手幫我們修車。返回西寧後，我因又凍又餓大病一場。但不等身體完全康復，我就趕到五百多公里之外的高原牧區，把這尊四臂觀音請回西寧。再過不久，這尊觀音也將在國家博物館面世，爲和諧社會的建設者們禳灾祈福！

在收藏佛像的滄桑歲月，我與金銅佛像結下不解之緣。我的床頭常年供奉着一尊永樂佛像，晚上不端詳佛像，睡覺也不踏實。有時深夜醒來，還要看看佛像纔能心神安寧。收藏佛像不僅净化了我的心靈，讓我懂得了人爲本、善爲上、和爲貴的道理，還讓我感悟到佛教造像的文化内涵和藝術魅力，激勵我爲保護民族文化遺産、建設和諧社會奉獻一己之力。

跨入己丑，我們將迎來共和國六十華誕，我也要以新的收藏成果向祖國生日獻禮，因爲收藏、保護佛像的激情依然在我心中澎湃。我堅信作爲中華民族文化載體之一的瑰寶——漢藏金銅古佛像，一定會在黨和政府的關心和重視下，得到更多群衆的珍惜和呵護，我更要爲此而不懈努力。

二〇〇八年十月一日

李巍（中國收藏家協會會員、金銅佛像收藏家）

Collecting Gilt Copper Buddhist Statues and Protecting the Cultural Heritage of Our Great Nation

Li Wei

The bright moon climbed high in Beijing autumn night.

Tomorrow, my dream of many years will be realized. I feel an upsurge of emotion when I see more than 20 rare gilt copper statues of Tibetan Buddhism donated to the National Museum of China. I try to hold back my tears but my tears roll like beads before exquisite Buddhist statues that are tranquil and peaceful. Although my eyes are dimmed with tears, I can still see a few senior monks chanting scriptures, propagating the Dharma, praying for my country and for our siblings with lively spirit and vitality.

It is my hope for several decades to donate the gilt copper statues to my country. This donation has comforted me and reminded me of my long journey to collecting these statues.

Although I am not a Buddhists, I respect and admire Buddha and his teachings since I was a child. My grandmother was a devout Buddhist. She set up a small shrine for worshiping Buddha in the living room of our home. It was part of my grandmother's daily practice to burn incense and kowtow to Buddha three times in every morning and every evening. When my mother died, I did not even reach my first birthday. It was my grandmother who adopted me and took great care of me. As I grew older, I gradually expelled my spiritual loneliness and came to believe that the infinitely merciful Buddha could deliver all living creatures from torment. I was imperceptibly influenced by my grandmother through her incense burning and praying. At the age of seven or eight, my grandmother took me to the White Horse Temple in Luoyang. All these things left a deep impression on me and later became my motivating force to collect and preserve Buddhist statues.

During the late 1960s, our people and nation were suffering from the cultural disaster, I was truly frustrated when I saw that temples and monasteries had been destroyed and Buddhist statues were ruined in the mass movement of ruining the old four and the Cultural Revolution. In winter of 1972, I travelled to Qinghai and lived in an ordinary household. Natural calamities and man-made misfortunes had made the family so poor that a six- or seven-year-old boy could only afford to wear shabby clothes when it was 20 degrees below zero. I could not bear to see him suffering in the cold. I gave my woolen vest and socks that I carried with myself to him. Before I left this family, the child's Chinese father and Tibetan mother thanked me over and over again and slid a packet into my handbag. For I did not know what was in my packet, I refused to accept it. Seeing me like this, the father of the child whispered to me, Please take it, Buddha will bless you! Upon hearing the word Buddha, I was stunned and took this packet. On my way back to Xining, I opened this packet without others around and found a small gilt copper Buddha statue. Pleasantly surprised, I hid this little Buddha statue, because it called up all the happy memories of the Buddhist statues in my childhood and lit up my passion for collecting Buddhist statue in my mind.

I began paying attention to Buddhist statues in 1970s. In the summer of 1973, I traveled to Xining and heard that a batch of Buddhist statues along with many scrap of iron and copper were to be melt down in the Xining Steelmaking Plant. I hurried to the Steelmaking Plant and one Tibetan veteran worker brought me to see a lot of wastes in scrap waste. Upon seeing the damaged and incomplete gilt copper statues to be melt down, I stood motionless and did not know what to say. The Veteran worker sighed, "What a sin, smashing even the Buddhist statues!" He also told me that all wastes were taken over in ruining the old four of the Cultural Revolution across the country. Under consent of this worker, I chose a few incomplete small statues, planning to get them repaired. This veteran worker was a devout Buddhist so when I held statues in my hands, he, muttering to himself, looked at me kindly for a long time with the palms of his hands joining together in a namaste gesture. I left all money and cigarettes in my pocket to this veteran worker. Before I left the Steelmaking Plant, I urged him to keep his eyes peeled to any Buddhist statues scattered among ordinary people. However, my wish would not be fulfilled this way, since I could not find anyone who dared to repair these broken statues. Up to now I am still puzzled by how my statue-collecting reputation could spread so far in the northwest Tibetan areas, albeit silently.

After the end of the Culture Revolution, Buddhist statues preserved by ordinary people appeared slowly in the market and soon become heatedly competed by collectors. I paid close attention to the market place of the trade of Buddhist statues and found that traffickers in antiquities entrusted by foreign agencies listed cultural relics as key collections. In order to keep the treasures away from the hands of foreign traffickers, my wife and I liquidated all our possessions and all three members of our family had to live very modestly for several years. Although I lived frugally, my fund for collecting Buddhist statues was always not sufficient. I was so helpless at one time that my mouth was full of blisters, for I could do nothing but watch many fine Buddhist statues fall into these traffickers' hands.

The shortage of funds stimulated me and gave me the incentive of engaging in business. It was very hard for me to make the decision of giving up my regular job. With support from my family, friends and relatives, I finally made up my mind to do business, hoping to earn enough money to collect Buddhist statues. After repeated investigations, I developed the Tao inkstone as a breakthrough in inkstone production and my business began from there.

The Tao inkstone was one of four famous inkstones in China. Its raw material comes from the Tibetan autonomous county of Tao. With the support of local government and the people of all ethnic groups, my Tao inkstone factory finally restored its traditional production technology and I recruited senior artisans for innovative works in selecting, modeling, composition and carving, which connected esthetic sentiment and cultural implications to Tao stone and inkstone pool. One batch of exquisite Tao inkstones bearing cultural implication after another soon opened the market in Hong Kong, Taiwan, Japan, Singapore and other Asian countries. Sometimes supply even fell short of demand. A lot of people, both Han Chinese and Tibetan, accumulated wealth in developing and selling Tao inkstone products. I have also done great business in Tao inkstone production and made good preparation for collecting Buddhist statues.

The market of trading gilt copper Buddhist statues is not a place without turbulences. During my time dealing, I found some statue collectors were actually local agents of foreign traffickers. They sometimes lower down the price to deceive the statue owners and sometimes elevated the price for competing with cultural heritage departments in the country. As a result with the cultural heritage departments lacking in funds, these statues were smuggled abroad or even lost in foreign lands. Once I saw that a small gilt copper statue sold by a foreign auction company was exactly the one I planned to collect but failed repeatedly because of the shortage of funds. I did not eat nor sleep very well for days with a broken heart. I vowed to myself that I would definitely retrieve the treasure even I were to be reduced to poverty and ruin. By borrowing money, I determined firmly to build a new wine factory, Sanxing Pile Old Wine. Because proper business management and good reputation, good quality wine was sold quickly. The business provided me with relatively great economic strength to compete with foreign traffickers. Once I got a phone call from China while travelling in Singapore and was informed that a rare Yongle statue was to be bought by foreign traffickers. Upon hanging up I bought a last minute ticket and flew back to China immediately. As soon as the plane landed, I flew on the last plane to Lanzhou without getting out of the Capital International Airport. The sky was studded with twinkling stars when the plane came down at Lanzhou Zhongchuan Airport. I ran out of the airport and jumped into the taxi I booked and rushed to Xining in an all-night trip. Finally, with all this effort, I bought this Buddha statue before the traffickers were able to loot it. Shortly after, the Buddha's solemn image will appear in the national museum of China officially for worship with reverence.

To accumulate funds for collecting Buddhist statues brought me into terrible financial predicament several times. To collect statues sometimes even put my life in danger. In autumn of 1989, I went to Qinghai pastoral area to collect one statue. Because of the muddy road, and it was getting late when I reached the pastoral area, I looked around and realized that there was no one in sight. Suddenly one Tibetan Mastiff attacked me in the dark. Although I was nearly 1.8 metres tall and wearing a thick coat, I was unarmed. I was forced to step back. In this crisis, thanks to a Tibetan amah, I luckily escaped while she scared away the Tibetan Mastiff.

Before the Spring Festival of 1996 in Qinghai, one fellow townsman told me that a countryman hoped that I could collect a statue of the four-armed Bodhisattva Avalokiteśvara. I rented a taxi cab in Xining, planning to arrive to my destination before lunch. However, the taxi cab broke down after running over 300 km from Xining to an altitude of over 3,000 meters. In penetrating high winds and heavy snow, the driver wrecked his brain and still could not repair the car. It was already 4:00 am with the temperature falling more than 30 degrees below zero. The food we carried with us was already finished and we were completely exhausted. The driver and I were frozen stiff from head to foot and our hands were too frozen to hold repair tools. Experience told us that if we continued to be frozen, we would freeze to death. For virtue was its own reward, thus when caught in a near-death situation, we saw a truck light from distant mountain. In trance, I felt the truck lights as Buddha light shining that dispelled my inner fear. I came to know we were saved. As the saying goes, "Men do not shed tears unless they are deeply in grief, " when the truck driver pulled up in front of us, my taxi driver and I could no longer hold back our tears. The truck driver told us he was a driver in an army in Tibetan plateau and when he heard we came to collect Buddhist statue and were stuck in trouble, he immediately helped us to repair the taxi. After returned to Nanning, I fell badly ill, freezing and hungry. But without having completely recovered, I had to travel another 500 km for the statue of the four-armed Bodhisattva Avalokiteśvara in pastoral plateau. Shortly afterward, this statue will appear in the national museum of China. It will be a symbol of blessings and a protector from all misfortunes for those who helps build a harmonious society.

In springs and autumns when I collected Buddhist statues, I was literally inseparable from the gilt copper Buddhist statues. One statue of the Yongle period is always displayed at the head of my bed. If I do not see it at night, I cannot sleep very well. Sometimes when I wake up in midnight, the sight of it alone can bring me to a calm and peaceful sleep. I believe that the collecting of Buddhist statues does not only purify my soul, but also makes me get a better understanding of the importance of humanity, kindness and harmony. These Buddhist statues have such cultural implications and artistic charm also spurred me to contribute myself to help build a harmonious society and to proserve our national cultural heritage.

Entering into the year of Yichou on Chinese lunar calendar, we are going to celebrate the 60th birthday of The People's Republic of China. I will give my newly collected present for our country's 60th anniversary. My passion for collecting and protecting Buddhist statues still rages in my heart. As a collector, I believe, Tibetan and Han Chinese gilt copper Buddhist statues will surely inspire people's love for the history and culture of our great nation. I hope this will also increase the attention from the party and government to protect and preserve our national treasure.

October 1st, 2008

Li Wei, The Member of China Association of Collectors

跋

保護金銅佛像　弘揚民族文化

གསེར་ཟངས་སྐུ་བརྙན་སྲུང་སྐྱོབ་བྱས་ནས།
མི་རིགས་རིག་གནས་དར་སྤེལ་གཏོང་དགོས།

屈全繩

根據李巍先生所藏金銅佛造像編輯的《漢藏交融——金銅佛像集萃》終於大功告成，即將付梓面世。這部光前裕後的圖集，是一株深深植根於中華民族文化沃土的佛苑奇葩。這株奇葩的綻放，生動地展示了佛教造像藝術動人心魄的無窮魅力，形象地表現了佛教造像藝術卓爾不群的神秘氣氛。這是中華民族文化根脉息息相通的又一歷史見證，是佛教文化薪火相傳的時代象徵，更是李巍先生保護佛像的真實記録。

「大樂之成，非取乎一音」。爲編輯這部《漢藏交融——金銅佛像集萃》圖集，學界方家同心戮力，厥功至偉。學界泰斗季羡林先生，紅學大家馮其庸先生，藏學名宿王堯先生，香港文化名人、藏傳佛教漢族大師談錫永先生，對圖集的編輯滿懷熱情，寄予厚望，不僅欣然接受圖集之顧問，還傾其心智，爲圖集題辭、賦詩、作序，增强圖集的歷史厚重感，充實圖集的文化内涵量。我們對前輩們以耄耋之年，爲弘揚民族文化再發扛鼎之力，表示崇高的敬意！對國家博物館及其館長吕章申先生，故宫博物院及其院長鄭欣淼先生，中国藏學研究中心及其總干事拉巴平措先生熱情支持圖集出版，表示衷心的感謝！國家級佛造像鑒定專家步連生、孫國璋、王家鵬等先生，以其嚴謹的治學態度，研究鑒定李巍先生收藏的佛像。這次擔任圖集學術顧問，更是鑽堅仰高，一絲不苟，爲圖集的出版付出了心血。故宫博物院藏傳佛教文物專家王家鵬研究員，長期從事故宫藏傳佛教文物的研究工作，在藏傳金銅佛像研究方面造詣精深。主編圖集期間，嚴格鑒定篩選佛像，逐尊深入考證研究，整體設計結構體例，全面指導照片拍攝，精心撰寫總論和全部文字説明，長年纍月，不辭辛勞。享譽國内外的佛學時俊，中國人民大學國學院副院長、漢藏佛學研究中心主任沈衛榮教授，留學海外近二十年，佛學造詣融通中西，此次兼任圖集副主編，夙興夜寐，暮史朝經，以其開闊的學術視野和深厚的學術功力，撰寫長篇專論，從漢、藏、蒙、滿的佛學歷史交融互補中，對佛教造像藝術的形成和發展進行了獨具見解的探討，對李巍先生所藏金銅佛像的藝術價值和學術意義給予充分肯定，對圖集譯文字斟句酌，嚴格把關，確保了譯文的質量和水準。正是由於諸多大家殫精竭慮，纔使這部圖集智望佛天，慧通法海，終於成爲當代一部難得的金銅古佛圖像新彙。

佛教文化是中華文明的重要組成部分。佛教自東漢初年傳入中國後，與儒家、道家等中國傳統倫理和宗教觀念相結合，滲透到中國社會的各個領域。有漢以來的中國哲學史、中國思想史、中國文化史、中國民俗史的大動脉中，始終涌動着中國佛學史的熱流。因此，説佛教文化是國學大厦的有機部分是言之有據的。

佛教造像作爲佛教傳承的重要載體，藴藏着極其豐富的文化内涵。馳名中外的克孜爾千佛洞、柏孜克里千佛洞、莫高窟佛教壁畫，譽滿天下的雲岡、龍門、麥積山、炳靈寺等寺院的佛教雕塑，以及長城内外、大江南北衆多寺廟中的各種佛像，無不閃爍着佛教文化發展的歷史輝煌——也爲後人研究佛教文化留下了彌足珍貴的實物。

佛教造像在我國有着廣泛的社會基礎。兩千多年來，規模不等、質地不同的各種佛像，不僅被供奉在晨鐘暮鼓、雕梁畫棟的寺廟中接受僧衆頂禮膜拜，而且也被百姓供奉庭堂，敬香祈福。特别是那些千尺斷崖上的古刹，峰巒環抱，臨流據險，天空雲蒸霞蔚，地上草木葱鬱，殿堂香烟繚繞，置身其境似有超凡脱俗之幻覺。幾十年來，李巍先生每到一地，總要尋訪這樣的佛土妙境，感受佛門的清静超然，并且常常流連忘返。

李巍先生不是佛教徒，但心境却很虔誠。他幼年喪母，生活坎坷，尋求心靈慰藉，消除精神孤獨——是他從小就有的願望。看到向來以慰藉僧衆爲己任的佛寺佛像，在十年動亂中却無法擺脱自身遭受浩劫的命運，李巍先生感到不可名狀的悲哀，繼而確立了即使傾家蕩産，也要設法保護佛像的決心。

李巍先生收藏保護佛像，是從發掘民間佛像資源中一步一步走過來的。在幾十年的寒來暑往中，他結識佛門高僧，探訪坍塌佛寺，尋覓流失佛像，經常輾轉於黄土高原，往返於戈壁雪域，出没於山村孤野，在日曬雨淋、風餐露宿甚至上門乞討的艱難跋涉中，與佛像結下了不解之緣，實現了夢寐以求的藏佛願望。

「精誠所至，金石爲開」。當李巍先生傾其心力、精力和財力收藏佛像的時候，他所至誠期盼的，就是讓這些標志人類文化歷史的燦爛明珠再現光輝，爲傳承佛教文化渲染風采，爲弘揚中華文明彰顯精神，爲構建社會主義和諧社會祈福禮贊。現在，圖集已經編就，他捐獻的二十二尊美奂絶倫的金銅佛像也將在國家博物館與世人見面，李巍先生多年的辛勤努力終於如願以償。滄海桑田，佛光輝映。歷史會記住這位爲保護佛教文化、弘揚中華文明而傾注畢生心血的民間佛痴。

盛世中華即將迎來甲子華誕，《漢藏交融——金銅佛像集萃》亦將開光面世。我們奉此圖集，向共和國六十周年大慶獻禮，向爲圖集補天柱地的所有前賢和時俊表示感謝！作跋至此，意猶未盡，遂吟小詩向李巍先生及其夫人鞠傳莉女士表示祝賀：

半生跋涉了初衷，永樂佛像舉世驚。茹苦含辛終有報，一朝重現展華容。

二〇〇九年三月一日於北京

屈全繩（原成都軍區副政治委員、中將、詩人）

Protecting Gilt Copper Buddhist Statues and Developing the National Culture

Qu Quansheng

The compilation and editing of *Sino-Tibetan Buddhist Interactions — A Treasury of Gilt Copper Buddhist Statues*, a volume of selected images of the gilt copper Buddhist statues collected by Mr. Li Wei, has finally been completed, and will be put into print and made available to the public soon. This volume of great Buddhist images will glorify our forefathers and enrich our posterity. It is a wonderful flower of the Buddha's garden deeply planted in the fertile soil of Chinese cultural traditions, the blooming of which bears witness to the close ties between Chinese and Tibetan Buddhist traditions and vividly demonstrates the beauty of the artistry; it also serves as a symbol of the new era of the spread of Buddhist culture. It also provides a true record of Mr. Li Wei's great contribution to the protection of Buddha statues.

For the compilation of the volume *Sino-Tibetan Buddhist Interactions — A Treasury of Gilt Copper Buddhist Statues*, a great number of scholars and experts have made concerted efforts and contributions. Mr. Ji Xianlin is one of the greatest scholars of our time; Mr. Feng Qiyong is a well-known scholar and artist and an absolute authority of the study in *The Dream of Red Chamber*; Mr. Wang Yao is a leading expert in Tibetological studies worldwide; and Mr. Tam Shek-wing is an oversea Chinese cultural celebrity and a great master of Tibetan Buddhism. They all showed great enthusiasm to and had high hopes on the editing of this volume. They did not only take the role of academic advisors for the volume, but they also made distinct contributions in various ways, for instance, by presenting calligraphy, poems and essays for inclusion in the volume. The involvement of these respectful scholars and experts enriches the cultural and historical significance of the volume. Here we like to sincerely express our great respect to these senior personalities who made contributions to carrying forward the cultural tradition of our great nation in their old ages. We would also like to express our heartfelt gratitude to the National Museum of China, especially its director Mr. Lv Zhangshen, for the great support to the publication of this volume. Mr. Bu Liansheng, Sun Guozhang, Wang Jiapeng, et al., state-level connoisseurs of Buddhist statue, carefully examined all gilt copper statues collected by Mr. Li Wei with great erudition and expertise. As the academic advisors of the volume, they made an intensive investigation in the pursuit of excellence, and have paid painstaking care for further improvement of the publication of the volume. Mr. Wang Jiapeng, a veteran expert in Tibetan Buddhist cultural relics from the Palace Museum, has long been engaged in the research works on Tibetan Buddhism cultural relics preserved in the Palace Museum, and specialized in the study of gilt copper statues of Tibetan Buddhism. During the long process of editing the volume, he investigated all Buddhist statues of Mr. Li Wei's collection, made a careful distinction and identification of the true identity and the exact date of these statues. He has also consulted a great number of literary sources seeking as evidence to support his identifications. He supervised the entire project and took the responsibility of selecting and describing all statues included in this volume. Professor Shen Weirong, a leading scholar of Tibetan Buddhist studies, associate dean of the School of Chinese Classics at Renmin University of China and director of the Research Center of Sino-Tibetan Buddhist Studies, has studied and worked abroad for nearly twenty years and has played a leading role in promoting the comparative studies of Chinese and Tibetan Buddhist traditions worldwide. This time, he took the role of an associate editor-in-chief of the volume, worked very diligently for contributing a lengthy treatise on the history of the interactions between Chinese and Tibetan Buddhist traditions. His thesis demonstrates his broad vision and profound academic ability. He gives full affirmation to the artistic value and academic significance of the gilt copper statues of Tibetan Buddhism collected by Mr. Li Wei. In addition, he made a contribution to decipher inscriptions in both Tibetan and Sanskrit scripts and improved the English translation of all texts in the volume. The success of the compilation of the volume is certainly the great product of the concerted efforts of all personalities mentioned above. Owing to their efforts could this volume finally become a brilliant piece of art demonstrating the greatness of gilt copper statues of Tibetan Buddhism.

Buddhist culture is an important part of Chinese civilization. Since its introduction into China in the early years of the Eastern Han Dynasty, Buddhism was integrated with Chinese cultural traditions such as Confucianism and Taoism, and deeply penetrated into the very essence of Chinese society. Since the Han Dynasty, Buddhist influences have been exerted into Chinese philosophy, ideology, culture and folklore. Therefore, it is an argument based on historical facts that Buddhism is an intergral part of Chinese cultural tradition.

As an important carrier of Buddhist tradition, Buddhist statues contain extremely rich cultural elements. The Kizil Thousand Buddha Caves, the Baizeklik Thousand Buddha Caves, the Wall Paintings in the Mogao Grottoes, the famous Buddhist sculptures of numerous Grottoes in Yungang, Longmen, Maiji mountain, Bingling si, to name a few places renowned at home and abroad, each statues sparkles with the historical brilliance of the development of Buddhist culture without exception and leaves us with great resources for the study of the Buddhist culture.

The art of building Buddhist statue has a comprehensive social foundation in our country. For over two thousand years, all kinds of Buddhist statues of different scales and materials are not only enshrined in the temples and monasteries with morning bell, evening drum, carved beams and painted rafter for worship, but they are also placed in the front courtyard of ordinary people to be worshipped and offered with burning incense and prayed to. Especially those ancient monasteries on the thousand feet high cliffs are surrounded by ridges and peaks, close to rivers and dangerous places, with rosy clouds slowly rising in the sky and flowers and plants flourishing on the ground. In the palace hall, with smoke coiling up from burning incense, you will experience a feeling of transcendence and free from vulgarity. For several decades, whenever Mr. Li Wei visits a place, he always seeks out such places of Buddha field to experience the Buddhist sense of tranquility and is often reluctant to leave.

Although Mr. Li Wei is not a Buddhist, he greatly appreciates the Buddhist teachings. He lost his mother early in his childhood and has lived a life full of hardship. Since his childhood, he actively seeks for the meaning of life and spiritual enlightenment. During the ten years of turmoil, Mr. Li Wei witnessed the unfortunate destruction of many Buddhist temples and monasteries. Mr. Li Wei felt an indescribable grief and was determined to make his utmost effort to protect Buddhist statues even at the cost of bankruptcy.

In his course of collecting and protecting Buddhist statues, Mr. Li Wei started from scouting for the Buddhist statue resources among ordinary people. In the decades of exploration, he made acquaintance with eminent Buddhist monks, visited collapsed temples and monasteries, and looked for lost Buddhist statues. He often commuted in loess plateau, travelled to and fro between desert and snowy regions, and hiked into mountain villages. In the hard trudge of being sun-scorched and rain-drenched, going through the rigors of living in the wilderness and even begging from door to door, he set up a firm karma with Buddhist statues and realized his long-cherished dream of collecting them.

While Mr. Li Wei devoted all his mental and physical efforts, energy and financial resources to collecting Buddhist statues, all he has been expecting is to be able to see them shine again like a beacon in human civilization, symbolizing the Buddhist spirit and passing on the Chinese culture to future generations. Now that his collection of gilt copper Buddhist statues is part of the National Museum of China, Mr. Li Wei's great efforts for decades have finally paid off. Time brings great changes to the world and the light of the Buddha can again shine like brilliant pearls. History will remember the great lover of Buddhist statues who devoted all his life to the course of protecting Buddhist culture and carrying forward Chinese civilization.

Our country is going to celebrate its sixtieth birthday, and *Sino-Tibetan Buddhist Interactions — A Treasury of Gilt Copper Buddhist Statues* is also going to be consecrated and open to the public. We present this volume to the sixtieth anniversary of the People's Republic of China and express our gratitude to all the scholars who have made contributions to the publication of this volume! Last, but not least I like to express my sincere congratulations to Mr. Li Wei and his wife Ju Chuanli for the publication of this wonderful book.

March 1, 2009, Beijing

Qu Quansheng, General and Poet

圖版索引

Index of Plates

30 吉祥天母｜152頁｜

29 喜金剛｜148頁｜

28 大威德金剛｜145頁｜

27 綠度母｜143頁｜

26 白度母｜140頁｜

35 六臂大黑天｜166頁｜

34 六臂大黑天｜162頁｜

33 騎鵬鳥護法｜160頁｜

32 白勇保護法｜158頁｜

31 寶帳怙主｜156頁｜

40 空行母｜180頁｜

39 喇呼拉護法｜177頁｜

38 財神大黑天｜174頁｜

37 金剛亥母｜172頁｜

36 金剛亥母｜168頁｜

45 高僧像｜192頁｜

44 宗喀巴｜190頁｜

43 蓮花生｜188頁｜

42 菩薩｜186頁｜

41 黃財神｜182頁｜

50 無量壽佛｜217頁｜

49 藥師佛｜214頁｜

48 旃檀佛｜206頁｜

47 格魯派高僧像｜198頁｜

46 咱雅班智達｜195頁｜

51 四臂觀音菩薩 | 220頁 |

52 彌勒菩薩 | 224頁 |

53 觀音菩薩 | 232頁 |

54 思惟觀音菩薩 | 236頁 |

55 思惟觀音菩薩 | 240頁 |

56 大持金剛 | 243頁 |

57 觀音菩薩 | 246頁 |

58 文殊菩薩 | 249頁 |

59 吉祥天母 | 253頁 |

60 寶帳怙主 | 256頁 |

61 馬頭金剛 | 260頁 |

62 四臂大黑天 | 264頁 |

63 紅閻魔敵 | 268頁 |

64 時輪金剛 | 271頁 |

65 大成就者毗盧巴 | 274頁 |

66 普賢菩薩 | 278頁 |

67 文殊菩薩 | 280頁 |

68 金剛手菩薩 | 284頁 |

69 持世菩薩 | 288頁 |

70 金剛薩埵 | 292頁 |

71 四臂文殊菩薩 | 295頁 |

72 大黑天 | 298頁 |

73 舞蹈菩薩 | 306頁 |

74 觀音菩薩 | 310頁 |

75 釋迦牟尼佛 | 316頁 |

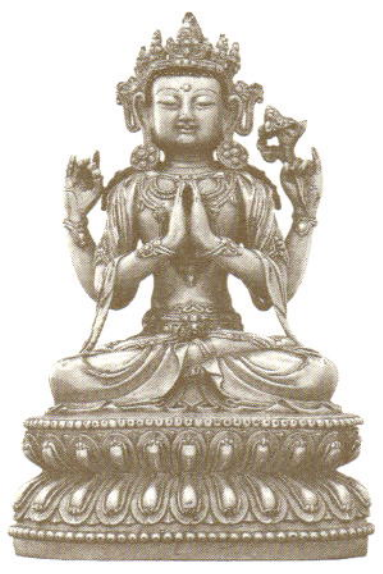

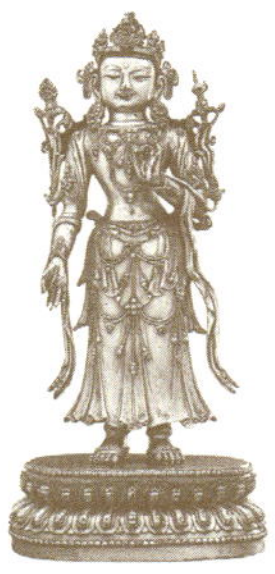

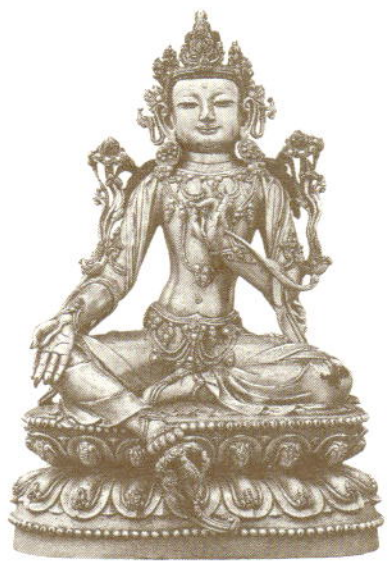

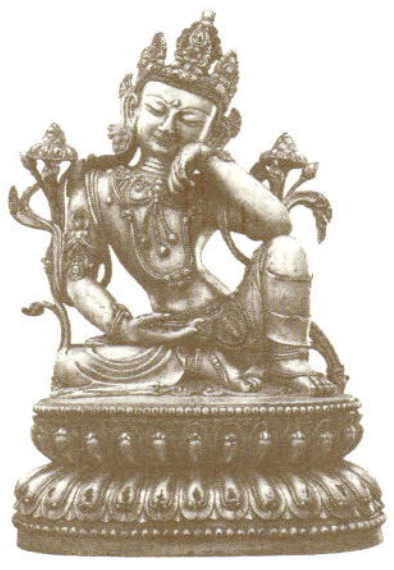

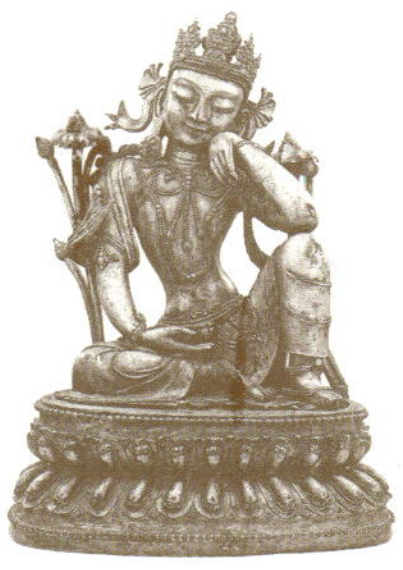

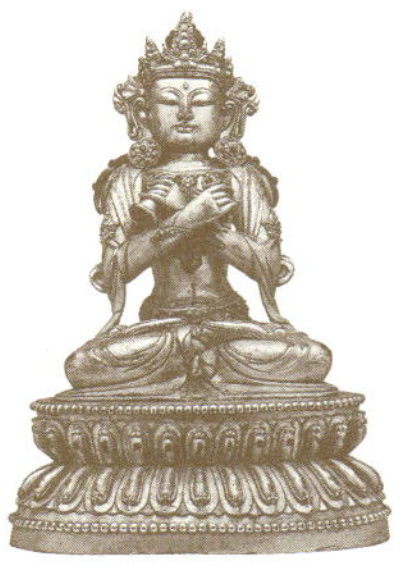

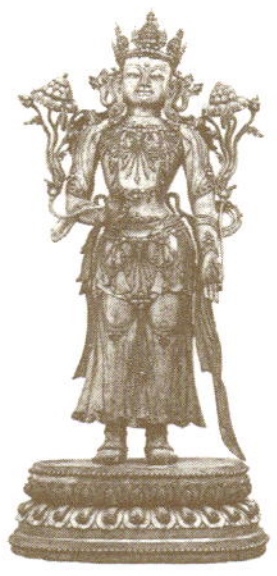

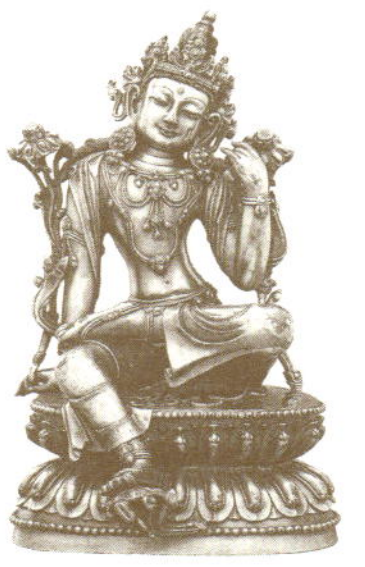

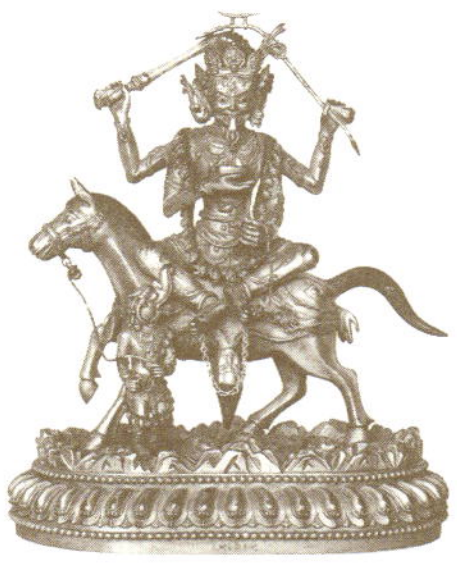

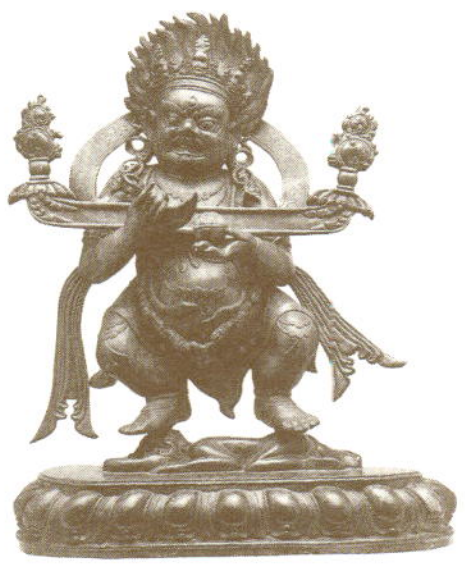

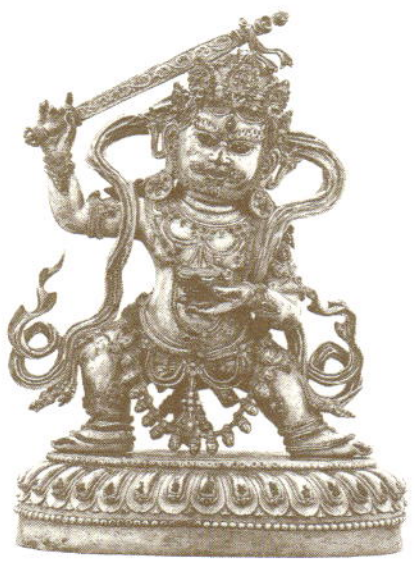

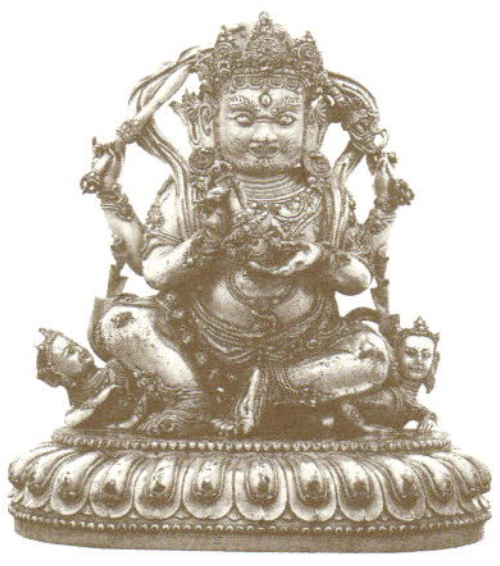

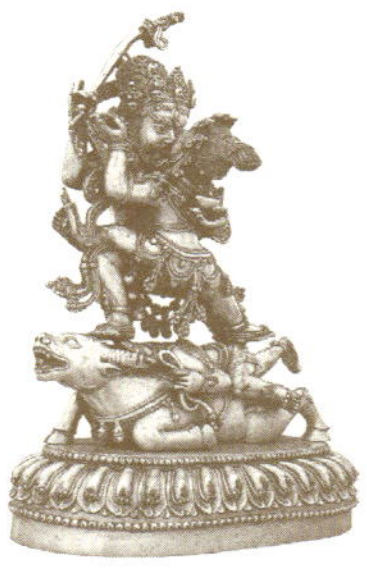

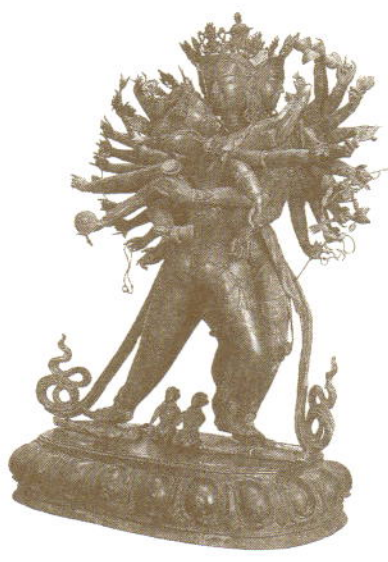

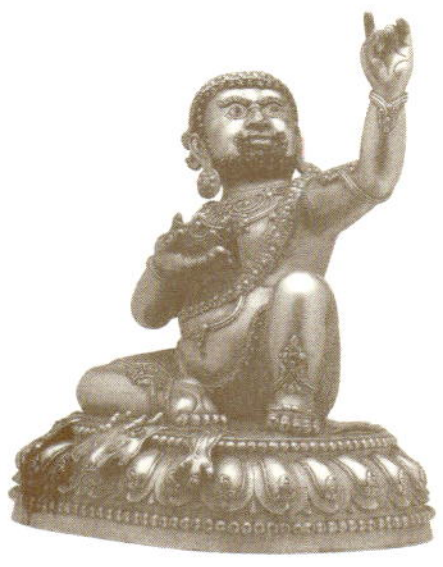

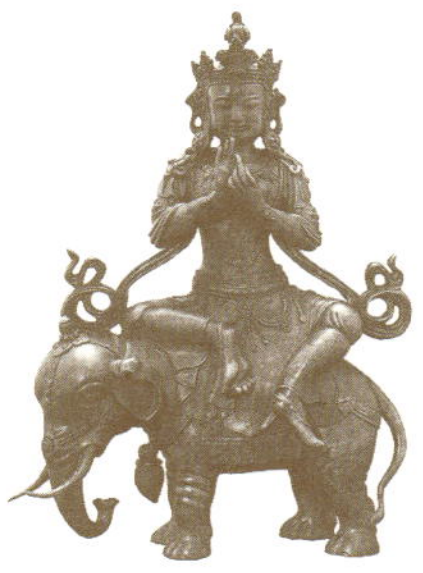

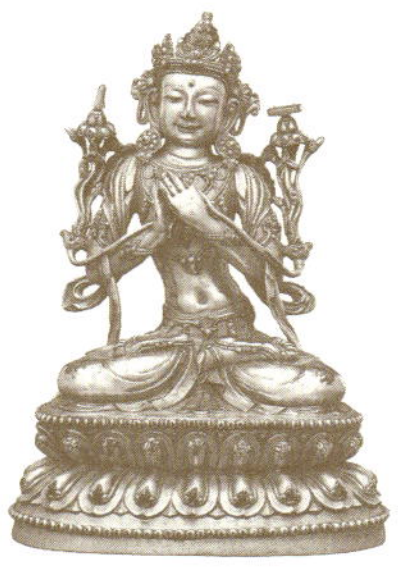

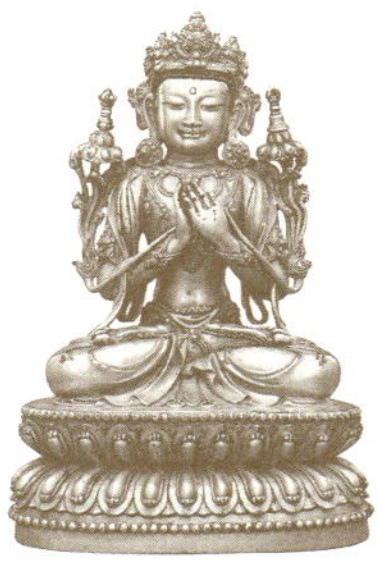

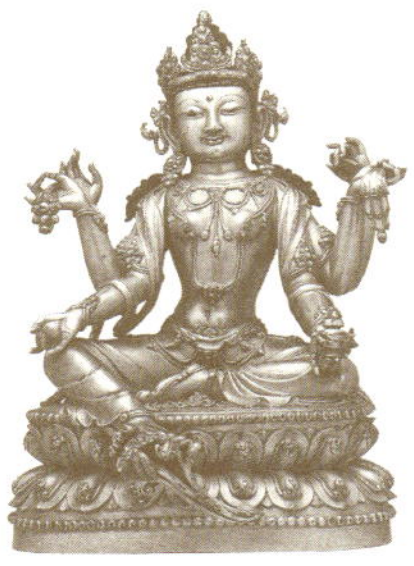

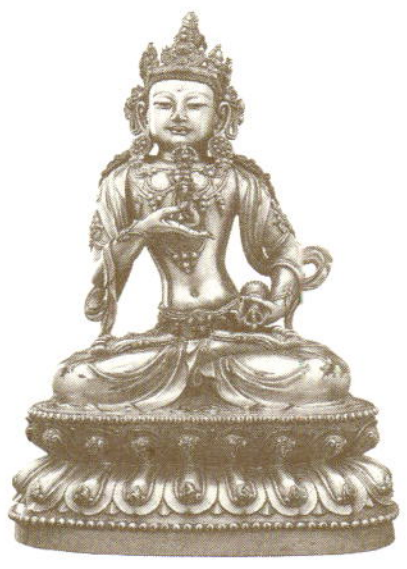

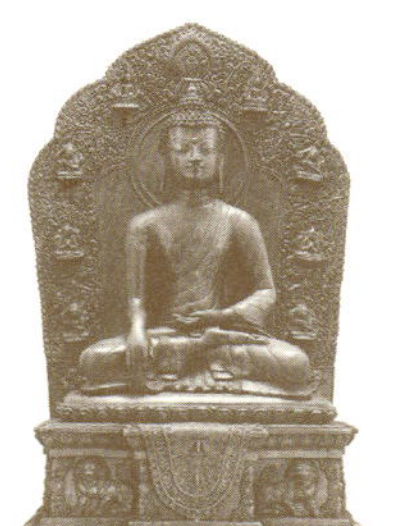

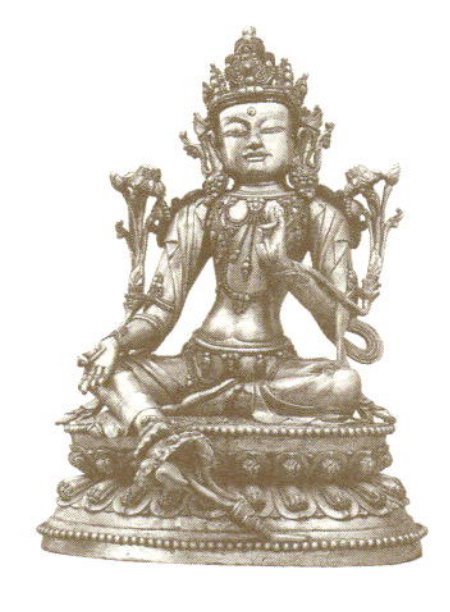

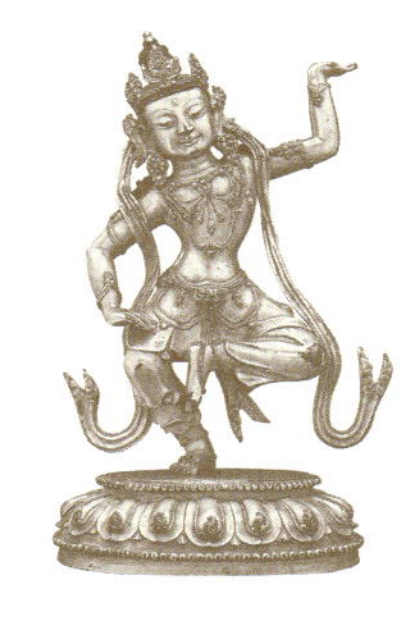

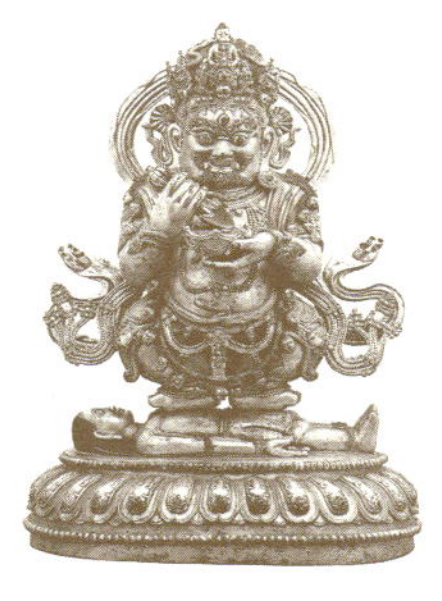

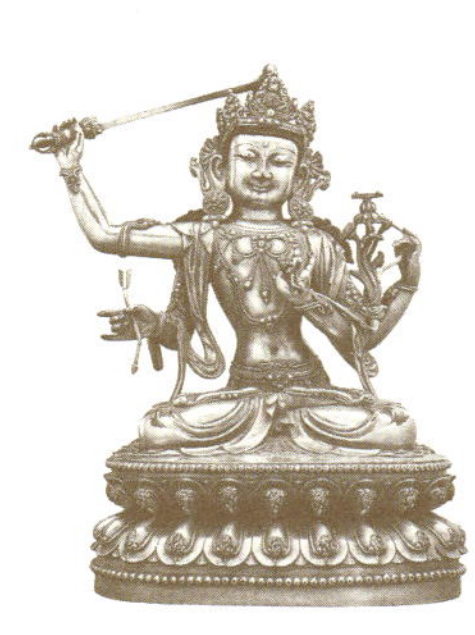

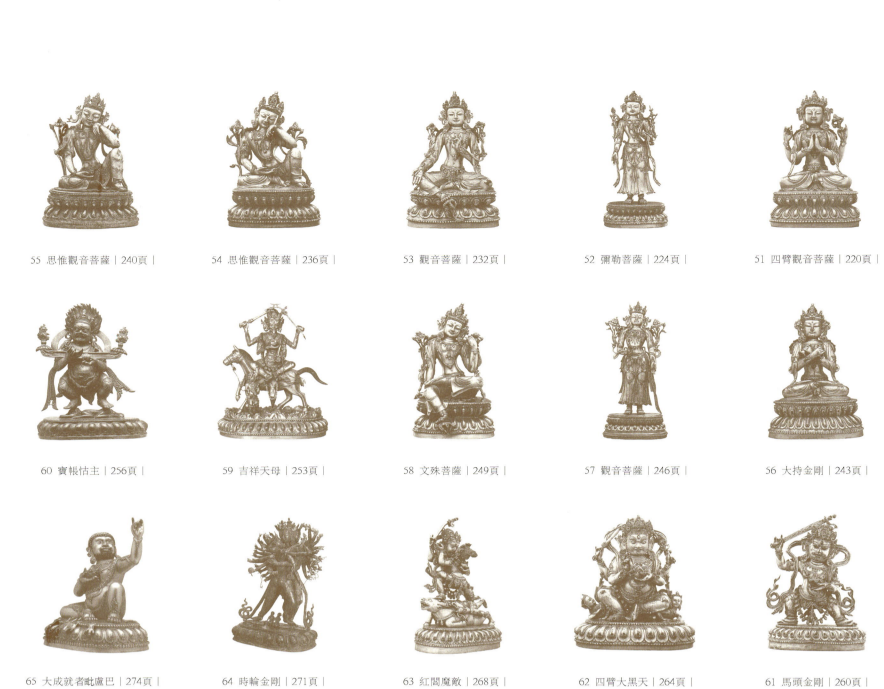

76 無量壽佛｜319頁｜

77 觀音菩薩｜322頁｜

78 財寶天王｜325頁｜

79 增長天王｜328頁｜

80 四臂觀音菩薩｜331頁｜

81 藥師佛｜334頁｜

82 四臂觀音菩薩｜337頁｜

83 彌勒菩薩｜340頁｜

84 彌勒菩薩｜342頁｜

85 彌勒菩薩｜344頁｜

86 宗喀巴｜347頁｜

87 思惟觀音菩薩｜351頁｜

88 四臂觀音菩薩｜354頁｜

89 四臂觀音菩薩｜358頁｜

90 觀音菩薩｜361頁｜

91 大黑天｜364頁｜

92 大持金剛｜367頁｜

93 釋迦牟尼佛｜370頁｜

94 釋迦牟尼佛｜374頁｜

95 釋迦牟尼佛｜377頁｜

96 彌勒菩薩｜379頁｜

97 紅閻魔敵｜382頁｜

98 馬頭金剛｜384頁｜

99 文殊菩薩｜386頁｜

圖書在版編目（C I P）數據

漢藏交融：金銅佛像集萃／王家鵬主編.—北京：中華書局，2009.9

ISBN 978-7-101-06944-0

Ⅰ.漢… Ⅱ.王… Ⅲ.佛像-中國-圖集 Ⅳ.B94-64

中國版本圖書館CIP數據核字（2009）第140578號

漢藏交融

——金銅佛像集萃

主　　編　王家鵬

副 主 編　沈衛榮

藏文翻譯　郭須·扎巴軍乃　吉美桑珠

英文翻譯　沈衛榮

文物攝影　趙秀文　劉志崗　趙忠路

責任編輯　朱振華　許旭虹

書籍設計　張志偉　知墨春秋設計工作室

文物監管　鞠傳莉　王珊珊

信息匯集　鄭　紅　汪　泱

出版發行　中華書局

印　　刷　北京雅昌彩色印刷有限公司

開　　本　889毫米×1194毫米　1/8

印　　張　53.5

版　　次　2009年9月

書　　號　ISBN 978-7-101-06944-0

定　　價　3980.00圓

Sino-Tibetan Buddhist Interactions
A Treasury of Gilt Copper Buddhist Statues

Chief Editor: Wang Jiapeng

Deputy Editor: Shen Weirong

Tibetan Translation: Guoxu · Zhaba Junnai Jigme Samdrub

English Translation: Shen Weirong

Photography of Cultral Relics: Zhao Xiuwen Liu Zhigang Zhao Zhonglu

Editor-in-Charge: Zhu Zhenhua Xu Xuhong

Design: Zhang Zhiwei Zhimo Chunqiu Design Studio

Supervision of Cultral Relics: Ju Chuanli Wang Shanshan

Information Collection: Zheng Hong Wang Yang

Publisher: Zhonghua Book Company

Printing: Beijing Artron Color Printing Co., Ltd.

Size: 889mm × 1194mm 1/8

Printing Format: 53.5

Edition: September 2009

ISBN: 978-7-101-06944-0

Price: 3980.00 RMB

本圖集金銅佛像收藏及出版投資人：李巍

དེབ་འདི་དང་ཟངས་སྐུ་ཉར་ཚགས་པ། པར་སྐྲུན་བཅས་ཀྱི་སྦྱིན་བདག་ནི་ལིས་ཝེ་ཡིན།

Li Wei: The sponsor of the Publication of the book and the owner of the collection of all statues included in this book.

海外聯絡：孫海明　高　楊

海外發行：俞維佳　蘇樹春

Oversea Liason: Sun Haiming　Gao Yang

Oversea Distribution: Yu Weijia　Su Shuchun